C0-CBZ-409

National Policy, Global Memory

BERGHAHN MONOGRAPHS IN FRENCH STUDIES

Editor: **Michael Scott Christofferson,** Associate Professor and Chair of Department of History, Adelphi University

France has played a central role in the emergence of the modern world. The Great French Revolution of 1789 contributed decisively to political modernity, and the Paris of Baudelaire did the same for culture. Because of its rich intellectual and cultural traditions, republican democracy, imperial past and post-colonial present, twentieth-century experience of decline and renewal, and unique role in world affairs, France and its history remain important today. This series publishes monographs that offer significant methodological and empirical contributions to our understanding of the French experience and its broader role in the making of the modern world.

Volume 1
The Populist Challenge: Political Protest and Ethno-nationalist Mobilization in France
Jens Rydgren

Volume 2
French Intellectuals against the Left: The Antitotalitarian Moment of the 1970s
Michael Scott Christofferson

Volume 3
Sartre against Stalinism
Ian H. Birchall

Volume 4
Sartre, Self-Formation and Masculinities
Jean-Pierre Boulé

Volume 5
The Bourgeois Revolution in France 1789–1815
Henry Heller

Volume 6
God's Eugenicist: Alexis Carrel and the Sociobiology of Decline
Andrés Horacio Reggiani

Volume 7
France and the Construction of Europe, 1944–2007: The Geopolitical Imperative
Michael Sutton

Volume 8
Shades of Indignation: Political Scandals in France, Past and Present
Paul Jankowski

Volume 9
Mitterrand, the End of the Cold War, and German Unification
Frédéric Bozo

Volume 10
Collective Terms: Race, Culture, and Community in a State-Planned City in France
Beth S. Epstein

Volume 11
France in the Age of Organization: Factory, Home and Nation from the 1920s to Vichy
Jackie Clarke

Volume 12
Building a European Identity: France, the United States, and the Oil Shock, 1973–1974
Aurélie Élisa Gfeller

Volume 13
General de Gaulle's Cold War: Challenging American Hegemony, 1963–1968
Garret Joseph Martin

Volume 14
At Home in Postwar France: Modern Mass Housing and the Right to Comfort
Nicole C. Rudolph

Volume 15
National Policy, Global Memory: The Commemoration of the "Righteous" from Jerusalem to Paris, 1942–2007
Sarah Gensburger

National Policy, Global Memory

The Commemoration of the "Righteous" from Jerusalem to Paris, 1942–2007

Sarah Gensburger
Translated by Katharine Throssell

Published in 2016 by
Berghahn Books
www.berghahnbooks.com

Originally published in 2010 by Les Presses de Sciences Po as
Les Justes de France. Politiques publiques de la mémoire

Translation by Katharine Throssell

This book was translated with the support of the
Fondation pour la Mémoire de la Shoah, Paris

Fondation
pour la
Mémoire
de la
Shoah

Translation support also provided by the
Direction de la Mémoire du Patrimoine et des Archives

Library of Congress Cataloging-in-Publication Data

A C.I.P. cataloging record is available from the Library of Congress

British Library Cataloguing in Publication Data

A catalogue record for this book is available from the British Library

ISBN: 978-1-78533-254-8 (hardback)
ISBN: 978-1-78533-255-5 (ebook)

To my daughter and her father,
who supported me in the writing of this book

CONTENTS

Acknowledgments

Because of the great diversity of fieldwork sites, languages, and disciplines mobilized in this research, this book received support from so many sources it would be impossible to name them all. My apologies to all those who have not been mentioned specifically; you have not been forgotten.

I would like to begin by expressing my deep gratitude to all those who agreed to meet with me and to tell their stories. I also thank the members of the French Committee for Yad Vashem. I hope that they understand my approach and will find in this book a new perspective on their practices and their environment. Many thanks also to the team at the Department of the Righteous of Yad Vashem in Jerusalem for welcoming me during the summer of 2003.

Finally, thanks to all the community groups: Hidden Children (France), Aloumim/Living Memory (Jerusalem), French Association in Honor of the Righteous among the Nations (Paris), Association of the French Righteous for Yad Vashem (Marseille), Claims Conference (New York), Chambon Foundation (Los Angeles), Children of the Holocaust (Warsaw), and the Jewish Historical Institute (Warsaw). To this list can be added the various political, administrative, and institutional leaders who met with me and sometimes even gave me access to their archives.

For their help and assistance I would also like to thank the teams at the Center for Contemporary Jewish Documentation and at the French Research Center in Jerusalem. A particular word of thanks to Sara Palmor for her assistance in the Israeli archives. For their language skills, Sara Baitel, Adrien Candiard, Nanou Gutman, Danièle Rousselier, and Miriam Ticktin. Although Agnieszka Niewiedzial was skilled in this also, she was above all a valuable research partner. I am very grateful to Katharine Throssell, who translated this book into English, and to Cynthia Schoch, who translated the first version of the introduction and of the first chapter. I also thank Magali Vautelin and my colleagues of the Institut de Sciences sociales du Politique (CNRS—UPOND—ENS Cachan) for their support.

Finally, I am grateful to the Fondation pour la Mémoire de la Shoah and the Direction de la Mémoire, du Patrimoine et des Archives for making possible the translation of the French version of this book.

Several colleagues helped me by providing comments and critiques during the writing of this book. I am grateful to the members of the former seminar on sociology of memory at CEVIPOF and particularly to Valérie Rosoux, Michèle Baussant, and Sandrine Lefranc. Thanks to Patrick Le Galès for his readings and his patience. Of course, an especially big thanks to Marie-Claire Lavabre, who has been so much more than my Ph.D. supervisor.

For their constant support and so much more, thanks to my parents and to Renaud.

Introduction

From "The Righteous among the Nations" to the "Righteous of France"

On 18 January 2007, the French president paid tribute to the "Righteous of France" and unveiled a plaque in their honor in the crypt of the Pantheon. This ceremony was the concrete realization of national recognition instituted by the law of 10 July 2000, the text of which defines the "Righteous of France" as those "who, risking their own lives and with no compensation whatsoever, took in, sheltered or defended one or more persons threatened with genocide" under the Occupation. This book aims to shed light on the process that brought about the creation of this new commemorative term.

The expression "Righteous of France" is explicitly borrowed from the Israeli term "Righteous among the Nations," a translation of the Hebrew *Hasidei Ummot Ha-Olam.* Since 1953, the state of Israel has used this rabbinical expression to refer to and honor non-Jews who "risked their lives to save Jews" during the Holocaust. Within the Yad Vashem Institute, the state authority in charge of commemorating the Holocaust, a special department manages the awarding of this title, which is decided by a commission that rules much in the same way as a criminal court does. To initiate the nomination procedure, two Jewish persons having directly received the help of non-Jews must petition the Israeli institute. Once the title is bestowed, the person recognized as Righteous among the Nations has his or her name engraved on a plaque in the Yad Vashem Garden of the Righteous in Jerusalem, and a representative of the state of Israel awards the person a certificate of honor and a medal.

The ceremony generally takes place in the country of which the person is or was a citizen; recognition can be posthumous. As of 1 January 2015, more than twenty-five thousand people had received this distinction, among them 3,853 French, 6,532 Poles, and 1,690 Belgians. In 1999, scarcely a year after the French Parliament had created the category, Belgium also instituted a "Diploma of the Righteous"; in Poland the "Polish Righteous" became eligible for war veteran status. In 2007, the year a commemorative ceremony was held at the Pantheon in Paris, twenty-one members of the Council of Europe Parliamentary Assembly signed a solemn tribute to the "Righteous" of Europe. In recent years, certain states have begun using this term to officially commemorate other genocides, such as in the Rwandan and Armenian cases. A "Garden of the Righteous" modeled after the Israeli original now exists in Yerevan on the site of the memorial of the Armenian genocide.

Making memory policies a topic for political science

As this brief presentation shows, analysis of the gradual institutionalization of the Righteous of France as a category provides material for a real case study of both contemporary public action and the current relationship between memory and politics in that "it is the set of questions one puts into it—and that are likely to be put to it—that forms a case."[1]

By studying the shift from the Israeli term "Righteous among the Nations" to the expression "Righteous of France,"[2] this book first sets out to advance a new topic for political science: memory public policies. Aside from a few recent studies,[3] political scientists have so far shown little interest in public actions that have to do with evoking the past.[4] However, the term "politics of memory" is currently used mainly by historians and sociologists in contemporary social sciences.[5] It oscillates between two meanings: it refers either to the political exploitation of the past in order to promote official memory through speeches and commemorations or to a diffuse memory of which speeches and commemorations are the public manifestations.

This study, however, sets out precisely to open up the black box of the public authorities' evocation of the past. The political nature of the exploitation of memory narratives by representatives of the state is not founded per se on the distance from factual truth as established by the work of historians.[6] It flows, like for any public policy, from the status of the public actors and institutions concerned as well as the objectives pursued and resources used. This analysis of the institutionalization of the Righteous of France category thus aims to provide a case study of a public policy of memory. It calls for public policy and public administration scholars to take these public policies dealing with the past more seriously.

However, in addition to examining a sector of public action that political science has neglected until now, this case study will touch on transversal issues. The research topic of the institutionalization of the Righteous of France category is constructed at the junction of the private and public spheres or, rather, at the point of passage from one to the other. Originally the expression of individuals' testimonies, the evocation and recognition of the Righteous has become a matter of state and adheres to a variety of calendars and trajectories. This dual interaction is at the very heart of the object of study here: between individuals, social actors, political actors, public authorities, and institutions but also between local, national, international, and transnational scales. It is conducive to undertaking a sociological study of the transnationalization of public policies, and this at various levels of public action.[7]

How do separate initiatives, stemming from actors occupying different spaces and operating in different periods, finally connect to produce a public policy? Symmetrically, what effects, in particular in terms of interest, do such policies have on the configuration of actors? In short, what respective roles do the mechanisms of transfer and translation of public policies play in the institutionalization of the term "Righteous" concomitantly in different countries? How do they play out on a global scale of which, precisely, the contours remain to be delimited and the nature determined? The approach here is therefore comparative; the institutionalization of the Righteous of France category is put in perspective with comparable phenomena observed in other countries, mainly Poland and Belgium. Particular attention is paid to the mechanisms[8] of appropriation and hybridization and the roles played by political institutions and the "institutional matrixes"[9] specific to each national configuration as well as the dynamics of Europeanization and globalization.

This volume thus provides a close analysis of the processes that inform these policies in order to explore the contexts, networks, and social actors as well as their practices and the social fabric of their interactions. It shows how the actors' logics are articulated with the institutions that structure them and that they modify in turn. In this respect it takes up "the institutionalist challenge"[10] discussed by Alec S. Sweet, Neil Fligstein, and Wayne Sandholtz: to explain the emergence of new institutions and, in this instance, of a new memorial category from its creation and codification to its shaping into an instrument of public action.

This study of a specific remembrance policy carefully identifies the types of motivations public policy actors can have. Much research has underscored the way in which the links between politics and memory are situated at the junction of symbolic practices and strategic practices.[11] Seeking to understand the institutionalization of the Righteous of France category offers a way to empirically study the articulation of "frames of meaning" and "logics of power"[12] at the heart of public action as well as the way in which institutions orient both. In particular, it raises the question of the relationship actors have with memory and especially the borderline between its instrumentalization and instrumentation: does politics instrumentalize the past to act on memories or is commemoration of the past first and foremost an instrument that serves policies of which the ultimate goal is anything but to influence representations of the past?

What is political about remembrance policies?

This last remark finally leads to an interrogation of the political nature of memory public policies. For instance, the study of the passage of laws aiming to commemorate the wars that France has been involved in since 1939 shows that these policies were usually adopted by consensus.[13] Similarly, in his analysis of the controversy surrounding the commemoration of the colonial past, Romain Bertrand has shown that with regard to highly polemical issues, remembrance policies are nevertheless enacted according to "the euphemizing mode of depoliticization."[14]

This mode would appear to be carried to the extreme in the case of the emergence of the term "Righteous of France." A total political and media consensus surrounded the ceremony at the Pantheon in January 2007. The law of 10 July 2000 was unanimously passed by both houses of Parliament. The present case study deals with this depoliticization and its corollary, the depoliticizing politics in which public actors who evoke the past regularly partake. Although the question of the relationship between public policy and democracy is currently a major research theme, it has particular resonance in the case of policies related to "memory."

Collective actors that regularly criticize public actions evoking the past do not so much denounce recourse to memory in principle, which is viewed as essential, as they do the interpretation(s) of history that are proposed on such occasions. The lack of any controversy in the case of the gradual institutionalization of the category Righteous of France merely underscores this state of affairs: studying it is a first step toward understanding. How did this shared belief in the capacity of memory as an instrument to act on contemporary society and improve its democratic nature emerge?

In France, a certain interpretative framework for the involvement of politics in the field of memory has come to hold sway in academia as well as in public debate following the controversy around so-called memory laws. The passage of these laws[15] was first criticized on the grounds that it was akin to dictating an official truth, a modern form of propaganda. At the same time, it was presented as being the result of campaigns by pressure groups, mainly described as communitarian.[16] The mechanism is moreover not specific to Parliament—even if by nature it is more attuned to memory clientelism; it is believed to affect all components of the state.[17] The multiplication of national commemoration days is particularly considered to be an indication of the rise of "communitarianism" and the shattering of the "national memory" into as many "competing memories."[18]

The institution of the national day devoted to the memory of victims of racist and anti-Semitic crimes committed by the French state and paying tribute to the Righteous of France has an important place in the debate. Never questioned by those who subscribe to this analysis, it nevertheless ushered in a period in which recourse to this instrument became increasingly frequent. When Parliament passed the law, it made use of an instrument it had not resorted to since the creation of the National Day of Remembrance of the Victims and Heroes of the Deportation in 1954.[19] Since then and up until 2006, five new dates have been added to the official calendar of historic memory.[20] The present volume offers a critical examination of the analysis presented briefly above through the study of one specific case. By paying particular attention to the intersection of state intervention and memories expressed by individuals, it provides a means of gauging the supposed social effects of remembrance policies.

This research was carried out over a long period and across several national spaces, which makes it a privileged case study of the question of social change common to studies on memory and analysis of public action. While with the former there seems to be, in France, a consensus regarding the "tyranny of memory" and the "regime of historicity"[21] that are said to characterize our contemporary societies, the ultimate horizon of the latter is the understanding of changes in the nature of politics. However, it remains to be seen to what extent the conclusions currently drawn regarding the change in politics as well as the transformation of memory "are the result of a change in reality, a change in representations of reality or a change in how the social sciences apprehend reality."[22]

Notes

1. Jean-Claude Passeron and Jacques Revel, eds., *Penser par cas* (Paris: Éditions de l'EHESS, 2005), 111.
2. The present volume is a partial reformulation of Sarah Gensburger, "Essai de sociologie de la mémoire. L'Expression des souvenirs à travers le titre de "Juste parmi les nations" dans le cas français: entre cadre institutionnel, public policy et mémoire collective"

(Ph.D. dissertation, EHESS, 2006). See Appendix 1 for a presentation of the methodology and corpus.

3. Romain Bertrand, *Mémoires d'empire. La Controverse autour du "fait colonial"* (Bellecombes-en-Bauges: Editions du Croquant, 2006). For an English review, see Sarah Gensburger, *Mémoires d'empire. La Controverse autour du " fait colonial,"* Romain Bertrand, ed. (Bellecombes-en-Bauges: Editions du Croquant, 2006); *National Identities* 10, no. 4 (2008): 453–55.
4. By way of example, there are no political scientists on the editorial board of the flagship review in *Memory Studies,* published since 2008 by Sage, nor are there many more among the contributors to the readers in this discipline that have emerged since 2005. The most important among these readers is Jeffrey K. Olick, Vered Vinitzky-Seroussi, and Daniel Levy, *The Collective Memory Reader* (Oxford: Oxford University Press, 2011).
5. Jeffrey K. Olick, *Politics of Regret: On Collective Memory and Historical Responsibility* (New York: Routledge, 2007).
6. For further details on this explicit epistemological position, which was already present in the work of Maurice Halbwachs, see Sarah Gensburger, "Fragments de mémoire collective: les Justes parmi les nations," in *La Topographie légendaire des Évangiles en Terre sainte (1941),* ed. Maurice Halbwachs (Paris: PUF, 2008), 99–112.
7. Patrick Hassenteufel, "De la comparaison internationale à la comparaison transnationale. Les Déplacements de la construction d'objets comparatifs en matière de politiques publiques," *Revue française de science politique* 55, no. 1 (2005): 113–32.
8. In this work, the term "mechanism" refers to the explication of causality; for a discussion of the term and approaches that use it, see Charles Tilly, "Mechanisms in Political Process," *Annual Review of Political Science* 4 (2001): 21–41.
9. Olivier Borraz and Patricia Loncle-Moriceau, "Permanences et Recompositions du secteur sanitaire, les politiques locales de lutte contre le SIDA," *Revue française de sociologie* 41, no. 1 (2000): 37–60.
10. Alec Stone Sweet, Neil Fligstein, and Wayne Sandholtz, *The Institutionalization of Europe* (Oxford: Oxford University Press, 2001), 3.
11. Jeffrey K. Olick, ed., *States of Memory: Continuities, Conflicts, and Transformations in National Retrospection* (Durham: Duke University Press, 2003).
12. Peter A. Hall and Rosemary C.R. Taylor, "Political Science and the Three New Institutionalisms," *Political Studies*, 44, no5 (1996): 936–957.
13. Claire Andrieu, "La Commémoration des dernières guerres françaises: l'élaboration de politiques symboliques, 1945–2003," in *Politiques du passé. Usages politiques du passé dans la France contemporaine,* ed. Claire Andrieu, Marie-Claire Lavabre, and Danielle Tartakowsky, 39–46 (Aix-en-Provence: Publications de l'Université de Provence, 2006).
14. Bertrand, *Mémoires d'empire,* 33–34.
15. For a list of these laws, see Appendix 2.
16. Françoise Chandernagor and Pierre Nora, *Liberté pour l'histoire* (Paris: CNRS Éditions, 2008).
17. René Rémond, *Quand l'état se mêle de l'histoire* (Paris: Stock, 2006).
18. On this point, see the numerous stands taken by members of the commission to reflect on the modernization of public commemorations; report made in November 2008, Appendix 2.
19. Law no. 54–415 of 14 April 1954 dedicating the last Sunday in April to the memory of the victims of deportation who died in concentration camps of the Third Reich during World War II.
20. For a list of the texts, see Appendix 2.

21. Pierre Nora, ed., "L'Ère de la commémoration," in *Les Lieux de mémoire*, vol. 3 (Paris: Gallimard, 1997), 4687–18; François Hartog, *Des régimes d'historicité. Présentisme et Expériences du temps* (Paris: Seuil, 2002).
22. Jacques Commaille, "Sociologie de l'action publique," in *Dictionnaire des politiques publiques*, ed. Laurie Boussaguet, Sophie Jacquot, and Pauline Ravinet (Paris: Presses de Sciences Po, 2004), 420. More broadly see also, Ian Hacking, *The Social Construction of What?* (Cambridge, MA: Harvard University Press, 2000).

Chapter 1

MEMORY AS AN INSTRUMENT OF FOREIGN POLICY?

The term "Righteous of France" refers directly to the title "Righteous among the Nations," which the state of Israel borrowed from Jewish religious tradition in order to honor the men and women who came to the aid of Jews during World War II. The expression arises from the double translation, both literally and metaphorically, found in Michel Callon's research.[1] To understand the dynamics that led to this term requires studying the original paradigm, that is, the actors, networks, processes, and contexts that presided over Israel's creation of the title Righteous among the Nations.

While, generally speaking, commemorations of the Holocaust have inspired a wealth of literature, the establishment of the "Righteous"[2] title has, on the contrary, aroused little interest.[3] The U.S. historian Peter Novick has studied it, however, considering at first that the "intention of most commemoration of the 'righteous minority' has been to damn the vast 'unrighteous majority'" before concluding, "Whatever the intention, this [the fortress-like mentality or suspicion of gentiles] seems to have been the consequence."[4] Such difficulty in discerning intention and consequence invites the researcher to take a dynamic approach in considering the political decision behind this linguistic creation not as a moment but rather as a process.

In search of the decision

The mechanisms leading to the creation of the title Righteous operated over a period of about twenty years. Was this type of instrument[5] intended to serve a new public policy pertaining explicitly to remembrance? Or does this instrumentation of the commemoration of non-Jewish rescuers fall within one of the standard areas of public action?

The legislative creation of the term "Righteous among the Nations"

In 1942, in the *Yishuv,* the Jewish community in Palestine, Mordechai Shenhabi, a Zionist activist from Russia, formulated a desire to preserve the memory of non-Jews who had helped Jews and bestow on them the title "Righteous among the Nations." His plan to create the Yad Vashem memorial—a monument and a name—included drawing up a "list of Righteous among the Nations who rescued people or protected property" in one of the destroyed communities.[6] The man who promoted the project gave no details of his intention. What's more, this particular mission holds only a marginal place in his overall undertaking.

Very quickly, however, Mordechai Shenhabi wanted to use this specific commemorative means as a diplomatic instrument. In 1947, he informed Golda Meir, then a member of the *Yishuv* political department, of the death of the king of Denmark and outlined the diplomatic benefits that could be derived from including this monarch among the Righteous.[7]

The project to establish the Yad Vashem Institute did not come to fruition until 1953. The prospect of a competing memorial being built in Paris and the refusal to see the "memory" of "Jewish Martyrdom"[8] established in another country decided the prime minister of the young state of Israel. The government drafted the bill for the Holocaust Martyrs' and Heroes' Remembrance [Yad Vashem] Law in 1953.[9] Unlike Mordechai Shenhabi's initial proposal, it made no provision for the commemoration of the "Righteous among the Nations."

The theme came up in the parliamentary debates that began in the Knesset on 18 May 1953. A member of Knesset (MK) from the Mapai,[10] the party in power, was introduced it. The idea of paying tribute to the Righteous was greeted with favor by all the participants, whatever their political persuasion. Several lines of cleavage appeared, however, with regard to the meaning to be invested in this category. The communist Mapam[11] wished to honor only those who had taken up arms in the course of collective worker action. The liberal General Zionists group[12] felt that rescue was primarily an individual act. Between military action and civilian engagement, between collective and individual actors, between the extreme left and right, the Mapai MKs occupied the middle ground in these debates, reflecting their position on the political checkerboard: "Murderers as well as rescuers came from all social strata. . . . All those who came to our aid are dear to us, and when the history of the Holocaust is written, an eternal monument will also be erected in honor of these Righteous among the Nations."[13]

The bill was brought before the Knesset Education and Culture Committee. The working group devoted none of their discussions to the theme of commemorating the Righteous, the idea seeming to have been approved in principle at the end of the first debate.[14] On 19 August 1953, the Knesset passed the amended text[15] by relative unanimity.[16]

The bill comprises eight articles. The first outlines the nature of the Yad Vashem Institute memorial and lists the nine themes that it should commemorate. The ninth and last paragraph refers to "the high-minded Gentiles who risked their lives to save Jews."[17] No other criterion was added to that of mortal risk. The phrasing settled none of the questions raised in the parliamentary debate. It gave rise to a new memorial expression that was defined (in order to gather consensus) in minimalist terms likely to produce protean, multiple, and evolving interpretations.

Manifestation of a cognitive framework

The legislative creation of the category the "Righteous among the Nations" is the result of a discontinuous process. Whereas the aspect of the Shenhabi project pertaining to the commemoration of the Righteous was absent from the text the government submitted to the Knesset, it cropped up again during parliamentary debates without the 1942 precedent even being mentioned. A decisional continuity emerged beyond the breaks that occurred in the decision-making chain. The strong and enduring presence of a cognitive framework shared by all of the actors in the decision-making process over the entire time explains the passage of this legislative provision.

The existence of such a framework appears first of all in the use of the expression "Righteous among the Nations" by all of the protagonists. In 1942, as in 1953, none of them felt the need to explain the origin of the term or explain the meaning given to it. In Jewish religious tradition, the Hebrew expression *Hasidei Ummot Ha-Olam* at first referred to pious non-Jews.[18] Use of the expression became widespread in the Middle Ages and ended up referring to non-Jews who were "friends" of the Jews and who, by their attitude, were an exception to the dominant hostility of the former with regard to the latter. When the Knesset members began using the expression in 1953 to honor the memory of those who had helped the Jews, despite the temporal discontinuity and the heterogeneity of its protagonists' political commitment, it thus came to refer to a specific conception of the relations between these two groups otherwise considered antagonistic. "The feeling of isolation and betrayal by Jews who, for many years, had lived amicably together with non-Jews under a non-Jewish government"[19] thus played a central role in the legislative borrowing of a religious expression.

In this respect, the measure concerning the Righteous is perfectly in keeping with the rationale presiding over political commemoration decisions. Adhesion to the idea of the "negation of exile,"[20] the assertion of the illegitimacy of a Jewish Diaspora community, is evidence of a cognitive framework shared by all Israeli MKs. During parliamentary debates, each speaker began with a reminder of the crimes perpetrated by the goyim. It is in view of those crimes that honoring those gentiles who helped the Jews was all the more necessary:

> It is a falsification of history to suggest that only Jews rose up and that no one else took part in the revolt. There are goyim who have our blood on their hands. But there are also rescuers. . . . It is true that we have heavy accounts to settle with goyim who lived by our blood. But rescuers were also from various walks of life.[21]

Eleven years earlier, this belief in the negation of exile already permeated the entire project conceived by Mordechai Shenhabi: the aim then was to make Jews of the Diaspora realize that the Genocide merely carried to an extreme the impossibility of a truly Jewish life in non-Jewish states.

The study of the legislative creation of the "Righteous among the Nations" category thus reveals once again the role of cognitive factors in the implementation of public policies. Rather than the existence of an "intention" as identified by Peter Novick, which would be in this case concealed behind a pretense of gratitude, the study of the legislative creation of the title "Righteous among the Nations" confirms that "the interests brought into play in public policies are expressed only through the production of frameworks of interpretation of the world."[22] In this case these are characteristic of Zionism and the Israeli political officials of the 1950s. The existence of these frameworks is explained in turn by a particular social morphology produced by the trajectories and social positions of the actors behind this legislative measure. The composition of the second Knesset as well as the social identity of Mordechai Shenhabi thus provided a social framework that held a particular point of view on the Holocaust and more broadly the history of Jews in exile.[23] Shenhabi, the instigator of the initial project for a commemorative institute, was born in 1900 in Czarist Russia, had been a militant in the Hashomer Hazair youth movement, and had lived in Palestine since 1919. Most of the MKs who sat on the Knesset in 1953 had a similar life trajectory: 67 percent of them were born in Eastern Europe and 79 percent had immigrated to the *Yishuv* between 1920 and 1940. Militant Zionists since the interwar period, they had a similar personal history and a largely common view of the Jewish condition in the Diaspora.

Comparison of the Israeli process with other projects envisioned by Diaspora Jews of the time confirms the power of this link between actors' social trajectories, a shared cognitive framework, and the decision to honor the Righteous among the Nations. First of all, in February 1945, two senior World Jewish Congress officials[24] (both citizens of the United States) had also made a proposal to create a Genocide memorial that in particular would include a "special room honoring non-Jews who saved Jews."[25] Although, like Mordechai Shenhabi's contemporaneous project, the location envisaged was in Palestine, the approach was the opposite. Its backers sought to remember the Holocaust while distancing it from the United States, where most Jews felt they were a part of the victorious America[26] and sought "acceptance by the Gentiles, and not confrontation."[27] Correlatively, the term "Righteous among the Nations" was not used, and the expression "non-Jews who helped the Jews" was favored instead.

The same mechanism was in operation in 1953. The very year in which Knesset members voted in favor of creating the title Righteous among the Nations, the Italian Union of Jewish Communities decided to honor with great solemnity Italians who helped the Jews. Representatives of Italian Jews sought to thank their country and thus reassert their own belonging to the national community.[28] On 17 April 1955, twenty-three "gold medals of merit" were awarded in a grand ceremony held in Milan. The recipients were from all sorts of religious backgrounds and walks of life. They were supposed to represent Italian society as a whole. The commemoration of non-Jews who had helped Jews in this case served as an affirmation of their collective belonging to the Italian nation. There, too, it was not the term "Righteous among the Nations" that was used but "Benemeriti" citizens "decorated for merit." Traditionally used by the Italian state to distinguish its great citizens, this term implies a conception of relations between Jews and non-Jews as cordial and friendly, hence radically different from that implied by the etymology of the term "Righteous among the Nations."

Short of speaking of an "unconscious intention," which is "a contradiction in terms (as is the notion of unconscious strategy),"[29] the study of the process of creating the legal category "Righteous among the Nations" requires a more complex analysis than the traditional frame for examining relations between memory and politics, as the notion of use of the past is not sufficiently operative. "If one looks at the processes of constructing meaning, it is impossible to reduce a policy to a set of organizational strategies, even if the analysis of these strategies is essential to understanding the concrete forms and mechanisms by which meaning is 'fashioned.'"[30]

An instrument lacking public action

Even if the enduring existence of the cognitive framework of negation of exile was a driving force behind the Knesset's creation of the category "Righteous among the Nations" over time, this fact does not explain the initial apparition and the ultimate disappearance of the strategic intention to make the commemoration of these rescuers an instrument of foreign policy.

The reason for this evolution lies in transformations in the international situation between 1940 and 1953. In the 1940s, *Yishuv* officials were looking for support for illegal immigration to the British Mandate for Palestine (known as *aliya bet*). They were working toward the creation of a Jewish state and needed the backing of the major, particularly European, nations and their governments. Mordechai Shenhabi was, moreover, not the only one at the time who envisaged commemoration of non-Jewish rescuers as a means of promoting these international negotiations. Meeting in Basel in December 1946, the Twenty-Second Zionist Congress passed a motion expressing the Jews' gratitude for the rescue efforts and humanism of the Italian people.[31] In exchange for its participation in restoring Italy's image, the Congress asked the government to back *aliya bet* and the creation of the state of Israel.

In 1953, *aliya bet* was long since finished. The state of Israel now existed and enjoyed the support of powerful countries in the international arena. The context and the problems facing the Israeli government had changed. The category Righteous among the Nations was not taken up by the public authorities to be used as an instrument for managing external state relations. As if the "grateful memory" was not in itself enough to justify the institution of a genuine policy, no public action was implemented to commemorate the "Righteous among the Nations" after the Knesset vote. The marginal status of this mission in fact became clear with the drafting of the law of 19 August 1953. Although guidelines were laid down for Yad Vashem to carry out its eight other commemorative tasks, the same was not true of that concerning the Righteous. Only paragraph 7 of article 7, which enables the Institute to lay down "such other provisions as the Minister may decide to be necessary for the maintenance of *Yad Vashem* as a memorial authority," gives it the possibility to establish a concrete procedure by which to honor the memory of the Righteous.

For nearly ten years, this possibility remained a dead letter. Government meetings pertaining to the ratification of the law did not deal with the issue,[32] and Yad Vashem activity reports make no mention of initiatives in this regard.[33] Even on 9 January 1962, the possibility of a concrete commemoration of the Righteous still did not appear in the commemorative institute's annual report and projects.[34] What's more, even though fifty years later the new memorial term "Righteous of France" was based partly on a translation of the original term "Righteous among the Nations," the translation of this memorial term did not give rise to any political decisions.

Even in the 1960s, official French and English translations of the law of 19 August 1953 still diverged somewhat. Whereas the former translates paragraph 7 as "les Justes parmi les nations qui ont risqué leur vie pour venir en aide à des Juifs," the latter speaks of those "high-minded Gentiles who risked their lives to save Jews." One uses the terms "Righteous" (*juste*), whereas the other is much closer to the notion of the "wise" or the "pious." Lastly, whereas the French formulation does not specify the non-Jewish identity of the individuals in question, it is explicit in the Anglo-Saxon version. Like the single article passed by the Knesset, this translation carries within it multiple and protean interpretations of the title Righteous among the Nations. The decision to create a new commemorative term thus cannot be reduced to a single intention pursued by successive protagonists. The procedural aspect of the political decision here appears with renewed force.

Even in 1960, although the title Righteous legally existed, it had no administrative substance. The year 1961, however, marked a turning point in the Parliament's disposition toward effective public action. In April, Yad Vashem organized a major ceremony on the occasion of Yom HaShoah (Holocaust Remembrance Day).[35] The official guest list mentioned the "Righteous among the Nations" for the first time.[36] Slightly less than a year before, Israeli premier David Ben-Gurion had announced to the Knesset the arrest and upcoming trial of Adolf Eichmann in Israel. The trial had begun a few days before. It was suspended for the occasion.

The commemoration of the Righteous and the ensuing controversies

Justice Moshe Landau presided over the tribunal before which the accused appeared.[37] Less than two years later, he would be appointed to head the Commission for the Designation of the Righteous among the Nations, which the state of Israel had set up in the meantime. Placed side by side, these raw facts seem to indicate that the holding of the trial was a major factor in the decision to effectively implement public action aiming to commemorate the Righteous among the Nations. What sort of role did the trial actually play?

The Righteous among the Nations at the Eichmann trial

The decision to hold the trial was a political one, the multiple and sometimes contradictory dimensions of which have been underscored by recent studies.[38] In putting Adolf Eichmann on trial, the Israeli prime minister intended once and for all to associate the victims of the Holocaust, as well as all Jews, with the Israeli state. He also meant to "cast shame on the world for having abandoned the Jews and incite the major powers to show greater support for the state of Israel."[39]

This second, more general aim went together with an extremely practical concern, however, which was partly contradictory: while Ben-Gurion was negotiating reparations with the Federal Republic of Germany, he wanted to dispel the fears expressed by his new partner of "seeing all Germans ostracized by the world's public opinion."[40] "Ben-Gurion was convinced that the strategic aim of making the FRG Israel's ally, required Israelis and Jews world-wide to perceive the 'new Germany' as a friendly state."[41] Ben-Gurion thus decided that a representative of this "other Germany," the Germany that was a friend of the Jews and Israel, would be called to testify. Heinrich Grüber, a pastor deported to Dachau for having helped the Jews, was chosen as a witness for the prosecution. He would later be designated Righteous among the Nations.

The Righteous among the Nations were indeed regularly mentioned during the trial. To prevent Israel's allies from enduring any negative diplomatic consequences of the event, the mention of the Righteous was first made in reference to the people and governments of the countries of Western Europe. It reflected David Ben-Gurion's adhesion to the ideology of *mamlakhtiyut,*[42] or "statism," based on the belief that relations with other countries could be grounded on "principles of equality, mutual aid and common interests rather than on moral responsibility or guilt."[43] The court began by discussing the French situation. Asked to describe how deportation was carried out in France, the historian and former Auschwitz inmate Georges Wellers concluded his testimony, prepared beforehand with the prosecutor, by reminding the court of "those Aryans who were guilty of providing assistance to Jews [and who] were made to wear a star on which was written: 'Friend of the Jews.'"[44]

Surprised by this indulgence, André Scemama, correspondent for *Le Monde* in Jerusalem, pointed out the care that the prosecution took in reporting the slightest initiative taken by the French Righteous among the Nations: "In the whole evocation of this French chapter during the Eichmann trial, the men of Vichy were not condemned. Darquier de Pellepoix, René Bousquet and Pierre Laval were all named, but more for their resistance in the end than their collaboration in the early years." Wellers, in answer to a question put by the ever-vigilant Judge Halevi inquiring about the role of the Vichy police, also said that on the whole they had tried to avoid the worst. It was noticed that the prosecution read out the famous protest by the Catholic clergy in Vichy in which was found the statement: "Jews are human beings, they are our brothers. No Christian can disregard this."[45]

Similarly, the deeds of the Belgians and Dutch were recalled, and the community mobilization of Italians, Danish, and Norwegians praised.[46] Again, such tributes astonished observers.[47] The journalist from *Combat* finally came to believe:

> What stands out is the discretion if not the indulgence shown by the prosecution with regard to collaboration with the Nazis in the occupied countries of Western Europe. It was only discretely mentioned. . . . Again yesterday, Thursday, Italy was praised for an even more meritorious attitude than little Denmark whose example demonstrated the possible actions when governments deep down adopted only a hypocritically complicit attitude.[48]

As agreed, Heinrich Grüber was called to the stand as one of the Righteous among the Nations. He expressed his desire that "these proceedings also contribute not only to clearing up the relations between Israel and Germany, but to helping humanity, humaneness."[49]

Such mentions during the trial were more sporadic as regards Eastern Europe. In his summary of the proceedings, Attorney General Gideon Hausner drew up a systematic list of the helpful non-Jews that he qualified as "Righteous among the Nations." No name was given; only nationalities were indicated, thereby underscoring the desire to establish a link between rescuer countries and countries that were friends of the state of Israel. Particular care was taken not to omit any of the countries that might have been involved:

> In the dark, horrible night which descended on Europe with Hitler's rise to power, there were also some rays of light. And the Jewish people will not forget its benefactors, just as it does not forget its mortal enemies. To this very day we speak with gratitude and admiration of the ancient Persian king, Cyrus, who made it possible for the exiles to return to their country. And we shall always remember those benefactors who tried to save at least a few. We shall never forget the noble-minded people of Denmark, the entire people, who labored at the risk of their lives, in order to save the Jews of Denmark. We shall never forget the kindness extended to us by the Royal house of Belgium, and by the Belgian underground, which tried to blow up trains in order to save Jews from deportation. We shall remember the Norwegian underground, which smuggled Jews into Sweden, while endangering their lives. We remember

> with gratitude how the Swedes granted asylum, and how their great son, Raoul Wallenberg, saved thousands of Jews in Hungary. We shall remember the French underground, which saved Jews. We shall not forget the Dutch people's show of solidarity when it put on the "mark of shame," as well as the strike it proclaimed in order to show its solidarity with the Jews, and the efforts of the Dutch Church, which acted openly, exposing itself to great danger. Nor shall we forget the Italian officials who thwarted Mussolini's evil designs, the priests in the Italian monasteries, and the simple people in that country, many of whom stood by the persecuted Jews. And those kindly Poles who were hiding Jews right in the middle of the valley of death, under fearful danger, braving the wave of hellish hate which enveloped all Poland; there were others also, there was the Polish underground, and there were ordinary people who helped, who concealed, who saved, who kept others alive. In Lithuania, also, we have heard about such people, we have heard about farmers' wives to whom Jewish mothers passed their children across the fence: "Please hide them until the storm blows over!"
>
> In Germany itself we heard about Dr. Grueber and his friends, about the spiritual efforts and the physical, deadly dangers braved by those who believed in man and in love for one's fellowmen, and they were inside Germany, they were common folk, as Grueber said, people who created an underground movement, one of whose aims was saving Jews. And since we do not condemn the righteous with the wicked—we shall know how to count the few just men from sinful Sodom. . . . And to end this chapter, Your Honors, I should like to mention what I may have left out before, when I spoke of the righteous gentiles in other countries: the Yugoslavs, the Greeks, and all those lovers of humanity in the conquered countries who fought against Satan at the risk of their lives, in order to save human beings from death.

As he concluded his summary, Gideon Hausner returned to his list of the Righteous to rectify an omission:

> And now a few comments in conclusion. I have been reminded that, among the list of satellite countries which stood later in the breach, and did not hand over the Jews, although at first they had cooperated in the crimes, there was also Bulgaria, and I have to mention this in order not to remain indebted to it. And I must also mention the German Grüber who intervened in order to save Jews, and whose deposition has been submitted to you here—the fearful description of executions by the Special Operations Units—I have to mention this.

To which presiding judge Landau replied, "If you wish to complete the list of these states, you must also mention Romania." Gideon Hausner acquiesced, expounding on this last example before again concluding on the fact that "in the end, despite the disaster which befell the Jews of that country in the camps of Transnistria, a large part was saved. Tens of thousands died, but hundreds of thousands were saved."[50] The purpose of citing the Righteous among the Nations at the Eichmann trial was not solely to mention the figure of Heinrich Grüber. The term was deliberately uttered by the attorney general as a veritable instrument of foreign policy. In that regard, in conducting the Eichmann trial, the Israeli government was driven by the same intent that Mordechai Shenhabi expressed when he envisioned the commemoration of the "Righteous among the Nations" in the 1940s.

The reactivation of an instrument of public action and the opening of a political window

The return to the instrumentation of this category, in spite of the discontinuity of the actors, stems from the diplomatic context of the Eichmann trial. As was the case in 1940, although under different circumstances and unlike in 1953, this event was problematic for Israel's diplomatic relations. Mentioning and commemorating the Righteous among the Nations seemed at the time to be an instrument that could provide a partial solution. Both the problem—improving Israel's foreign relations—and one of its possible solutions—honoring the Righteous—already existed in the 1940s. But at the time, the political structure of an embryonic state with no formal status was not conducive to effectively implementing a public policy to commemorate the Righteous among the Nations. In 1963, the creation of a concrete procedure for nominating the Righteous indicates that a change had occurred. Which actors—political, social, or in public opinion—took advantage of the opening of a window of opportunity for the promotion of an administration in charge of commemorating the Righteous?

Prior to the trial, the Yad Vashem Institute and the attorney general's office worked together closely to prepare the court sessions.[51] A number of individual and institutional reactions to the trial ended up finally prompting the Yad Vashem Institute directorate to implement this particular commemorative mission. These unexpected reactions were all in keeping with the event in that they suggested using recognition of the Righteous as a diplomatic instrument.[52] As soon as Adolf Eichmann's capture and upcoming trial were announced, the government and the Yad Vashem Institute received phone calls and letters requesting recognition of the merits of the Righteous among the Nations.[53] In March 1961, for instance, a British Jewish woman wrote to Ben-Gurion to recount the deeds of her fellow countryman Charles Coward, who helped Jews inside the Auschwitz camp. In so doing, she expressed her feeling of symbolically belonging to the Hebrew state and her desire to see it enjoy international standing. She thus asked:

> Would it not be appropriate for our country to show its gratitude by a trip to its sunny coast—with VIP treatment—a word from you, favorable travel conditions, a visit of the country? . . . The state of Israel should reward such noble acts. All great states have their own methods to show "gratitude for services rendered." I'm sure that we are not lacking them.[54]

Her diplomatic request was exemplary of other letters received and was sent on to Yad Vashem.

However, the pressure placed on the Institute mainly came from outside institutional initiatives that were perceived as competitors. One member of the Yad Vashem Directorate summed up the situation in 1962, "Until now no institution showed any concern for the Righteous, and now suddenly everyone's interested in them."[55] Events had occasionally been organized in the United States to honor the memory of non-Jews who helped the Jews during the Holocaust in the past,[56] and the American Jewish Joint Distribution Committee founded the Institute for Righteous Acts.[57] But the principal competing initiative came from the World Jewish Congress. During its plenary session in August 1961 in Geneva, it announced the creation of the World Council of Righteous among the Nations[58], with a mission to honor the memory of these rescuers. Its members came from the Jewish Diaspora but also and especially the Israeli government and political personnel, such as the presidents of Israel and the Knesset.[59] The stated intention of its backers was also rooted in foreign policy and the need, following the Eichmann trial, to restore dialogue between Israel and foreign, particularly European, countries. In May 1962, Yad Vashem president Aryeh Kubovy expressed before his board his hostility toward the congressional project:

> Mr. Reiss, member of the World Jewish Congress, contacted me and told me that in August 1961 the organization had decided to set up a World Council of Righteous among the Nations. I'd read about it at the time but didn't give it much thought. By law it is our duty to take care of those who rescued Jews.[60]

A year earlier, in May 1961, Aryeh Kubovy himself had turned to the initiatives of the American Jewish organizations for inspiration.[61] The urgency with which the concrete modalities of commemorating the Righteous were decided indicates that they were conceived by an institution first of all seeking to assert its specificity and defend its territory. As one of its officials told the president of the World Jewish Congress in 1963: "Yad Vashem is inflexible as regards its prerogatives in relation to the question of the Righteous among the Nations."[62] Although the paragraph in the law of 19 August 1953 instituting the title Righteous holds a minor place and does not make use of the diplomatic instrumentation imagined by Mordechai Shenhabi, it remains the principal justification for the Yad Vashem Directorate's claim to have the exclusive prerogative of recognizing the Righteous. The Institute thus, to its own benefit, closed the political window opened by holding the Eichmann trial.

In February 1962, Yad Vashem created an administrative department dedicated to the mission of commemorating the Righteous. David Alcalay, already the head of a large department,[63] was made its director. Established primarily to occupy ground that others had sought to invest, the new "department of the Righteous" took time to determine the concrete modalities of its activities. First they agreed to plant a tree in the name of each Righteous person as a symbol of the Institute's new mission. By this choice, the Yad Vashem Directorate highlighted its specificity with regard to the World Jewish Congress, which, in view of its status as a transnational organization, had no sovereign territory on which to proceed solemnly with such plantings. More fundamentally, by this decision, a long-standing national insignia with patriotic connotations was invoked.

In Israel, "trees carried an even greater symbolic value: they became an icon of national revival, symbolizing the Zionist success in 'striking roots' in the ancient homeland."[64] This choice further reflected the political decision to use state action with the Righteous as an instrument of foreign policy. In 1962, the Jewish National Fund had been planting forests in memory of the dead for years.[65] Yet, although the Fund was a Yad Vashem trustee, the Institute's Directorate did not call on its expertise. Now wishing to assert its prerogatives in the disputed question of commemorating the Righteous, the Institute acted alone to establish an Avenue of the Righteous[66] and thus reinforce its role.

The government approved each stage of the implementation of the new public action. The director general of the Ministry of Foreign Affairs was in charge of the dossier, while the selection of the Righteous for the inauguration of the Avenue of the Righteous involved teams in charge of external relations for the prime minister's office.[67] The choice of persons to be honored was a political decision made by the president of Yad Vashem and ratified by its executive board.[68] Their personality was not taken into account at the time because ultimately they were merely representatives of their country. At that stage, the policy set in motion had to do mainly with foreign relations and not with memory and remembrance.

The only criterion retained was that of the presence of the Righteous on Israeli soil. The awardees had to be able to attend the planting of their tree so as to make the inauguration of the avenue a media event.[69] Selection was thus carried out in a makeshift fashion. When it was not done by word of mouth, names were drawn from newspapers or requested from associations whose members lived in Israel but who came from former European communities. Out of the twelve people selected, half lived permanently in Israel. The others, most of them Polish, sojourned there by invitation from the Jews they had rescued.

The Avenue of the Righteous was inaugurated on 1 May 1962, Yom HaShoah. The eleven Righteous chosen were referred to by their nationality: on the plaque placed beneath their tree their country of origin was specified next to their name. Fifteen years after Mordechai Shenhabi had drawn her attention to the question, Golda Meir, who had since become minister of foreign affairs, represented the Israeli executive.[70] The decision to create an Avenue of the Righteous on the premises of Yad Vashem gave rise to a new instrument of foreign policy.

Controversy and amendments to the public action

The list of the Righteous at first included twelve names. Arriving in Israel a few days beforehand to plant his tree,[71] Oskar Schindler was not present at the ceremony.[72] His case had become the object of controversy. While some of those he had helped accused him of financial opportunism, others considered him to be an extraordinary rescuer, a controversy that put the Yad Vashem Directorate and the Israeli government in an uncomfortable position.[73] The prime minister intervened directly to try to reach a consensus,[74] but the scandal was such that official recognition of Oskar Schindler was delayed. He had to wait one week in order to plant his tree with the utmost discretion.

This episode prompted the government to alter its procedures. On 10 July 1962, the Yad Vashem president acknowledged it publicly: "Doubts have been expressed in some cases and since we envision publishing a Dictionary of the Righteous among the Nations, we have decided to set up a commission to assess the merits of each individual case."[75] One week later, during a meeting of the Institute Directorate, he more clearly explained the role the controversy surrounding the Schindler case played in changing the modalities of this new public action: "Up to now we have assumed that if survivors invite their rescuers to Israel and nominate them as Righteous persons, their request should be accepted. The resulting situation is rather awkward and we must avoid another Oskar Schindler case."[76]

Commemoration of the Righteous could not remain a political decision made in the framework of Israeli foreign policy.[77] The memory of gratitude to an individual or group was no longer enough to legitimate official recognition, a pretext for diplomatic action. Yad Vashem's use of the category Righteous among the Nations henceforth had to take into account the full depth of different social actors' memories of and viewpoints on the past, even if they happened to diverge.

To put an end to the controversy, Yad Vashem set up a commission functioning according to collegial principles. Moshe Landau, formerly the presiding judge of the Eichmann trial, became its chairman.[78] While waiting for it to be established officially, administrators continued to decide tree plantings. They continued down the avenue as eminent non-Jews who had helped Jews visited the country. In August 1962, the visit of French member for Parliament Eugène Van Der Meersch was handled directly by the Ministry of Foreign Affairs.[79] In September, the announcement of the upcoming visit of the director general of the Belgian Foreign Affairs Ministry induced his Israeli counterpart to organize the planting of a tree in his name.[80]

These diplomatic tree plantings became more frequent as the process of putting together the Commission was protracted. In opposition to those who believed care should be taken so that most of its members were knowledgeable about the Holocaust, especially members of survivor organizations, were those who believed specialists were not essential. The Commission's primary role was to determine the criteria for designating the Righteous. Its members should have the ability to judge. Specialists could be called on to give an opinion on a case by case basis depending on the context.[81] The Commission's final makeup, like the debates taking place within it, reflected its status: halfway between memory and justice.

On the grounds that the Ministry of Foreign Affairs "was closely linked with this business of the Righteous among the Nations,"[82] it was immediately decided that a ministry official would sit on the Commission. The Yad Vashem Directorate also had to accept the presence of a representative from the World Jewish Congress, with which an agreement was signed stipulating that Congress would be responsible only for providing financial aid to needy Righteous.[83] In order for the Commission to reach a consensus that would bring the controversy surrounding the Schindler case to a close, the government appointed six members of survivor organizations, deported and partisans, and five practitioners of the law, either judges or lawyers, to sit alongside the institutional representatives.[84] With the former presiding judge and attorney general of the Eichmann trial in its ranks, the Commission for the Designation of the Righteous among the Nations had the appearance of a tribunal and seemed to be a true corollary of the Beit Haam courtroom. It held its first meeting on 1 February 1963.

The government's decision, nearly ten years later, to assume responsibility for the mission of commemorating the Righteous that had been attributed to Yad Vashem by the Knesset in 1953 was obviously a complex and serpentine process. It was made possible by the existence of a window of opportunity that up until then had remained partly closed. At the time it was established, the members of the Designation Commission shared the government's aim of making the title Righteous an instrument of foreign policy.

Forty years later, Moshe Landau still considered this mission to be a diplomatic consequence of the trial: "I accepted the responsibility because after Eichmann's sentence, I considered it necessary to restore equilibrium to the international climate. We had to show that we did not look upon the world around us with hostility but that we would be capable of distinguishing between those who had persecuted us and those who had helped us."[85] The fact nevertheless remains that due to its collegial nature, the existence of a structure for collective deliberation established a new field of public action that was potentially distinct from the foreign policy of which the title Righteous could no longer be merely an instrument.

From political decision making to public policy implementation

"The further one moves from the public decision, the less what occurs is suited to analysis of public policy."[86] Conversely, it seems reasonable that the further back in time the original decision goes, the better the researcher can grasp the social substance of the public action and view implementation of the policy as a process in which interactions between actors both within and outside the public sphere play a driving role. What were the factors involved in the decisions made by the Commission for the Designation of the Righteous among the Nations? And, correlatively, what remained of the initial diplomatic objective once the Commission was set up?

Instrumentation of public action and instrumentalization of memory

The title Righteous among the Nations took a more formal shape once the Commission set to work. In addition to planting a tree, recognition entitled the Righteous person to a medal and a certificate of honor issued exclusively by the Ministry of Foreign Affairs.[87] On 1 February 1963, at the Commission's inaugural session, the Yad Vashem president reiterated the government's diplomatic intention. He intended to point the way for the experts who agreed to take part:

> I have heard that some are afraid that recognizing a large number of Righteous would give younger generations the feeling that other nations were heroes, unlike the Jewish people. But I believe that here we have a great opportunity to cherish these people. Furthermore, it is important from a political standpoint. By cherishing them, we will then become a friend of their friends and their country.[88]

Two years later, in 1965, he continued to take pride in the fact that bestowal of this distinction would potentially create "thousands of friends" that would "give rise to love and respect for Israel." But this time he expressed his regret at not being able to honor the Ministry of Foreign Affairs' request to grant the title to eminent visitors.[89] The initial political decision to make the title Righteous a diplomatic instrument ran up against the limits of implementing public action. As Philip Selznick observed with regard to the Tennessee Valley Authority,[90] the process of institutionalizing the commemoration of the Righteous altered the goals set by the original political decision. Once formed, and in the absence of any real legal codification, the Commission claimed its total independence.

Its members managed to decide according to their conscience and usually notwithstanding pressure from the government or from the Institute's executive board.[91] Refusing to lay down a priori recognition criteria, they adopted the principle of building the doctrine on precedent. In the wake of the controversy surrounding Schindler's attitude, the absence of financial reward was quickly added to the legal criterion of having taken a risk as a prerequisite for nomination. A new codification gradually arose out of the Commission's deliberations that was organized on the model of court proceedings. The Commission demonstrated its members' resolve to rule on elements attested by direct "testimonies" of help provided during World War II. The central place given to memories finally made the "witnesses"—Jews who felt they had been saved—the unexpected users of this new category of public action.

The aftermath of the Oskar Schindler case is perhaps the best illustration of this process. Since May 1962, pressure was put on the Yad Vashem Directorate to rehabilitate Schindler's reputation. Finally, on 16 July 1963, during the Commission's first work session, the Institute's president pleaded in favor of the case. Moshe Landau and most of his colleagues nevertheless remained inflexible. Landau stated, "As a judge, [I needed] to hear both versions of the story to make a decision."[92] After hearing out the witnesses, the Commission favored the version that considered Schindler an opportunist motivated by financial gain. His nomination thereby escaped a directly political usage despite the repeated insistence of the Institute's president. Oskar Schindler was not recognized finally until 1993, with the joint nomination of his wife Emilie to the title Righteous and only one week following Steven Spielberg's visit to Israel to prepare the film that would make this German an international figure.[93]

The Commission's institutional emancipation from initial policy decisions made the political authorities gradually lose interest in this commemorative means, which had ceased to be an instrument of foreign policy. Ultimately and consequently, the little attention paid to the activity of recognizing the Righteous among the Nations by the Yad Vashem executive or by the successive Israeli governments meant that the Commission's independence was rarely put to the test.

Almost from the time it was formed, the Commission was not given the means to fully assume its mission by either the Israeli leadership or the Institute's sponsors.[94] As early as 1964, Moshe Landau in vain requested a specific budget so that Institute civil servants could conduct research and recognition of the Righteous could enjoy wider publicity.[95] Since that time, and despite the many changes at the head of the Israeli state as well as the Institute Directorate, the Commission's operating budget and the very existence of the Department of the Righteous has continued to be periodically called into question. The political authorities treated the work of the experts with such offhandedness that its president Moshe Bejski resigned in 1995, having been a member of the Commission since its inception.[96]

The evolution of the Avenue of the Righteous forcefully illustrates the process of political marginalization of individual and concrete commemoration of the Righteous among the Nations. In 1990, the Yad Vashem Directorate suspended tree plantings on the site set aside for this purpose.[97] Lack of space due to the deluge of nominations was argued to justify this decision. Plantings were replaced by names engraved on the Walls of Honor in what is now called the Garden of the Righteous. Five years later, the Institute's Directorate finally decided to limit and then to do away with these honorary engravings. Only the Commission's threat to bring the matter before the nation's court to settle the dispute made the Directorate back down.[98] Up to the mid-1990s, having been transformed by the collective management of the Commission, the diplomatic instrument of the tree planting, and the commemoration of the Righteous more broadly, was progressively abandoned by the political authorities.

The political authorities altered their stance, finally considering the Righteous symbolic figures and the term an abstract category rather than an institutionalized title over which they had lost all control. This redefinition alone was enough to make the mention of the Righteous a political instrument once again. The meaning of the term thus became twofold: the expression "Righteous among the Nations" refers to people recognized individually by the Yad Vashem Commission; and at the opposite, this lexical category is subject to a more political interpretation dictated by circumstance and thus liable to give rise to a variety of interpretations, appropriations, and translations.

This dual meaning appears clearly in the Yad Vashem Directorate's response to the request from the Israeli ambassador in Santo Domingo in 1993. The diplomat suggested bestowing the title Righteous on this state for having offered to accommodate 100,000 Jews in 1938. After outlining the official procedure for awarding the title Righteous, the Institute's president advised the ambassador to move the issue to the "political realm": "It would be preferable to address your request to the prime minister, who, when the opportunity presents itself, will publish a letter of recognition recalling Santo Domingo's offer to welcome Jews during a difficult time."[99] The use of the title Righteous among the Nations thus altered the very contours of the instrument of public action that it was conceived as.

Because remembrance policies are often considered a means of propaganda for a state that makes use of the past, it is striking to note that here the effective implementation of remembrance actions liable to channel memories was accompanied by a decline in the involvement of political officials. As soon as the policy no longer provided a means of pursuing diplomatic aims but instead mainly had to do with an institutional management of memories expressed by individuals, it no longer seemed to interest the Israeli government. By 1993, commemoration of the Righteous among the Nations was only rarely used for diplomatic purposes to foster rapprochement and dialogue with foreign states, even abstractly or symbolically. The government's and the Parliament's interpretation of the existence of the Righteous and the political role given to evoking them had changed.

Change in cognitive framework and transformation of the public action

Even though a number of memorial actions conducted by the Israeli authorities since the mid-1970s can still be linked to the foreign policy arena, they reflect a qualitative change as regards the signification such commemoration is supposed to assume. A Righteous person is now not so much perceived or presented as a channel through which to reconcile states, as a person who is well disposed toward Israel but isolated within countries that are hostile to it. As had been the case in 1953, it was the Knesset, in passing a new law, that would bring about the evolution of the political meaning not so much of the title but of the very category "Righteous among the Nations."

The "Message to the Righteous among the Nations," sent in October 1973 after the Yom Kippur War, is a sign of this evolution. Signed by Gideon Hausner, the former state prosecutor during the Eichmann trial who had become president of the Yad Vashem Council, this letter revealed a break from his oral summary at the Eichmann trial. The conception of the Righteous as physical persons identified by name, as isolated individuals in a hostile foreign environment in which they had to "make their voice heard," replaced that of partner states or at least of respectful interlocutors, which could be honored via their citizens who were Righteous among the Nations. This shift in meaning went along with a shift from the political to the humanitarian register in qualifying acts of rescue:

> Dear Friend, the state of Israel, where Holocaust survivors have found shelter and a homeland, is once again the brunt of a perfidious attack from the Arab states whose leaders once again state their aim to destroy the country and annihilate its inhabitants. The Egyptians and the Syrians launched their attack on the very day of Yom Kippur, the Day of Forgiveness, the Jewish people's most sacred day, the same day that the Nazis too, at a time when they dominated Europe, chose to step up their atrocities—deporting Jews to extermination camps and perpetrating mass executions in the ghettos and other Jewish population centers. In this hour of ordeal, we remember with gratitude that in the darkest days in the history of humanity you stood by persecuted Jews, risking your life, driven by a natural human sentiment. Your noble actions in those times encourage us in our struggle to live and maintain our existence as a free people in our homeland. From the bottom of our hearts we are convinced that today, as in the past, you stand by us and that your magnificent action will be a luminous example for many. In these hours of ordeal for the state of Israel, we are sure you will make your voice heard and express your support for us by all avenues open to you.[100]

The transformation of the political interpretation of the category "Righteous among the Nations" in turn reflects the deep modifications of the Israeli political class's frames of interpretation of the world since the Yom Kippur War.

> Proponents of *mamlakhtiyut* [statism] had claimed that the Holocaust and other instances of Jewish persecution at gentile hands were an inseparable part of Diaspora life, of no relevance at all to conditions in Israel. The new approach, however, saw in the Holocaust the prime manifestation of the gentiles' evil and hostility toward the Jews, which was now being expressed in their attitude toward modern Israel. . . . The statist approach maintained that "overemphasis" on the Holocaust could divert attention from the main task of fortifying and building up the state of Israel. It might also damage the state's vital interests in the sphere of foreign relations, particularly relations with Germany. According to the new, post-Six-Day War approach, which became even more popular after the Yom Kippur War, the very opposite [is] true: the best interests of the state [are] served by preserving and fostering the memory of the Holocaust among Jews and non-Jews alike. Such a policy reminds the rest of the world that it owes the Jewish people and its state a moral debt. . . . The doctrine [has been] further reinforced after the Likud came to power in May 1977. From this time on, the Holocaust [has been] increasingly appealed to as positive proof of gentiles' hostility toward the Jews.[101]

Beginning in the mid-1970s, and more clearly in the 1980s, the Righteous became, for both the Yad Vashem Directorate and the Israeli political leadership, exceptions to the general hostility of non-Jews and their countries toward Israel. Carried to its extreme, this view of the past led to the territorialization and the settling of the Righteous in the Hebrew state. As the procedure for bestowing the title Righteous was no longer considered an instrument of public action soon after it was established, such redefinition took other avenues.[102] In the Israeli parliamentary regime, as in 1953, Knesset members tackled the question themselves. In January 1985, a Likud MK tabled a bill to confer symbolic citizenship on the Righteous.[103]

The law authorizes "Yad Vashem to confer honorary citizenship of the state of Israel upon the Righteous among the Nations, and commemorative citizenship if they have passed away, in recognition for their action."[104] The provision was passed unanimously. A special commission with limited membership and this time mainly made up of state officials was created. The bestowal of citizenship was symbolized by a specific certificate signed by the president of Yad Vashem and the chairman of the special commission. In June 1987, the Parliament invited the Righteous living in Israel to the Knesset, where its members all rose in their honor.[105] Although this symbolic reinterpretation of the figure of the Righteous was favored by the Likud's having a majority, it aroused no opposition.

Israel's adoption of the Righteous went together with the institution of a social action program. At the end of 1985, a popular television program showed the poverty affecting the Righteous living in Israel and sparked a new controversy. Several bills by Knesset members of various political persuasions were tabled in response.[106] The government finally resorted to regulatory procedures[107] and granted financial assistance to needy Righteous.[108] Burial of the Righteous on Israeli soil is the ultimate form of national appropriation, which can be considered virtually a conversion.[109] In 1974, just after the Yom Kippur War, the Yad Vashem Directorate granted Oskar Schindler's request to be buried in Jerusalem.[110] In the late 1980s, with the rise in deaths of the Righteous, a special plot of fifteen vaults was finally allocated to them in Tel Aviv's main cemetery at the behest of the city's mayor and in agreement with Yad Vashem and the religious authorities.[111]

Israel's institutionalization of the commemoration of the Righteous among the Nations stretched over the period between 1942 and 1986. It was used by the successive governments as a means of defining the relations, and by the same token the boundaries, between Israel and the rest of the world. It wavered between recourse to a formal title and mobilization of a symbolic category, between foreign policy and memory policy, between the quest for a harmonious relationship between Israel and non-Jewish states and the emphasis on exceptions to the supposed hostility of non-Jews toward Israel.

Contrary to Peter Novick's remarks, Israel's decision, part of a process over time, cannot be tied to one or more discrete intentions. It was a complex process driven by interactions between political strategies, cognitive categories, and institutional configurations. The conclusions reached by James G. March and Johan P. Olsen as regards the development of political institutions apply almost literally to Israel's implementation of the category "Righteous among the Nations." It is "less a product of intentions, plans and consistent decisions than incremental adaptation to changing problems with available solutions within gradual structures of meaning."[112]

In 1986, the structure of the meaning that presided over the political mobilization of the category "Righteous among the Nations" made them Israeli citizens, while the official procedure for awarding the title Righteous as an instrument was neglected by the public authorities. This initial chapter takes stock of Israel's territorialization and appropriation of the Righteous, which seem radically incompatible with any public policy transfer in this regard. Yet in 1988, only two years after the law conferring Israeli citizenship on the Righteous was passed, the number of annual recognitions of French citizens underwent a significant and lasting increase, to the point of ushering in a new commemoration regime.

Notes

1. Michel Callon, "Some Elements of a Sociology of Translation: Domestication of the Scallops and the Fishermen of St Brieuc Bay," in *Power, Action and Belief: A New Sociology of Knowledge?* ed. J. Law, 196–223 (London: Routledge, 1986).
2. Unless stated otherwise, for greater readability the titles "Righteous among the Nations" and "Righteous" will be used interchangeably.
3. Gabriele Nissim's authorized biography of Moshe Bejski gives a partial account of the vote on the law of 19 August 1953; it does not take this moment as a specific object of analysis. Gabriele Nissim, *Il tribunale del bene: la storia di Moshe Bejski, l'uomo che creò il Giardino dei giusti* (Milan: Mandadori, 2003) and, more recently, Kobi Kabalek, "The Commemoration before the Commemoration: Yad Vashem and the Righteous among the Nations (1945–1963)," *Yad Vashem Studies* 39, no.1 (2011): 169–211.
4. Peter Novick, *The Holocaust in American Life* (New York: Houghton Mifflin, 2000), 180.
5. Pierre Lascoumes and Patrick Le Galès, eds., *Gouverner par les instruments* (Paris: Presses de Sciences Po, 2004).
6. Shenhabi Project, Yad Vashem Archives (YV), AM1/313. The Shenhabi Project has extensively commented on by historians, in particular, Tom Segev, *The Seventh Million: Israelis and the Holocaust* (Jerusalem: Keter Publishing, 1991). However, none of these historians discusses the article concerning the Righteous. For more detail, see Kabalek, "Commemoration before the Commemoration."
7. Letter of 23 April 1947, YV, AM1/293. In this regard, the king of Denmark symbolized his government's opposition to the arrest of Danish Jews, the large majority of whom were finally spared thanks to the population's mobilization. Jacques Sémelin, *Sans armes face à Hitler* (Paris: Payot, 1998 [1989]), 193–94.

8. Orna Kenan, *Between Memory and History. The Evolution of Israeli Historiography of the Holocaust, 1945–1961* (New York: Peter Lang, 2003), 45–47.
9. Bill no. 161 of 25 March 1953.
10. The Zionist Worker Party, which was founded in 1930.
11. The Israeli Communist Party, which grew out of a split with the Mapai in 1948. It differed from the Israeli Communist Party in its collectivist, Marxist ideology and its lasting attachment to Stalin. It rejoined the Mapai in 1968.
12. Founded in 1961, this group, one of the two ancestors of the Liberal Party, allied with Herut (the Israeli right-wing party, which was the ancestor of Likud) in 1965.
13. Statement by Yona Kesse, 229th Knesset session, 18 May 1953, Archives of the Knesset (AK), 25/s/2.
14. Minutes of the government meeting of 12 August 1953, Israeli National Archives (INA) and minutes of the Education and Culture Committee meeting of 27 July 1953, AK, 25/s/2, 1655.
15. AK, Amendment 162A to the Holocaust Martyrs' and Heroes' Remembrance (Yad Vashem) Law.
16. The Herut abstained; see Yechiam Weitz, "Political Dimensions of Holocaust Memory in Israel," *Israel Affairs* 1, no. 3 (1995): 129–45.
17. 296th Knesset session, 19 August 1953, Knesset proceedings; the full and exact wording of this paragraph is in the official translated version.
18. Eugene Korn, "Gentiles, the World to Come and Judaism: The Odyssey of a Rabbinic Text," *Modern Judaism* 14 (1994): 265–87.
19. Dalia Ofer, "The Strength of Remembrance: Commemorating the Holocaust during the First Decade of Israel," *Jewish Social Studies* 6, no. 2 (2000): 29.
20. *Shelilat ha-galut* in Hebrew. The term is preferred here to the more commonly used "negation of the Diaspora" (*shelilat ha-gola*) because—although it implies the same condemnation of the Diaspora now that the *Yishuv*, soon to be the state of Israel, existed—it does not consider the past of the Jewish diasporic existence worthless. Unlike *shelilat ha-gola, shelilat ha-galut* united all Israeli political officials of the early years; see Yael Zerubavel, *Recovered Roots. Collective Memory and the Making of Israeli National Tradition* (Chicago: University of Chicago Press, 1995), 21.
21. Yona Kesse, 229th Knesset session, 18 May 1953, AK, 25/s/2.
22. Pierre Muller, "L'Analyse cognitive des politiques publiques: vers une sociologie politique de l'action publique," *Revue française de science politique* 50, no. 2 (2000): 193.
23. For biographical information as well as the Latin spelling of Knesset member names, see www.knesset.gov.il.
24. For a suggested conceptualization of the conflicts and possible divergences between Jewish organizations and the state of Israel, see Shmuel Sandler, "Towards a Conceptual Framework of World Jewish Politics: State, Nation and Diaspora in a Jewish Foreign Policy," *Israel Affairs* 10, nos. 1–2 (2003): 301–12.
25. From an article in *Gesher*, a quarterly journal dealing with questions related to national life, July 1958, fourth year, published by the Israeli office of the World Jewish Congress.
26. Maurice Kriegel, "Trois Mémoires de la Shoah: États-Unis, Israël, France. À propos de Peter Novick, L'Holocauste dans la vie américaine," *Le Débat* 117 (November–December, 2001): 61–62.
27. Mooli Brog, "In Blessed Memory of a Dream: Mordechai Shenhavi and Initial Holocaust Commemoration Ideas in Palestine, 1942–1945," *Yad Vashem Studies* 30 (2002): 321.
28. Paola Bertilotti, "Italian Jews and the Memory of Rescue (1944–1961)," in *Resisting Genocide. The Multiple Forms of Rescue*, ed. Jacques Semelin, Claire Andrieu, and Sarah

Gensburger, 127–44 (New York: Columbia University Press, 2010); Rebecca Clifford, *Commemorating the Holocaust: The Dilemmas of Remembrance in France and Italy* (Oxford: Oxford University Press, 2013).

29. François Héran, "Rite et Méconnaissance. Notes sur la théorie religieuse de l'action chez Pareto et Weber," *Archives de sciences sociales des religions* 39, no. 85 (994): 144.
30. Pierre Muller and Yves Surel, *L'Analyse des politiques publiques* (Paris: Montchrestien, 1998), 32.
31. Bertilotti, "Italian Jews."
32. Minutes of the government meeting of 15 November 1953, INA.
33. Central Zionist Archives (CZA), Z6/1828. Regarding the Institute's early years, see Mooli Brog, "Victims and Victors: Holocaust and Military Commemoration in Israel Collective Memory," *Israel Studies* 8, no. 3 (2003): 65–99; Kabalek, "Commemoration before the Commemoration."
34. CZA, Z6/2030.
35. Created in April 1951 and set on Nissan 27, this day was formerly titled "Day of the Commemoration of the Genocide and the Ghetto Uprising." In April 1959 it took its new name of "Yom HaShoah," Holocaust Remembrance Day.
36. It was celebrated on 13 April 1961. Yad Vashem annual report for 5721 (1960/1961), CZA, C6/420.
37. Due to the crowd it drew, the trial was held in the auditorium of the new Beit Haam Theater in Jerusalem.
38. Especially Hanna Jablonka, *The State of Israel vs. Adolf Eichmann* (New York: Schocken Books, 2004); Hanna Jablonka, "After Eichmann. Collective Memory and the Holocaust since 1961," *The Journal of Israeli History* special issue 23, no. 1 (2004): 1–17; Leora Bilsky, *Transformative Justice. Israeli Identity on Trial* (Ann Arbor: University of Michigan Press, 2004); Shoshana Felman, *The Juridical Unconscious: Trials and Traumas in the Twentieth Century* (Cambridge, MA: Harvard University Press, 2002); Lawrence Douglas, *The Memory of Judgment. Making Law and History in the Trials of the Holocaust* (New Haven: Yale University Press, 2001).
39. Annette Wieviorka, *Le Procès Eichmann* (Brussels: Editions Complexe, 1989), 16.
40. "It would be unfair to ostracize all Germans in the world's public opinion," Dr. Adenauer stated with regard to the Eichmann trial, *Le Monde*, 12–13 March 1961.
41. Roni Stauber, "Realpolitik and the Burden of the Past: Israeli Diplomacy and the 'Other Germany,'" *Israel Studies* 8, no. 3 (2003): 115.
42. Nir Kedar, "Ben-Gurion's Mamlakhtiyut: Etymological and Theoretical Roots," *Israel Studies* 7, no. 3 (2002): 117–33.
43. Eliezer Don-Yehiya, "Memory and Political Culture: Israeli Society and the Holocaust," *Studies in Contemporary Jewry* 9 (1993): 146.
44. Reported in "Un Témoin français évoque les horreurs du camp de Drancy," *Le Figaro*, 10 May 1961. Georges Wellers was deported from Drancy to Auschwitz in convoy 76 on 30 June 1944.
45. "Le Cauchemar des Juifs français évoqué au procès Eichmann," *Le Monde*, 11 May 1961. The "protest by the Catholic clergy" alludes to His Grace Jules-Géraud Saliège's pastoral letter read on Sunday, 23 August 1942, in the churches of his diocese (pastoral letter of the archbishop of Toulouse, Toulouse, 1945).
46. Trial proceedings 34–36, Eichmann trial, Archives du Centre de documentation juive contemporaine (CDJC), DCCLV-34-DCCLV-36.
47. "Au Process Eichmann. Un Témoin explique comment le Danemark réussit à sauver la plupart des Juifs," *Le Monde*, 12 May 1961; "Eichmann. Trois Pays franchement hostiles aux menées antijuives: Danemark, Norvège et Italie," *Le Figaro*, 12 May 1961.

48. "Le Massacre des Juifs norvégiens, italiens et allemands au procès Eichmann. Un Grand Nombre furent sauvés grâce à la Suède et au peuple italien," *Combat*, 12 May 1961.
49. Trial proceedings no. 41, Eichmann trial, CDJC, DCCLV-41.
50. Trial proceedings no 113, prosecution's closing speech, CDJC, DCCLV-113, Dd1.
51. Annual report 1960/1961, CZA, C6/420.
52. On the various consequences of the Eichmann trial, see Anita Shapira, "The Eichmann Trial: Changing Perspectives," *The Journal of Israeli History* 23, no. 1 (2004): 18–39; Yechiam Weitz, "The Holocaust on Trial: The Impact of the Kasztner and Eichmann Trials on Israeli Society," *Israel Studies* 1, no. 2 (1996): 1–26.
53. Minutes of the Yad Vashem Directorate meeting, 2 May 1961, CZA, C6/420; memo of 31 December 1962, YV, AM6/946.
54. Letter from Mme Anne R. to the prime minister, 21 March 1961, Archives of the Yad Vashem Righteous Department (YVRD), File Charles Coward.
55. Minutes of the Directorate meeting, 31 July 1962, CZA, C6/424.
56. The American Jewish Joint Distribution Committee was the main architect; Archives of the Joint (AJDC), "Christians Who Helped Jews (Hassidei Haumot)," no. 4159. Currently known as the "Joint," it was founded in 1914 to help the Jews in Palestine and Europe during World War I; Yehuda Bauer, *American Jewry and the Holocaust: The American Jewish Joint Distribution Committee, 1939–1945* (Detroit: Wayne State University Press, 1981).
57. Institute for Righteous Acts. Documentation and research center on rescuers of Jews under Nazism, Statutes of the Institute for Righteous Acts, AJDC, "Christians Who Helped Jews."
58. Minutes of the General Assembly meeting of the World Jewish Congress, 20–23 August 1961, Geneva, CZA, C6/85.
59. World Council for the Commemoration of the Actions of the Righteous by the World Jewish Congress, Commemoration and Esteem report, October 1962, Tel Aviv, YV, 116 946.
60. Minutes of the Yad Vashem Directorate meeting, 15 May 1962, CZA, C6/424.
61. Minutes of the Yad Vashem Directorate meeting, 2 May 1961, CZA, C6/420.
62. Letter from Mark Uveeler to Nahum Goldmann, 11 March 1963, YV, AM1/1184.
63. He was already head of the Testimonial Forms Department, which collects pages of testimony, known as the DAF-ED, regarding victims of the Genocide.
64. Yael Zerubavel, "The Forest as a National Icon: Literature, Politics and the Archeology of Memory," *Israel Studies* 1 (Spring, 1996): 60.
65. Also known by the acronym KKL (Keren Kayemeth Leisrael), the NJF historically constitutes an executive arm of the Jewish people for the development of the Jewish state; Walter Lehn, *The Jewish National Fund* (New York: Kegan Paul International, 1988). Founded in 1901, it set about purchasing parcels of land. Together with the Jewish Agency, they formed the two national institutions of the embryonic state that was the *Yishuv*. As soon as 1945, and independently from the title Righteous awarded by Yad Vashem, some people also appealed to the fund to plant trees in memory of those they considered their rescuers.
66. Minutes of the Yad Vashem Directorate meeting, 15 May 1962, YV and JNF-KKL, 5/27270.
67. Letters from Yad Vashem to the department of inquiry of the Minister of Foreign Affairs, 29 December 1961 and the information center for the department concerned with foreign relations in the prime minister's office, 10 January 1962, YVRD, File Charles Coward.

68. Letter from Aryeh Kubovy to Martin A. Gosh, 31 January 1965, YVRD, File Oskar Schindler.
69. List of the Righteous found at that time in Israel, YVRD, File Alphonse and Emilie Gonsette, Belgium.
70. The analysis of the ceremony is based on two articles (*Haaretz*, 2 May 1962; *Maariv*, 16 May 1962) and two administrative documents (memo of 31 December 1962 by David Alcalay, YV, AM6/946; Minutes of the Yad Vashem Directorate meeting, 15 May 1962, YV).
71. More than three hundred of the Jews on the list, including Moshe Bejski, future president of the Commission for the Designation of the Righteous, were living in Israel at the time. See Nissim, *Il tribunale del bene*, 102.
72. "A Man from Cracow . . . ," *Haaretz*, 2 May 1962.
73. Memo from M. Karamish, 29 April 1962, YVRD, File Oskar Schindler.
74. Letter from the president of Yad Vashem to the prime minister's military secretary, 3 August 1962, YVRD, File Oskar Schindler.
75. "Time Is Running Out. Opening Address at the Fifth Session of the Fifth Council, 10 July 1962," *Yad Vashem Bulletin*, 12 December 1962, p. 102.
76. Minutes of the Yad Vashem Directorate meeting, 17 July 1962, CZA, C6/424.
77. While the Yad Vashem Directorate and the government were looking for a solution, other disputed cases came to light, e.g., YVRD, File Asen Ruben Dimitrov.
78. Statement by the president of Yad Vashem, minutes of the Yad Vashem Directorate meeting, 15 May 1962, YV.
79. Letter from David Alcalay to Aryeh Kubovy, 24 August 1962, YVRD, File Eugene Van Der Meersch.
80. Planting a tree on Yad Vashem Avenue of the Righteous by Leon Platteau of Belgium, YVRD, File Leon Platteau.
81. Minutes of the Yad Vashem Directorate meeting, 17 July 1962, CZA, C6/424.
82. Minutes of the Yad Vashem Directorate meeting, 3 July 1962, CZA, C6/424.
83. Letter from Aryeh Kubovy to Nahum Goldman, 6 November 1962, minutes of the Yad Vashem Directorate meeting, 17 July 1962 and 31 July 1962, CZA, C6/424. This aid was managed by the Conference on Jewish Material Claims against Germany, 1951–2001, 50 Years of Service to Holocaust Survivors, New York, NY, CJMCAG, 2001, pp. 13–15. At that date, and since 1963, the organization has spent 2,615,890 dollars (Claims Conference 2002 Annual Report).
84. Moshe Landau, before the public commission presided on by Aryeh L. Pincus, set up by the government at Yad Vashem's request to examine the Institute's tasks and redefine its goals, 24 May 1965, YV, AM1/1185/2.
85. Nissim, *Il tribunale del bene*, 117–18.
86. Pierre Favre, "Qui gouverne quand personne ne gouverne?" in Pierre Favre, Jack Hayward, and Yves Schemeil, eds., *Être gouverné. Études en l'honneur de Jean Leca* (Paris: Presses de Sciences Po, 2003), 264.
87. Exchange of correspondence on the subject between Donia Rosen, head of the Righteous Department, and Max Nurock, official at the Ministry of Foreign Affairs, 21 January 1974 to 5 January 1975, YVRD, File Jean Marius and Amélie Imberdis, no. 795, title awarded on 4 January 1973.
88. Minutes of the first meeting of the Commission, 1 February 1963, YV.
89. Aryeh Kubovy before the public commission presided over by Aryeh L. Pincus on 24 May 1965, YV, AM1/1185/2.
90. Philip Selznick, *TVA and the Grass Roots* (Berkeley: University of California Press, 1949).

91. Report, drafted at the request of Aryeh Kubovy, of the conversation between David Alcalay and Moshe Landau, 31 December 1962, YV, AM1/394.
92. Minutes of the Commission meeting, 16 July 1963, YVRD, File Oskar Schindler.
93. Minutes of the Commission meeting, 24 June 1993 and the meetings of 18 July 1967 and 17 October 1974, YVRD, File Oskar Schindler.
94. Statement made by Aryeh Kubovy before the public commission to examine the work of Yad Vashem, 4 October 1964, CZA, C6/428 and "From the Activities of Yad Vashem. The Public Commission for the Examination of Yad Vashem Activities," *Yad Vashem Bulletin*, December 1965.
95. Moshe Landau before the public commission presided over by Aryeh L. Pincus on 24 May 1965, YV, AM1/1185/2 and YV, AM1/1185/3.
96. Letter from Lucien Lazare to Louis Grobart, 26 December 1994, Archives of the French Committee for Yad Vashem (CFYV), "Correspondances avec Lucien Lazare, 1992–1996."
97. YV, AM2/1007.
98. Letter from Lucien Lazare to Louis Grobart, 3 July 1995, CFYV, "Correspondances avec Lucien Lazare, 1992–1996."
99. Letter from Yad Vashem to the Israeli ambassador to Santo Domingo, YV, AM2/1007.
100. Dated October 1973, signed by Gideon Hausner, president of the Yad Vashem Council, and Dr. Haim Pazner, president of the executive board. Starting in 1966, Yad Vashem in fact had a two-headed directorate (YVRD, File Suzanne Rodi-Boyer, no. 126, title awarded on 25 April 1965 and File Oskar Schindler).
101. Don-Yehiya, "Memory and Political Culture," 151.
102. A similar process is underway with the organization of school trips to Poland. See Jackie Feldman, *Above the Death Pits, beneath the Flag: Youth Voyages to Poland and the Performance of Israeli National Identity* (New York: Berghahn Books, 2010).
103. Bill drafted by Dov Shilansky, "Holocaust Martyrs' and Heroes' Remembrance Law, Amendment, Conferring Honorary Citizenship on the Righteous among the Nations," tabled on 7 January 1985, AK.
104. This provision was added to paragraph 4 of the second article of the martyrs and heroes law of 3 April 1985, *Knesset Proceedings*, also YV, AM2/1110.
105. Eva Fogelman, *Conscience and Courage. Rescuers of Jews during the Holocaust* (New York: Anchor Books, 1995 [1994]), 303.
106. Three bills in this regard were tabled between 6 January and 3 March 1986, AK.
107. Believing that the number of Righteous was too small to justify the passage of a law. Subsequently, four bills were nevertheless again tabled between 21 May 1990 and 30 May 1994.
108. The government officially agreed to assume this charge on 2 May 1986, YV, AM6/942. The World Jewish Congress then transferred to Yad Vashem a portion of the funds earmarked for the assistance of needy Righteous. In April 1986, Yad Vashem estimated that there were thirty-eight Righteous persons living in Israel. Letter from Mordechai Paldiel to Mr Livnat, 5 April 1986, YV, AM6/943.
109. In an agreement the minister of finance notified Moshe Bejski (chairman of the Commission for the Designation of the Righteous) of, 14 April 1986, YV, AM6/942.
110. Minutes of the meeting of 17 October 1974, YVRD, File Oskar Schindler.
111. Letter from the grand rabbi of Tel Aviv/Jaffa to the mayor of Tel Aviv, 5 October 1992, YV, AM2/1007.
112. James G. March and Johan Olsen, *Rediscovering Institutions. The Organizational Basis of Politics* (New York: Free Press, 1989), 94.

Chapter 2

Memory Entrepreneurs and the French Space

The shift of the "Righteous among the Nations" title from Israel to France

Since 1988 there has been a continual increase in the annual number of French nominations for the "Righteous among the Nations" title, and this has effectively marked the first stage of the institutionalization of the commemoration of the Righteous in France. Who were the people who revived this title? Who invested it with their own meanings and fought for its application in France from 1988? What were the nature and the cause of these individuals' mobilization? Once established, public action instruments are liable to provide political entrepreneurs with opportunities for action that vehicle dynamics of institutionalization that were unforeseen and unintended by those who conceptualized them at the beginning.

The relationship between social actors, memory, and politics has not attracted the attention of specialists in political entrepreneurs, interest groups, experts, or mobilizations, or other collective actors until now. However, certain authors, particularly sociologists and historians, studying memory rather than politics, have taken an interest in it.

Over the past fifteen years or so, a canonical critical reading of Maurice Halbwachs's sociological theory on memory has led to the emergence of a concurrent paradigm. The new paradigm shifts the focus from society and its representations (supposedly the sole scale and object of Halbwachs's thinking) to actors and their practices (seen as being of little interest to the author of *La Mémoire collective*[1]). This development explains the success of notions such as memory entrepreneurs, agents, and other actors of memory.[2] Michael Pollack, the sociologist and author of

L'Expérience concentrationnaire, was one of the first to coin the term "memory entrepreneur."

In 1990, he proposed a study of the "framing of memory" operated by "professionalized actors." Pollack set out to "follow Howard S. Becker's analysis of 'moral entrepreneurs' and, by analogy, [to] speak of memory entrepreneurs, who can be divided into two categories: those who create common references and those who ensure they are respected."[3] Other authors similarly speak of "agents of memory" to refer to those who "commemorate" and "control images of the past."[4] Reading between the lines, we can see that this raises the question of the political nature of this undertaking. Are memory entrepreneurs in fact political entrepreneurs? Inversely, are the policies that they aim to influence part of memory policy or other sectors of public action?

Pollack's conceptualization does not, however, provide a consideration of the processes behind the mobilization of these entrepreneurs or of the type of rationality that they implement. Jay Winter and Emmanuel Sivan partially address this question. They emphasize the leading role in recollection that is played by individuals determined to act. In so doing, they question the origin of these peoples' initiative: "He or she acts, not all the time, and not usually on instruction from on high, but as a participant in a social group constructed for the purposes of commemoration."[5]

Neither *homo pyschologicus* (a person of private memory) nor *homo sociologicus* (a person of socially determined memory) to whom Halbwachs is said to have paid exclusive attention, this *homo actans* is said to have a central and primary role in the evolution of commemoration as well as, ultimately, the implementation of all remembrance policies. "What is missing in the sociological approach is the appreciation of remembrance as a process, dependent upon groups of people who act over time. It is this collective enterprise through which *homo agens* creates and maintains. If rehearsal is the key to remembrance, agents count."[6]

Understanding the transfer of the category "Righteous among the Nations" from Israel to France supposes that we begin by identifying those who were the first to translate this term and exploring the nature of their involvement.

The mobilization of actors for the remembrance of the Righteous

In order to understand "the desire for memory" that can be expressed by states, political parties, or administrations, we must first ask ourselves who is acting: "which generation, which spokesperson and with what legitimacy?"[7]

From the mid-1980s, the activity of the Department of the Righteous at Yad Vashem regarding French cases went through an internal transformation due to the initiative of external social actors. This external mobilization put forward an interpretation of the Righteous category and pursued objectives that were contrary to the perspectives of both the Israeli government of the time and the leadership of the commemorative institute.

The group of Francophone Volunteers for the Department of the Righteous at Yad Vashem

In 1985, the year the Righteous were made Israeli citizens, several Jews who had previously served as witnesses for the Yad Vashem Commission decided to mobilize to obtain greater recognition for the Righteous in France and to increase public awareness. As citizens dissatisfied with the public action instruments set up by the state of Israel, they sought to influence both its interpretation and its utilization.

One woman we interviewed recounts the beginnings of her involvement with the movement for the commemoration of the Righteous in France in these terms:

> I remember having been to the embassy in Paris with a friend, Jacques Pulver, who knew that there were medals for the Righteous that had been sent, so files had most certainly already been set up directly with Yad Vashem in Israel. And these medals were lying in a drawer at the Israeli embassy. And very few of these medals were awarded because the embassy felt that it was not its responsibility to do so. And that's when things started to become more organized in France.[8]

At the beginning of the 1980s, Jacques Pulver was indeed interested in the title Righteous among the Nations, initially as a witness. In 1983 he put together an application for recognition as Righteous for the main person responsible for smuggling his wife and children into Switzerland during the Occupation of France.[9] Two years later, in 1985, his friend Denise Sikierski began the process of honoring the two residents of Marseilles who had helped her during the war.[10] On both of these occasions these two friends noted Yad Vashem's lack of interest in the evocation or concrete recognition of the Righteous in France.[11] At the time, Jacques Pulver considered it "absolutely inadmissible" that there were "approximately thirty medals still lying in drawers in the Israeli consulate in Paris (some for several years)"[12] because of the Institute's and the Israeli diplomats' lack of interest in this task.

Initially, faced with what they considered the "total indifference" of the Department of the Righteous, Jacques Pulver and Denise Sikierski organized a tree-planting ceremony for a French Righteous woman,[13] attracting as much attention as possible to the event. However, they rapidly decided to undertake more long-lasting action to change the situation and created a group called the Francophone Volunteers for the Department of the Righteous at Yad Vashem.[14]

These Volunteers gave themselves the objective of accompanying the witnesses (rescued Jews bearing witness to the actions of their rescuers) when filing their application and giving their testimonies. They began by renewing all the files that were stalled at the time.[15] Intent on making their actions well organized, they wrote and disseminated French-language instructions on "how to set up a file for the title of Righteous among the Nations to submit to the commission" and on the "details to include in the testimonies." In so doing, they formalized, for the first time, the procedure of the activities of the Commission for the Designation of the Righteous among the Nations.

The Volunteers worked hard to make sure the files conformed as closely as possible to the Commission's expectations and were thus favorably received as often and as quickly as possible. They also aimed to encourage more people to ask Yad Vashem to honor the memory of their French rescuers. In order to do this they wrote a leaflet that was distributed in all areas covered by the Central Consistory of France.[16] Its wording was explicit: "From 1939 to 1945, a great number of non-Jews risked their lives to help us or save us from the Holocaust. Testify!" Alongside this, Francophone Volunteers systematically contacted any person that they had heard, or believed, had helped rescue—or had themselves rescued—Jews in France during the Occupation.[17]

This group of Volunteers was also responsible for organizing the ceremonies in which the medals and certificates were awarded to the Righteous. They sought to transform this rare, semiprivate, and almost individual event into a regular, public, and collective commemoration. In Israel, the event was organized at the Mount of Remembrance, the Volunteers aiming to give it as much resonance as possible. In France, they sought to obtain "the maximum media coverage and presence of local, regional, and sometimes national authorities." In order to achieve this, the Volunteers systematically contacted the dignitaries of the Jewish community as well as French political and civil society leaders. As early as July 1986, and in order to make up for what they considered lost time, they organized a ceremony at the Israeli embassy in Paris for "ten medals that had been waiting for a long time and for significant persons" and another in the south of France at the general consulate in Marseille, where there were also many "long-suffering"[18] awards.

Shared experience, group reunion, and desire for action

Thus, at the end of 1985, several individuals came together to encourage testimonies and attributions of the title and to make the commemoration of the Righteous in France a major public event. Before determining the possible effects of this collective action on initial Israeli public action and on French political authorities, as well as on their possible hybridization, we first need to understand the nature and causes of this mobilization. This requires the analysis of the social positions of these actors and the type of rationality governing their engagement.

Born between 1910 and 1924,[19] the Francophone Volunteers for the Department of the Righteous at Yad Vashem were young adults during the Occupation, and in 1985 they were all recently retired. They were all born in France (with the exception of Jacques Pulver, who was born in Belgium and later immigrated to France), where they spent the duration of the war. Above all, they were also all former members of the Jewish Scouts and Guides (Eclaireurs Israélites de France) from the "Sixth" group, a clandestine civil resistance movement engaged in saving Jews[20]; so they had already participated in collective action together during the war. As such, they all had previously testified in favor of a French person in at least one application for "Righteous" status.

These individuals who decided to act on memory were thus from the same generation both in space and time as well as in terms of their lived experience. They had a shared past, which they also shared with many non-Jews, potential Righteous, who had accompanied them during the war in their fight to save their Jewish brothers and sisters. The imprint of this shared past thus constitutes one of the keys to understanding their decision to act together to promote the public commemoration of the Righteous in France.

However, the weight of the past is not sufficient to fully understand all their engagement. Indeed, the involvement of Jews from different Jewish resistance movements in the recognition of the Righteous in France was not a new phenomenon.[21] In 1969, some of them had already attempted to form a group to work for the nomination and the celebration of these French people, but without success.[22] Finally, alongside this, the individual testimonies of many of these future Volunteers—among them Denise Sikierski and Jacques Pulver—were unsuccessfully solicited in the 1970s.[23]

The 1980s can be distinguished from the two previous decades in that this was when the former members of the Jewish resistance were reunited. While the leaders of these various networks wrote their memoirs, one after another, they joined forces.[24] In 1985, the organization Veterans of the Jewish Resistance in France was created in Paris in order to "unite the members of the former Jewish resistance organizations."[25] Jacques Pulver became the vice-president and the representative of this group in Israel, particularly at Yad Vashem. The mobilization of Francophone Volunteers for the public recognition of the Righteous in France is thus precisely contemporary to this reconstitution of the network of former members of the Jewish resistance in France. It found its origin in this change in the social fabric.

Although the Francophone Volunteers did indeed constitute a social group with the goal of pursuing the common objective of commemoration, it seems that the formation of the group was initially based on the preexistence of a broader social group. Contrary to the analysis of Jay Winter and Emmanuel Sivan, *homo sociologicus* takes precedent over *homo actans* here. As was the case during the vote on the 1953 law in the Knesset, the social positions and trajectories of the actors structured their representations of the past and guided their engagements in the realm of memory.

Entrepreneurs and transmitters of memory

Cognitive factors—which are quite directly explained here by the evolution of morphological data—played a leading role in the original mobilization of social actors for the public commemoration of the Righteous of France. However, the fact remains that, once established, the group of French Volunteers indeed acted as "entrepreneurs" in launching the process. As a result, it is important to investigate the element of reflexivity these actors had regarding their action and, by extension, the nature of this action.

In describing the preparation of these ceremonies, Jacques Pulver made his objectives clear. Evoking the past was not an end in itself; it was once again to serve diplomatic goals. The situation he encountered initially seemed "prejudicial to the good reputation of the country" of Israel, while the organization of the medal-giving ceremonies had to show that "the people of Israel and the Jews are not ingrates." In other words "the efforts undertaken [were to] improve the image of Israel within the French population."[26] When Edouard Simon, one of Pulver's colleagues, organized an important ceremony at the Hotel de Ville in Paris in March 1989, he hoped that "with its particular prominence, it would be good for Israel."[27]

Rapidly, in view of Israel's lack of interest in the formal attribution of the title of Righteous, the consuls and ambassadors became concerned about the potential spending associated with the increased recognition of the Righteous in France. Jacques Pulver lamented this reaction. He expressed his expectations and his objectives like this:

> The Embassy has no budget for the "Righteous" and is worried about the expenses (?) that it will incur due to the flood of medals to award. [The

ambassador] has written to [the director of the Department of the Righteous] to ask for a contribution from Yad Vashem. Of course Yad Vashem doesn't have the money to finance the Ministry of Foreign Affairs. It should be the other way around, but there it is.[28]

It is striking to observe that these new actors' reinvestment of the public action instrument set up by the Israeli government in 1962 reactivated its original diplomatic objectives. In this respect the Francophone Volunteers weren't so much entrepreneurs of memory—although they shared their past and memories with each other and with the Righteous—as entrepreneurs of Israel's foreign affairs. These memory entrepreneurs were thus in fact political entrepreneurs whose instruments for action were commemoration and memory.

However, the meaning of this reinvestment of the title Righteous as a policy instrument was not perfectly identical to its original form. Unlike in 1962, the diplomatic orientation was not absolute here; it was only addressed to France. The Volunteers sought to become intermediaries between the public action of Israel and the public—but also political—space in France. Therefore they chose to publish the accounts of the ceremonies they organized in the review *France–Israel.* This desire to shift the Israeli category toward France appears clearly in Jacques Pulver's description of what he considered a successful ceremony:

Bringing together hundreds, sometimes thousands, of people, prefects,[29] members of parliament and senators, regional representatives, mayors from all parties, Resistance members and veterans, with the band playing Hatikva[30] and the Marseillaise. A parade through the town, with French and Israeli flags entwined.[31]

Once again the specific social and spatial position of the Francophone Volunteers helps explain the reinterpretation of the instruments and the objectives associated with them. Indeed, although the establishment of the group "Veterans of the Jewish resistance in France" played an important role, the resulting association did not accommodate the Volunteers' initiative. The Volunteers had their own singularities. They were also characterized by the fact that some of them lived in Israel, others in France, and most of them in both, working with partners from the two countries together.

In this respect, the national and geographic situation of Jacques Pulver is a good example. As the leader of the Volunteers, Pulver had a stable address in both France and Israel. His correspondence with his comrades is peppered with his incessant travels between the two countries. It is as though this double belonging was—among all his other characteristics—what made his action legitimate. It is systematically mentioned by his former partners in their interviews. Pulver is presented as the one "who lived half in Israel—and half in France, at the time."[32] Likewise, Denise Sikierski went back to live in Israel in 1979 (after several years in Brazil), but she only found out about the title of Righteous during a trip to France in 1984. Similarly, her engagement as a Volunteer led her to leave Jerusalem in 1987 to spend a year in France. The shift of the category of "Righteous among the Nations" from the Israeli context to the French context is mirrored by the geographical shift of its protagonists.

The mobilization of the Volunteers is thus situated at the crossroads of the Israeli space and the French space. The passage from one to the other is what inspired these individual political entrepreneurs to reinvest the title of Righteous with meaning. Thus, in the context of the Gulf War, Jacques Pulver specified to one of the Volunteers living in France, "I believe enough in the importance of what we are doing together to continue in spite of everything, and also in spite of my disgust for the attitude of *our* French leaders (or perhaps 'because of' it)."[33] Whereas the carefulness in organizing the ceremonies aimed to improve Israel's image, encouraging the increase in the number of attributions of the title Righteous to French citizens aimed to promote that of France. Although honoring the Righteous in other countries would have contributed just as much to the reputation of Israel overseas, it was not among the objectives that Pulver and his friends pursued—even when it concerned Francophones. If "the rescue happened in Belgium," "in principle it [was] of no concern [to them]."[34]

From 1987 on, Pulver evoked the fundamental role of his observation "of the insufficient number of French people among the 'Righteous among the Nations'"[35] in his commitment to this cause. In 1990 he discussed it again: "[We have] observed the shameful backwardness of France compared to Holland, or even Poland. A backwardness that we will not make up because in Holland, 2200 people were recognized at the end of 1989, and in France only 680. But we will do better."[36]

In the mid-1980s, a group of individuals thus decided to promote the commemoration of French citizens through the title Righteous among the Nations. Although these social actors had explicit objectives, it appeared once again that their definition and the means chosen to obtain them resulted from the social (and geographical) trajectories and morphological positions of the actors. The complex rationality at work from the very beginning articulated cognitive determinants and the pursuit of strategy, on one hand, and memory and politics, on the other. It is in this precise sense, and because the Francophone Volunteers were primarily *homo sociologicus* according to Winter and Sivan's typology, that they undertook to act upon memory and in so doing became engaged in the public action area of Israeli diplomacy in France and that of France in Israel.

The institutionalization of the term "Righteous" in the French space

It is now necessary to explore the impact that the mobilization of these Volunteers had on public policy in France and Israel. The Volunteers did not explicitly target French leaders with the goal of creating autonomous French public action regarding the Righteous. However, they did express, on several occasions, their desire to see the state of Israel become more involved in awarding the title of Righteous to French citizens.

The mobilization of these Volunteers was progressively institutionalized to the point of transforming the functioning of Yad Vashem itself, in terms of its nomination of French Righteous. Indirectly, and to a certain degree involuntarily, these social actors became the vectors of the transfer of Israeli public action to France, where it then genuinely took root.

The institutionalization of action by Francophone Volunteers in Israel

In a context where the management of Yad Vashem had given very little credit—literally and figuratively—to the Department of the Righteous, the Volunteers instantly received a warm welcome. When Pulver and his friends decided to take action, the director of the Department had been in place for three years. He gave them both encouragement and access to the archives. He found in them a new means of developing the activity of his department and, as in any administration, further justification for its existence. Moreover, like the Volunteers themselves, he had an intimate connection with the acts of which they wanted to preserve the memory. He was Francophone himself, having fled from Belgium to France during the war, where his parents, who had come from Poland, had found refuge. In 1988, thanks to one of the Volunteers, he found the French priest who had smuggled him into Switzerland with his family and was able to apply for him to be recognized as Righteous.[37]

Progressively, and with a certain amount of independence due to Israeli authorities' lack of interest, the director of the Department formally integrated the Volunteers into his team. They thus became an extension of the administration, although they were not an official emissary of the Institute. The Volunteers used the "Yad Vashem: Department of the Righteous" letterhead from as early as 1988.

The Commission for the Designation of the Righteous, itself regularly called into question by the management of the Institute, in turn came to give credit to these Volunteers. Two of them even joined the Commission as Francophone rapporteurs. From 1987, its president granted several Volunteers the authority to certify signatures and receive depositions from witnesses. Up until then, these acts had been performed solely by Israeli embassies or consulates. Pulver was also authorized to occasionally award the medals in France, in the name of the Commission, in instances when Israeli diplomats were unable to attend the ceremonies. Finally, from the 1990s onward, the Commission allowed (exceptionally and on a case by case basis) Volunteers other than Pulver to play this role. Thus, between 1986 and 1990 there was a durable reactivation of a public action instrument by a group of individuals in the form of the title Righteous. It was progressively institutionalized until it formed the French branch of Yad Vashem's activity in the commemoration of non-Jews who had helped Jews during the war.

The institutionalization of the action of Francophone Volunteers in France

However, this institutionalization was limited to the Department of the Righteous and the Commission for their designation. In 1992 the Israeli embassy in Paris still had little interest in its role in commemorating the Righteous, to the point where it lost several files. Pulver continued to hope, in vain, for a minimum of support from the chairman of Yad Vashem.[38]

The total lack of subsidies for the action of the Volunteers is one demonstration of the Institute's leadership's lack of interest. The Volunteers had to cover all the costs associated with their initiatives themselves.[39] On several occasions Pulver evoked the numerous practical difficulties he encountered in this area, before finally ironically commenting that soon he'd "have to clean the hallways at Yad Vashem."[40]

This situation emerged with particular force in 1988. In that year, Yad Vashem and the Israeli government decided to create an official representation in France[41] from scratch. Its goal was to "promote the creation of a French Committee of Friends of Yad Vashem, who would form a link between French Jews and Yad Vashem." Although the Volunteer group had already been operating for two years, this project was distinct in two important ways. First it exclusively focused on the relations between the Institute and the "Jewish community in France," whereas Pulver and his friends addressed all French and Israeli citizens (in keeping with their political objectives). Second, and as a result, the commemoration of the Righteous was not something the Committee was responsible for in the eyes of its promoters.[42]

The statutes of this new organization were registered on 15 March 1989 at the prefecture in Paris.[43] The French Association for the Remembrance and Teaching of the Shoah,[44] referred to as the "French Committee for

Yad Vashem," was recognized as the only official representation of Yad Vashem in France.[45] Its main objective was to collect funds to finance the major projects of the Institute, none of which concerned the Righteous. From this perspective, the Committee[46] was exclusively directed at Jews and did not really seek to create links with the rest of the population in France.[47] It therefore did not set up any partnerships with organizations outside the Jewish community, nor with the French administrations responsible for the commemoration of the past. The creation of this association was not intended to encourage transfers from Israel to France but instead to serve as a vector for transfers—both financial and symbolic—from France to Israel.

The formation of the Francophone Volunteer group and the establishment of the French Committee for Yad Vashem were thus perfectly contemporary. These organizations represented two independent and parallel extensions of Yad Vashem. In the first case, the extension was partial and informal. In the second, it was official and all-encompassing—except for tasks relating to the Righteous among the Nations, itself marginal within the Institute's activities. However, these two organizations would progressively come together to encourage the shift of the category of the Righteous from Israel to France. The analysis of this dynamic, which might initially seem long and straightforward, is fundamental for an understanding of the process of institutionalization that ultimately occurred as a result.

Starting in 1990, only two years after its creation, the Committee was faced with the Jewish community's lack of responsiveness. It became, in turn, an inefficient instrument for action and was liable to be subject to reinvestments and reinterpretations. The effects of the action by the Volunteers finally came to fill this void. Between 1990 and 1992, talks on a possible rapprochement were held between the leaders of the organization and Jacques Pulver, on one hand, and the chairman of Yad Vashem, on the other[48]; they considered the possibility of incorporating the Volunteers into the Committee.

Alongside this, also at the beginning of 1990, the Francophone Volunteers acquired a new recruit. Through the intermediary of the rabbi of the Mouvement Juif Libéral de France (Liberal Jewish Movement of France),[49] Jacques Pulver was put in contact with Louis Grobart. Grobart had been saved by a couple from the Grenoble region during the war[50]; now a recently retired pharmacist, he was looking for a Volunteer activity. Pulver thus initiated Grobart into the group and the "disciple" followed in the footsteps of his "master."[51] He took the place of Edouard Simon, who died in 1993,[52] as the leader of the Volunteers in France. Thus the socialization of a new category of these entrepreneurs began. In 1991, Grobart was officially appointed to his new mission by the director of the Department of the Righteous.

From 1992, following the death of several of the Francophone Volunteers, among them Jacques Pulver himself, the group was progressively dissolved. Only Lucien Lazare, still a Francophone member of the Committee for the Designation of the Righteous, continued his activity from Jerusalem, where he still lives today.[53]

As the French Committee struggled to make progress, and as some of its founders passed away, Louis Grobart found himself alone in Paris—the only one left to carry on the Volunteers' project. Informally starting in 1994 and then officially from 1995 on, he became a member of the French Committee, in which he created and directed the new Department of the Righteous.[54] This was also the year that the Israeli diplomatic services in France took their first initiatives regarding the attribution of the title Righteous. The communications officer at the embassy in Paris produced a brochure presenting the action of Israel and the Committee in favor of the recognition of the Righteous[55] to be distributed during the medal ceremonies in France.

Between 1986 and 1995 the mobilization of the Volunteers thus became more institutionalized. In so doing it transformed both Yad Vashem's use of the title Righteous in the French context and the official representation of the Institute in France. Benefitting from this new foundation, the project ultimately became independent of its initiators and experienced its own dynamic of institutionalization. Thus, although Grobart declared his own quantitative ambition—to "double the number of Righteous in France in five years"[56]—he did not express any of the political diplomatic objectives pursued by his predecessors.

The process led to a progressive transfer of the attribution of the title Righteous from a strictly Israeli space to a French one. This shift in public action relating to the Righteous can be clearly seen in the places that Pulver and Grobart respectively chose for the ceremonies to honor those who helped them personally during the Occupation. In 1984, Pulver organized a ceremony to honor the woman who helped his family cross into Switzerland,[57] and he had it held in Jerusalem, where he lived for half of the year. In 1995, his successor chose the French Senate and Paris—the town where he was born and still lives—as the site for the medal ceremony honoring the teachers of Isère who had taken him in during the Holocaust.

The establishment of a French configuration

The ultimate institutionalization of the Volunteers' activity within the official representation of Yad Vashem in France was accompanied by the organization of two successive ceremonies, held for the first time in a place representing the French nation as a whole. These events marked the beginning of this Israeli public action being shared with representatives of the French state. The French Senate was the site of a medal ceremony on 28 March 1995, as was the National Assembly on 19 January 1994. On this occasion the then president of the Assembly stood next to the Israeli ambassador to award the medals and diplomas to the Righteous who were honored that day. He then delivered a speech to thank these people for having "contributed to preserving France's honor, even as it was compromised by the Vichy government."[58]

As we can see in these two major ceremonies, even though the mobilization of Volunteers did not lead to a direct and formal public policy transfer from Israel to France, it did sporadically but regularly call on French public figures. It was thus at the origin of a process of their progressive socialization to the title Righteous and its symbolic potential.

Only the beginnings of this social construction of the title Righteous as a reference for the French citizens who helped the Jews, and for the period of Occupation more broadly, can explain why the project of the Volunteers endured even as those who initiated it disappeared. Between 1986 and 1995, the "Righteous" category was implanted in the French space to the point where it provoked interest and commitment and generated opportunities. At that time, a nascent configuration of social and public actors was being constructed around the title Righteous among the Nations.

Establishing the title Righteous as a reference category

The mobilization and the action of the Volunteers indeed produced several social effects. The first can be seen in quantitative terms. More witnesses turned to the title Righteous to honor the memory of those who they considered to be their rescuers. In 2003, Denise Sikierski said she was convinced that the Volunteers' action had an "unprecedented impact" in this area.[59]

There is indeed a strong connection between the date when the Volunteer group was formed and the increase in the annual number of nominations for the title Righteous in France. In 1990, Pulver himself remarked, "In the last three years, the number of French citizens recognized as Righteous has increased substantially thanks to our action. It meant ninety-seven medals were awarded in 1989 alone, compared to 310 over 23 years (from 1963 to 1986)."[60] As we have seen, in 1988 the number of annual nominations increased substantially for the first time, jumping from twenty-two to fifty-three. This turned out to be a long-lasting increase.

On 1 January 1987, the total number of French citizens recognized as Righteous was 434, yet it reached the figure of 3,925[62] at the beginning of

Table 1. Number of Righteous recognized in France, by year of nomination[61]

Year of nomination	Number of Righteous recognized in France by the Yad Vashem Commission
1983	21
1984	39
1985	35
1986	27
1987	33
1988	76
1989	153
1990	109
1991	93
1992	116
1993	94

2016. In the past thirty years, nearly eight times as many people have been honored as in the first twenty-four years of the title's existence.

However, from a qualitative perspective, the correlation cannot be made according to a mechanism for the trigger and control of memory but rather through a continual process of channeling recollections. The methodic publicity the Volunteers gave to the Righteous title neither created nor prescribed a narrative of the past, nor did it create a new memory. Instead it progressively made the title attributed by Yad Vashem a shared reference and a legitimate framework within which to discuss those who had helped Jews in France during the war.

The example of the attribution of a collective title to the village of Le Chambon-sur-Lignon shows this social channeling of memory that resulted from the Volunteers' actions in France. In 1979, Philip P. Hallie published the first book to tell the story of Le Chambon-sur-Lignon, *Lest Innocent Blood Be Shed.*[63] The review of the French translation published in the *Arche,* a monthly magazine on French Judaism, caused a torrent of letters from former refugees telling their stories.[64] On 17 June 1979, a plaque was erected in the village in the name of "the Jewish refugees of Le Chambon-sur-Lignon and surrounding towns."[65] This plaque ceremony had no connection to Yad Vashem, and this first public recognition of the past did not lead to the propositions for the Chambonnais to be recognized as Righteous. This honorific title did not serve as a vector for the expression of this rediscovered memory.

One year later, Pierre Sauvage made a documentary called *Weapons of the Spirit*. Sauvage was born and then hidden in Le Chambon during the war but discovered his birthplace only later, once he had become an American citizen. He made contact with other children who had lived in hiding in this village[66] and built a network of veterans of Le Chambon. The organization Friends of Le Chambon was created in Los Angeles in 1982,[67] with Sauvage as its president. At first, its organizers only rarely solicited the title Righteous or the Yad Vashem Institute as part of their activities. Although the Friends of Le Chambon did finally ask the Department of the Righteous to award a collective recognition to the village as a whole, they did not want to conform to the formal rules for the attribution of the title, which stipulate that only the individual recognition of a large number of village members could eventually lead to honoring the village as a whole.[68]

It was only the mobilization of the Volunteers that caused the title Righteous to become such an essential reference in channeling these memories from the private into the public sphere. When Jacques Pulver and Denise Sikierski observed the emergence of this remembrance, they produced a specific document "Former Le Chambon Refugee Questionnaire."[69] Overall, out of the sixty-seven people from the area around Le Chambon recognized on 1 January 2004, fifty-four (80 percent) had their nominations initiated and managed by the Volunteers. Moreover, the Volunteers had actively worked to obtain the collective recognition of Le Chambon-sur-Lignon.

The transmission of memory that was made possible by the action of the Volunteers led first to the installation of a memorial to the village in the Avenue of the Righteous in Yad Vashem and second to the towns of the Le Chambon area being granted a collective certificate of honor. This was awarded on 14 October 1990 during a grand official ceremony. Representatives of Israel stood alongside the Volunteers and the Friends of Le Chambon as well as the delegate for the Rhône-Alpes region of the Representative Council of Jewish Institutions in France (CRIF), the pastor of Le Chambon (a mainly Protestant village), the president of the regional and departmental councils, and the mayor of Le Chambon.[70]

The dynamic of institutionalization and the establishment of a specific French configuration

As the Volunteers slowly channeled the recollections of potential witnesses, they simultaneously interacted with a wide range of actors—most notably elected officials and state representatives. In so doing, they associated French political authorities with their project—on the occasion of these events—and progressively socialized them to the use of the title Righteous among the Nations.

Like the increase in the number of nominations, the increase in the number and frequency of ceremonies was also the work of the Volunteers. Between 1988 and 1993, forty-eight ceremonies were held in northern France.[71] In the space of four years there were 50 percent more ceremonies than in the seventeen years between 1966 and 1984. This evolution can be attributed directly to the system put into place by the Volunteers, who systematically organized a ceremony for each certificate and medal to be officially awarded. In their eyes, "anything is better than sending them by the post, or letting them collect dust in a draw until the recipients are dead."[72]

In addition to this quantitative evolution, the activity of the Volunteers transformed the ceremonies in qualitative terms. Ceremonies are now held in town halls and other republican sites rather than in diplomatic buildings or Jewish community sites—either cultural or religious. Out of the forty-eight ceremonies organized between 1988 and 1993 by the Volunteers in the northern part of France, thirty-one took place in a town hall or prefecture; only five were held in synagogues. Although many of them took place in villages and small towns, several town halls in major cities held these events too. The mayors invited all the local representatives, as was the case in Chambéry, Limoges, Grenoble, Lille, and Lyon in 1990 and in Nancy, Clermont-Ferrand, and Belfort in 1991. From 1989 on, the town hall in Paris was also the backdrop for major medal ceremonies; and in 1990 the town hall of the tenth arrondissement of Paris accepted the Volunteers' request, as did the town hall of the third arrondissement in 1991 and the town hall of the sixteenth in 1992.

Through the mobilization of the local public authorities that it provoked, the ceremonies and their organization began to turn the title Righteous (and the interpretations that it gave rise to) into a potential instrument for public action in France. Following the ceremony recognizing René Bessède[73] as Righteous, which was organized by the Volunteers in the town hall in Caussade, the municipal council of the village decided to name the market building adjacent to the town hall after him.[74] In this example, the title Righteous was literally implanted in the French landscape through a durable toponymic change.

The institutionalization and organization of the Righteous of France

Through regular but sporadic interactions with a wide range of social actors, among them public officials, the Volunteers made the title Righteous a widespread reference. In so doing, it became a marker around which a configuration of actors, interests, and interpretations emerged.

This mechanism can be clearly seen in the fate of the decision made by several Righteous to form an organization in the mid-1970s. During this period, some of the French Righteous joined together to assist the nomination of some of their fellow citizens. The statutes of the organization the Righteous among the Nations, French Section were registered at the Prefecture of Police in Paris on 21 October 1981.[75] The objective was to speak in the name of the French Righteous in order to "promote and preserve the spirit of all those who saved persecuted Jews, at risk to their own lives."[76] The founders were also involved in the friendship movement between Jews and Christians and the local sections of the France-Israel Society. However this double collective foundation was not enough to ensure the survival of this group. It failed to provoke any real interest among broader French society, particularly among public actors who had been contacted by the group. From 1983 on, the group had significantly declined.

A second group emerged in 1986. The statutes of this new association, the French Association for Yad Vashem: Marseille-Paris-Jerusalem, were registered at the Prefecture for the Bouches du Rhône on 28 August 1986.[77] This group was initiated by two Righteous from Marseille, and in 1987 they were joined by Jeanne Brousse, one of the founding members of the 1981 group. Her request for the transfer of unused funds from the previous organization to this newly created one demonstrates the proximity between the two projects.[78] Exclusively open to the French Righteous and their descendants, the French Association for Yad Vashem: Marseille-Paris-Jerusalem intended primarily to "speak in the name of the 'Righteous among Nations' when necessary" and to "honor, in collaboration with the French and Israeli Consulates, all those awarded with the title Righteous among the Nations.'" [79]

The difference between the 1981 configuration and that of the new group meant the latter was able to survive where the former had disintegrated. Although there were 167 members according to the president,[80] in reality the group was organized and run by just a few Righteous. Its activities consisted mainly of attending the medal ceremonies,[81] which provided an opportunity to speak publically in the name of the group.

In 1987, and unlike 1981, the French Association for Yad Vashem thus benefitted from the impetus provided by the Volunteers—with whom it was in regular contact. With the two projects mutually reinforcing each other through their activities, at the end of 1988 their respective roles began to crystalize within an emerging configuration of actors. While the Francophone Volunteers were responsible for the nominations and ceremonies, extending the activities of the Israeli Institute onto French soil, the French Association for Yad Vashem: Marseille-Paris-Jerusalem represented the French Righteous and organized activities that brought them together. Jacques Pulver recognized this mission when he responded to the proposal of the Reims rabbi to organize a national meeting of the Righteous in 1992, stating, "Above all, make no decision concerning the Righteous without the prior agreement of Mr. Beltrami and Mr. Grimaldi,"[82] the two Righteous in charge of the French Association for Yad Vashem.

In the mid-1980s, social actors sharing a particular experience and social position at the crossroads of French and Israeli space came together to demand the recognition of more French citizens as Righteous among the Nations. In so doing they shifted the Israeli category into the French context. In particular, these Volunteers sought to improve the image of Israel in France and vice versa. But they did not seek the creation of autonomous French public policy for the recognition of the Righteous in France. Although the request for sporadic participation by official representatives in the medal ceremonies demonstrates a form of belonging to French space, it was above all a means of attracting attention to the event.

In 1995, a Department of the Righteous was formally integrated into the French Committee for Yad Vashem, thus extending and formalizing the Volunteers' action. The year 1995 therefore also marks an important step in establishing the French context of the reference of the title Righteous. It marks the transformation of this title into a cognitive category open to reinterpretation, conflict, and convergence. From this point on, the term escaped the control of those who had introduced it into the French context. It became a social resource and the object of competing interests.

Thus, in 1995, the French Committee for Yad Vashem insisted that the French Association for Yad Vashem: Marseille-Paris-Jerusalem change its name to avoid any confusion. The latter thus became the Association of the Righteous of France for Yad Vashem.[83] This new title was the first appearance of the expression "Righteous of France." At the same time, the status of the Committee evolved substantially. It was now the object of increasing demands from correspondents of various nationalities, statuses, and social characteristics,[84] and French public actors appeared among them with increasing regularity.

Notes

1. For more details, see Sarah Gensburger, "The Righteous among the Nations as Elements of Collective Memory," *International Social Science Journal*, nos. 203/204 (March–June 2012): 135–46.
2. Gary Alan Fine, "Reputational Entrepreneurs and the Memory of Incompetence: Melting Supporters, Partisan Warriors, and Images of President Harding," *American Journal of Sociology* 101, no. 5 (1996): 1159–93; Robert S. Jansen, "Resurrection and Appropriation:

Reputational Trajectories, Memory Work, and the Political Use of Historical Figures," *American Journal of Sociology* 112, no. 4 (2007): 853–1007; Barry Schwartz, "Memory as a Cultural System: Abraham Lincoln in World War II," *American Sociological Review* 61, no. 5 (1996): 908–27; Barry Schwartz and Robin Wagner-Pacifici, "The Vietnam Veterans Memorial: Commemorating a Difficult Past," *The American Journal of Sociology* 97, no. 2 (1991): 376–420.

3. Michael Pollak, "Mémoire, oubli, silence," in *Une Identité blessée. Etudes de sociologie et d'histoire* (Paris: Métailié, 1993), 30. The reference to Howard Becker refers to Chapter 8, "Moral Entrepreneurs," in *Outsiders. Studies in the Sociology of Deviance* (New York: Free Press of Glencoe, 1963), 147–65.
4. Vered Vinitzky-Seroussi, "Commemorating a Difficult Past: Yitzhak Rabin's Memorials," *American Sociological Review* 67 (2002): 46.
5. Jay Winter and Emmanuel Sivan, *War and Remembrance in the Twentieth Century* (Cambridge: Cambridge University Press, 1999), 9–10.
6. Winter and Sivan, *War and Remembrance*, 29.
7. Marie-Claire Lavabre, "Du Poids et du Choix du passé," *Cahiers de l'IHTP* 18 (1991): 185.
8. Interview with Liliane Klein-Lieber, 3 April 1998, Paris.
9. Archives of the Department of the Righteous of Yad Vashem, DRYV, File Rolande Birgy, no. 2613, title awarded 27 May 1983.
10. DRYV, File Emilie alias "Hélène" Guth, no. 3210 and Hermine Orsi, no. 3211, titles awarded 29 April 1985.
11. Private archives provided by Fanny Wertheimer (Wertheimer Archives), particularly a summary titled "Medals and Certificates of Honor Awarded to the 'Righteous among the Nations' and Tree-Plantings at Yad Vashem," written by Jacques Pulver, 19 February 1990, addressed to Jules and Fanny Wertheimer by then new members of the group.
12. Letter to Emmanuel Racine, 29 September 1987, YV, AM6/945.
13. DRYV, File Marie-Rose Gineste, no. 3256, title awarded 24 October 1985.
14. Although this group had no other formal status than its informal attachment to Yad Vashem, it appears constantly in the files, particularly through the use of a stamp "FRANCOPHONE VOLUNTEERS for the Department of the Righteous at Yad Vashem." E.g., DRYV, File Georges Seurre, no. 3786, title awarded 28 March 1988. For the sake of readability, in this chapter the group is referred to alternately as the "Francophone volunteers" or simply the "volunteers."
15. E.g., DJYV, File Andrée Pelissier, no. 3781, title awarded 23 December 1987.
16. The Israelite Central Consistory of France was set up by Napoleon to administer Jewish worship in France. It remains the official representative institution for French Judaism.
17. E.g., Archives of the French Committee for Yad Vashem, Paris based, FCYV, File Roger Darcissac, no. 3905, title awarded 14 November 1988.
18. Wertheimer Archives, "Remise de médailles . . . ," 19 February 1990. This description was confirmed by several reports of ceremonies held between 1986 and 1993, which were addressed to other volunteers; it was also confirmed by interviews with Denise Sikierski, 24 June 2003, Jérusalem; Fanny Wertheimer, 2 February 2000, Paris; Lucien Fayman, 21 June 2000, La Cadière d'Azur; and various interviews with Lucien Lazare between 2003 and 2008.
19. The founding members were Edouard Simon, born 1910; Jacques and Monique Pulver, both born 1914; Lucien Fayman, born 1916; Alfred Lazare, born 1923; Denise Sikierski, Liliane Klein-Lieber, and Lucien Lazare, all born 1924.
20. The term "Sixth" refers to the organization of Jewish scouts called the Eclaireuses et Eclaireurs Israélites de France, the "Israelite Pathfinders." They were active in the operation of clandestine actions for the survival of Jewish children and adolescents in

France. The name comes from the inclusion of scouting as the sixth section of the fourth division of the General Union of French Israelites, the only Jewish organization authorized and created by the Vichy regime. "Les Eclaireurs Israélites de France dans la Guerre," *Le Monde Juif*, no. 161, January–February 1998.

21. From the beginning, when the official nomination procedure was created, many witnesses were former members of various networks. E.g., DRYV, File Magdelein-Louise Charretier-May, no. 473; Charles, Joséphine, and Gaston Baud, no. 1277; Antoinette Masserey, no. 1532; Zwolakowski, no. 200; Oswald and Léa Bardone, no. 579.
22. The initiative of Léon Poliakov, DRYV, Dossier Bardone, no. 579, title awarded 8 September 1970.
23. DRYV, File Pastor Jean-Séverin Lemaire, no. 1039, title awarded 19 February 1976; File Juliette Vidal, no. 518, title awarded 2 January 1969.
24. Léon Poliakov published *l'Auberge des musiciens. Mémoires* (Paris: L'Harmattan, 1998); Robert Gamzon, alias Worried Beaver [Castor soucieux], *Les Eaux claires. Journal 1940–1944* (Paris: EIF, 1998); Frédéric Hammel, alias Camel [Chameau], *"Souviens toi d'Amalek": témoignage sur la lutte des Juifs en France 1938–1944* (Paris: CLKH, 1982); René Kapel, *Un Rabbin dans la tourmente* (Paris: Editions du CDJC, 1986); Lucien Lazare, *La Résistance juive en France* (Paris: Stock, 1987).
25. Statute no. 7436 8P, 31 October 1985, Prefecture of Police, Paris, Office of Associations.
26. Letter addressed to Emmanuel Racine to be communicated to the executive president of Yad Vashem and the minister of foreign affairs, 20 September 1987, YV, AM6/945.
27. Letter from Edouard Simon, 4 March 1989, DRYV, File Pasteur Boegner, no. 2698, title awarded 21 June 1988.
28. "Medal ceremony . . . ," 19 February 1990 and again in 1992, letters from Jacques Pulver to Fanny Wertheimer, 26 January and 5 May, Wertheimer Archives.
29. In France, the prefect is the state's representative in a particular region; the corresponding administration is the prefecture.
30. Israeli national anthem, titled "Hope."
31. "Medal ceremony . . . ," 19 February 1990, Wertheimer Archives.
32. Interviews with Liliane Klein-Lieber, 3 April 1998 in Paris and Lucien Fayman, 21 June 2000, la Cadière d'Azur.
33. Letter from Jacques Pulver to Fanny Wertheimer, 12 February 1991, Wertheimer Archives. My emphasis.
34. Ibid. 29 December 1991, Wertheimer Archives.
35. Letter from Pulver to Jean Louis Trèves, 16 January 1987, DRYV, File Boccard, no. 3601, title awarded 4 March 1987.
36. "Medal ceremony . . . ," 19 February 1990, Wertheimer Archives.
37. DRYV, File Abbot Simon Gallay, no. 4363, title awarded 19 September 1989.
38. His mindset can be seen in his report of the Yad Vashem Committee, which met the day before: "Mr. Racine told his colleagues how the ceremony [in the sixteenth district of Paris] took place, and he emphasized the fact that this action in favor of the Righteous was the most important aspect of Yad Vashem's activities. He made an impression on the members of the committee but I am not sure that he convinced Dr. Arad [executive president of Yad Vashem]. But it is still useful and positive." Letter to Fanny Wertheimer, 14 April 1992, Wertheimer Archives.
39. "Remise des médailles . . . ," 19 February 1990, Wertheimer Archives.
40. Letter from Jacques Pulver to Fanny Wertheimer, 2 November 1992, Wertheimer Archives.
41. Letter from Emmanuel Racine to Sylvain Caen, 5 May 1988, FCYV, "French Committee for Yad Vashem" files.

42. Letter from Emmanuel Racine to Sylvain Caen, 19 May 1988, FCYV, French Committee for Yad Vashem" files.
43. Association Française pour le Souvenir, la Mémoire et l'Enseignement de la Shoa. Statute no. 89249 P, Prefecture of Police, Paris, Office of Associations.
44. Letterhead of the paper used by Sylvain Caen and the Committee until 1995, FCYV, French Committee for Yad Vashem files.
45. Letter from Sylvain Caen to Cynthia Haft, 2 June 1989, FCYV, French Committee for Yad Vashem files.
46. To help readability, the terms "Committee" and "French Committee" will be used interchangeably to refer to the French Committee for Yad Vashem.
47. Brochure published in 1990 by the French Committee for Yad Vashem, Wertheimer Archives.
48. "Medal Ceremony . . . ," 19 February 1990, letters from Jacques Pulver to Fanny Wertheimer, 23 March 1990, 4 May 1990, and 13 May 1990. Also a letter from Fanny Wertheimer to Jacques Pulver, 13 February 1992, Wertheimer Archives.
49. The rabbi was himself sheltered during the war by two Righteous, DRYV, File Georges and Juliette Allenbach, no. 4185, title awarded 27 August 1989; sermon of Rabbi Daniel Farhi, preached 7 April 1994 for Yom HaShoah, *L'Arche*, May 1994, no. 444.
50. On 22 May 1994, Louis Grobart obtained recognition for the teachers from Isère who sheltered him. FCYV, File Marie-Louise and Prosper Coiraton, no. 6121, title awarded 22 May 1994.
51. Louis Grobart's own words, interview, 30 May 2000, Paris.
52. Correspondence between Jacques Pulver and Mordecai Paldiel, particularly the letter of 20 September 1992, FCYV, "Correspondances avec Mordecai Paldiel 1992–1996."
53. Lucien Lazare, *Le Tapissier de Jérusalem. Mémoires* (Paris: Seuil, 2015).
54. Letter from Louis Grobart to Mordecai Paldiel, 1 May 1994, "Correspondances avec Mordecai Paldiel 1992–1996," FCYV.
55. A trained historian, Marc Knobel had just been appointed communications officer and made contact with the French Committee in order to improve their cooperation. Participant observation and interview with Marc Knobel, 12 February 2004, Paris.
56. Letter from Louis Grobart to Lucien Lazare, 18 March 1993, FCYV, "Correspondances avec Lucien Lazare. . . ."
57. DRYV, File Rolande Birgy and interview with Denise Sikierski, 25 June 2003, Jerusalem.
58. "Des Justes à l'Assemblée Nationale," *L'Arche*, no. 438, March 1994.
59. Interview with Denise Sikierski, 24 June 2003, Jerusalem.
60. "Remise de médailles . . . ," 19 February 1990, Wertheimer Archives.
61. See Appendix 1 for an overview of the construction of these data.
62. http://www.yadvashem.org/yv/en/righteous/statistics.asp.
63. Philip P. Hallie, *Lest Innocent Blood Be Shed: The Story of the Village of Le Chambon and How Goodness Happened There* (New York: Harper and Row, 1979).
64. *L'Arche* published them in April, May, June, July, and August 1980.
65. Archives of the Center of Contemporary Jewish Documentation (CDJC), DCCCIII-4, document no. 35.
66. Interview with Pierre Sauvage, 4 March 2004, Paris; also two anonymized interviews with individuals hidden as children in Le Chambon, 16 and 17 October 2003, New York.
67. The actual name of the organization is the Le Chambon Foundation. Inaugural interview for the U.S. version of *Weapons of the Spirit*, http://www.chambon.org/weapons_en.htm.
68. The vice president of Yad Vashem finally reminded them, "The attribution of the title 'Righteous among the Nations' is the jurisdiction of Yad Vashem, appointed by the state

of Israel. Yad Vashem will not have its attitude or its chronology dictated by an outside source." Letter to Pierre Sauvage, 18 July 1984, DRYV, File Magda Trocmé.

69. E.g., DRYV, Files Barraud, no. 3833, title awarded 28 March 1988; Abel, no. 3832, title awarded 28 March 1988; Heritier, no. 3792, 28 December 1987, FCYV, File René and Simone Cordon, no. 4021, title awarded 16 November 1988.
70. See, e.g., the report in the article published by Ilana Cicurel in *L'Arche*, November 1990. Letter from Jacques Pulver to Fanny Wertheimer, 1 June 1990, Wertheimer Archives.
71. The volunteers organized their activities by zone: the northern part of France, southern France, the Savoie region, and the Swiss border zone.
72. Letter from Jacques Pulver to Fanny Wertheimer, 3 March 1990, Wertheimer Archives.
73. DRYV, File Renée Bessède, no. 4423, title awarded 26 October 1989.
74. *Tribune Juive*, 23 November 1990.
75. Under French law, nonprofit organizations and community associations are subject to the Law of 1901, which requires that they obtain juridical personality through incorporation, which involves registering their formation at the Prefecture of Police.
76. Statute no. 55.336, Prefecture of Police, Paris, Office of Associations.
77. Statute no. 16.363, Prefecture of Police, Bouches du Rhône, Office of Associations.
78. Letter from Jeanne Brousse to the Prefect of Police, 21 October 1987, attached to statute no. 55336.
79. Rules of procedure of the French Association for Yad Vashem, Marseille-Paris-Jerusalem, Chapter VIII, Righteous among the Nations Group, Article 23, Paul Grimaldi Archives.
80. Interview with the group's president Ivan Beltrami, 18 March 2003, Marseille.
81. The distribution of circulars replaced the organization of a statutory general assembly. Circulars 1–12, from 1993 to 2004, provided by Ivan Beltrami.
82. Letter from Jacques Pulver to Fanny Wertheimer, 11 November 1992, Wertheimer Archives. This distribution of roles is also described in a letter from Jacques Pulver to Sylvain Caen, 30 April 1991, FCYV, file "FCYV."
83. Circular no. 4/96, Beltrami Archives. The discussions that led to this change are reported on in circulars 1–5, 1993 to 1997, The French Association for Yad Vashem: Marseille-Paris-Jerusalem, which became, starting in 1995, the Association of the French Righteous for Yad Vashem, Beltrami Archives. This request appeared for the first time in 1991.
84. Circulars no. 1–12, from 1993 to 2004.

Chapter 3

Memory Public Policy and Transfers

The translation of the term "Righteous among the Nations"

In 1995, the social configuration of the commemoration of the Righteous in France changed significantly. In that year, President Chirac paid a specifically French homage to the French Righteous among the Nations for the first time. He praised this France that:

> Is present, one and indivisible, in the hearts of these French citizens, these "Righteous among the Nations," who at the darkest moment of agony, as Serge Klarsfeld writes, at the risk of their live, save three-quarters of the Jewish community resident in France, and give life to its better qualities: humanist values, values of freedom, justice and tolerance, on which French identity is founded, to which we remain bound in the future.[1]

This discourse signaled a break with the policy of his predecessor, François Mitterrand, who in 1994 had refused to receive the French Righteous at the Elysée Palace (in the context of a documentary about the Righteous in Europe[2]).

This hitherto unprecedented use of the term "Righteous among the Nations" by the French head of state provided both legitimacy and opportunity that deeply altered the number, identity, and configuration of the actors involved in the commemoration of the Righteous in France. Through the interactions, shared anticipations, and mutual interests of these heterogeneous actors, this presidential discourse led to the sustained development of public action for the commemoration of the Righteous among the Nations in France. We will see in this chapter that it then ultimately led to the birth of the Righteous of France category. To understand the institutionalization of this expression it is necessary to explore the turnaround that occurred in 1995, by attempting to deconstruct the microprocesses that were behind the progressive transfer of this public policy from the Israeli state to the French state.

Two intermediary questions emerge here. Given that the commemoration of the Righteous initially appeared as part of Israeli foreign policy, what public policy sector was it associated with for the French protagonists appropriating it? Was memory a genuine object of policy this time? Or was it first and foremost an instrument for broader public action of which the area of relevance still needs to be established? In other words, what is the balance between instrumentation and instrumentalization? Between memory as an instrument of public policy and the instrumentalization of the past?

Finally, the existence of a formalized Israeli procedure for the nomination of the Righteous leads us to question the tools and means used by the French state to appropriate the expression and to propose a French translation of it: the "Righteous of France" (Justes de France). It is important to specify the mechanisms by which social effects can be produced by public action instruments that imply neither binding norms nor budgetary commitments.

The appropriation of the term "Righteous among the Nations" by the French state

Contemporary analysis of public policy transfers ordinarily emphasizes the role that global elites play in this process. As we saw in the previous chapter, the mobilization of transnational actors in the form of the Francophone Volunteers indeed constitutes the main factor in the shift of this title from the Israeli context to the French one. However, the appropriation of this category by the French government was not one of these entrepreneurs' objectives; instead, their commitment focused on raising awareness about Israel's policy of recognition. So how did the reference to the Righteous become part of the French political agenda? Given that transfers of this kind of public policy most often occur in crisis situations, to what extent does the use of the term "Righteous" correspond to the emergence of a public issue? Finally, and perhaps most importantly, how did the mobilization of this category become a possible solution for the presidency (which had previously refused to use it)?

Jacques Chirac's socialization to the term "Righteous among the Nations"

The socialization to the title of Righteous, launched by the work of the Francophone Volunteers that we described in the previous chapter, also affected Jacques Chirac. Of course Chirac was among the parliamentarians present at the National Assembly for the ceremony organized by the French Committee for Yad Vashem in 1994. But in his particular case this process of familiarization was not limited to this one occasion; it went back much further.

In July 1986, Chirac, then mayor of Paris, was invited to speak at the commemoration of the Vel' d'Hiv Roundup[3] organized each year by the Representative Council of Jewish Institutions in France (CRIF). In this speech he presented a reading of the events of World War II based on an opposition between the attitude of the state and that of civil society. While recognizing the responsibility of the attitude of the state in the deportation of Jews, he also paid homage to the "sincere sympathy of all French people, and their active solidarity from the moment it became clear that the Jewish families who fell into German hands were destined for death."[4] Chirac did not use the term "Righteous among the Nations" to refer to these French people who helped the Jews; in 1986 the action of the Francophone Volunteers had only just begun. But the interpretative framework that would enable the reuse of the title was already present in his discourse and representations when he was still the mayor of Paris.

The following year, in 1987, Chirac encountered the Israeli title for the first time. As prime minister of France, he laid the foundation stone of the French section at the Valley of the Destroyed Communities at Yad Vashem, and on this occasion he visited the Avenue of the Righteous. In 1989, once again mayor of Paris, Chirac was called upon by the Francophone Volunteers to hold the first major medal ceremony to be staged in France, at the Paris Town Hall. The speech that Chirac delivered during this ceremony already contained the elements—even the lexical ones—that would be used in the declaration of 16 July 1995.[5] In May 1995, when the president and his advisors came to power, they had thus already been strongly socialized to the title of Righteous and its symbolic potential.

Historical memory of the Occupation and controversy

At the time of Chirac's election, the situation was critical. The policy of remembrance that had been in place since the end of the war had been a source of controversy for a number of years. After 1945 it had traditionally emphasized the French Resistance as the incarnation of the "true France," to balance out the weight of defeat and collaboration. National heroes were thus defined by their engagement in armed combat and honored as such with the status of voluntary combatant in the Resistance.[6] Actions taken to help civilian populations, particularly Jews, were given no legal recognition. As recently as 1988 the Administrative Tribunal in Bordeaux reaffirmed that, although commendable, "the saving of Israelites threatened with racial persecution" did not legally constitute resistance.[7]

Yet since the beginning of the 1990s, this historical memory[8] of the occupation, this canonical narrative of the past (decreed by the state since the liberation) has been the subject of social contestation. As the prestige of the Resistance declined,[9] the question of the responsibility of the French state in the deportation of Jews became more pressing.

On 13 April 1992, the dismissal of the case against the former member of the pro-Nazi group Milice, Paul Touvier, by the court of appeals in Paris led to widespread protest.[10] Using petitions, these social actors, using the name "Vel d'Hiv Committee," addressed a solemn request for justice to the president: "On the occasion of the fiftieth anniversary of the Vel d'Hiv Roundup, 16 and 17 July, we ask the president of the Republic, the head of state, to officially recognize and proclaim that the French state of Vichy was responsible for persecutions and crimes against the Jews of France."[11] François Mitterrand refused to grant this request. This decision, as well as the Vichy past of the president himself, provoked a fierce controversy. The event crystalized the challenges to the postwar memory policy.

What had become a public problem was then solved. In February 1993 a presidential decree made 16 July—the anniversary of the Vel d'Hiv Roundup—"a national day of commemoration of the racist and anti-Semitic persecution carried out under instruction of the authority of the so-called 'Government of the French State' (1940–1944)."[12]

The establishment of this day cannot only—or even directly—be explained by the existence of pressure groups. In this case it does not correspond to the initial request made to the French president, which focused on justice rather than memory. In December 1992, however, the president of the CRIF continued to express his desire to see both houses of Parliament officially perform the recognition of responsibility that was expected of them. Yet the national day did provoke a minimal consensus. In this respect it seemed to constitute a specific public action instrument producing specific social effects.

Only the polysemy vehicled by this event enabled it to reach its goal. Although the president felt that he had not granted the request for the recognition of France's responsibility, those who had made the request were satisfied and declared they couldn't "ask for much more."[13]

While the creation of an official day of memory does appear, for the first time, to be a genuine instrument to resolve so-called memorial issues, and although it did appease the controversy, it did not break with the official narrative of postliberation memory policy. Yet in 1992, at the heart of the controversy, there was a different, and unsuccessful, proposal for a bill that mobilized a redefinition of the historical memory of the Occupation. Written by Jean Le Garrec, a Socialist MP, this text proposed the "recognition of 16 July as a national day to commemorate the persecutions and racist, anti-Semitic, and xenophobic crimes perpetrated by the Vichy regime."[14] Proposing a transitional official narrative, it recognized France's responsibility in the deportations but also simultaneously paid homage to the civilians who took the Jews' defense: religious authorities, humanitarian organizations, and the general population.

The expression "Righteous among the Nations" was not used in this context, but in order to reconstruct a dichotomous narrative references were made to the actions that render individuals eligible for this title. This dichotomy allowed for the simultaneous recognition of two visions of France: one that had a role in the deportations and another that was able to salvage the honor of the nation. However, in 1992, Jean Le Garrec (along with other French MPs) had not yet discovered the existence of the Israeli category or the symbolic potential of its possible translation to the French context. In any event, Le Garrec was unable to get the text past his parliamentary group, and his solution was refused.[15] The president's opposition to the transformation of the historical memory of the time meant that the bill was never voted upon.

Translation of the term "Righteous among the Nations" and the outcome of the controversy

In this context, the arrival of Jacques Chirac marked the beginning of a new era. Changes to the members of the presidential institution led to a change in public policy in this area.[16] The election of May 1995 in particular was characterized by the arrival of a new generation in power. Unlike his predecessor (but like Jean Le Garrec), Jacques Chirac was a child during World War II. This generational belonging, until then unprecedented in the presidency, led him to see the controversy in a new light. As leader of the Rally for the Republic (RPR) party, the political heir of the Gaullist movement, Chirac decided to put an end to the historical memory that had been one of the pillars of the culture of his own political tradition.

This decision meant that the president's advisors were confronted with a major difficulty. They anticipated a negative reaction from French citizens if they were presented with only the recognition of France's responsibility in the deportation. A positive counterpoint was deemed necessary to offset this reaction. The statement made by one of the writers of the July 1995 declaration clearly reveals the reasoning behind this:

> In fact, when [Chirac] became president of the Republic, Christine Albanel soon came to see me [and said], "The President is going to make an announcement about the 1942 Roundup and the instructions are very clear, the president has to do what Mitterrand did not: recognize the responsibility of the state." And we couldn't go so far in recognizing the responsibility without also saluting those who represented the eternal France, who incarnated a certain idea of France. You know, the president is a conciliator, he brings people together. And you can't take a hard line without compensating for it by emphasizing positive actions. Otherwise you can't be a conciliator. It was a terrible time, but there was also a France that saved people.[17]

This reference to those "who saved people" as a kind of compensation was already present in the 1986 speech by the mayor of Paris for the commemoration of the Vel d'Hiv Roundup. Nine years later it took the form of the "Righteous among the Nations" in the presidential discourse, written by the same advisors for the anniversary of the same event.

In his speech on 16 July, now a national day of commemoration (since the 1993 decree), the president of the Republic operated a slippage between the vision of France as a nation, marked by patriotism and accused of defeat and submission to the enemy, and France as the birthplace of human rights, guilty of crimes against humanity. He thus recognized France's responsibility in the deportation of Jews, before making the Righteous among the Nations the central characters in this new historical memory of World War II:

> I want to remember that the summer of 1942, which revealed the true face of "collaboration," unquestionably racist in the wake of the anti-Jew laws of 1940, would be for many of our countrymen a jumping off point for a vast movement of resistance. I want to remember all the Jewish families tracked down, but shielded from the ruthless investigations of the occupier and the Milice, by the heroic and fraternal action of numerous French families. I like to recall that a month earlier, at Bir Hakeim, the Free French Forces under General Koenig heroically held out against the Italian and German divisions for two weeks. Of course mistakes are made, there are faults, there is a collective fault. But there is also France, a certain idea of France, honest, generous, faithful to its traditions, to its genius. This France has never been in Vichy. For a long time it has not been in Paris. It is in the sands of Libya and wherever the Free French Forces are fighting. It is in London, embodied in General de Gaulle. It is present, one and indivisible, in the hearts of these French citizens, these "Righteous among the Nations," who at the darkest moment of agony, as Serge Klarsfeld writes, at the risk of their life, save three-quarters of the Jewish community resident in France, and give life to its better qualities: humanist values, values of freedom, justice and tolerance, on which French identity is founded, to which we remain bound in the future.[18]

The use of the Israeli title "Righteous among the Nations" in the discourse of the head of state on 16 July 1995 is the result of a conscious desire to find a solution to this controversy, a solution that might be accepted by the French people. The reference to the Righteous was explicitly used by the presidential speechwriters to perform a function hitherto fulfilled by the simple mention of the Resistance. Together the Resistance and the Righteous provided a counterweight to the recognition of collective responsibility and incarnated the "true" France. This incarnation was based on an implicit syllogism: there are French people—Righteous among the Nations—who helped the Jews, three-quarters of the French Jewish population survived, therefore it was the majority of the French population that assisted—most often anonymously—the Jews and the 1,366 people officially recognized as Righteous are a mere fraction of the total.[19]

However, the strategic mobilization of the category Righteous is not purely rational. It is embedded in the representations of the president and his ghostwriters, who were progressively socialized to the existence of the Israeli distinction between 1987 and 1995. "The term [Righteous] came naturally" to the writers, who had the impression they "had always known it."[20] Other expressions, from "French people who saved Jews" to "civilian Resistance members who fought against the deportation of Jews," would have been a similar counterweight and covered the same concrete facts (as they did in Chirac's 1986 speech or in Le Garrec's bill in 1992).

The process at work here thus corresponds to the use of limited rationality. If Lucien Nizar insisted on the importance of the socialization of social partners to allow for a change of economic policy,[21] a similar socialization, a progressive familiarization also seems to play a role in this process. But this time it is inversed, it emanates from civil society and plays out on political leaders. Moreover, along the lines of the notes and reports that Florian Charvolin revealed as being involved in political decision making,[22] the discourses and editorial choices played a dynamic role in the presidential decision to appropriate the Israeli expression "Righteous among the Nations." In this case, the passages and expression present in the 1986 speech were also present in the 1989 speech and were then reused in the 1995 declaration. The latter also reuses fragments of phrases from the speeches of the presidents of the two houses during the ceremonies in 1994 and 1995. The presidential 1995 declaration would in turn be reused, almost word for word, in other later speeches.

However, the French president reinterpreted the term based on this early socialization, clearly extrapolating on the link between the honor of France and the Righteous among the Nations, which was of course present among the Francophone Volunteers. The appropriation of the Israeli category by the French state implied a total reversal of meaning. As we saw in the first chapter, since 1973 the Israeli state had considered the attitude of the Righteous toward the Jews to be an exception to the generally hostile attitude of most non-Jews. Yet the way it was evoked—or rather invoked—in France made these individuals symbols of the solidarity of the whole French population with the fate of the Jews.

The presidential appropriation of the title Righteous therefore gives it another meaning. Chirac provided a translation of the term, literally because the term originally came from Hebrew but also and above all figuratively. Once again, the prior socialization of the actors involved in this public policy shift allowed for the construction of this new meaning of the term. The role of these specific interactions in this dynamic can be clearly seen in the comments of Christine Albanel,[23] the main writer of the speech of 16 July 1995. Here the existence of a shared network among the social actors in this sector was held up in support of this translation and the use of the survival statistics concerning French Jews:

> Well, the theme of the Righteous, I've always known about it. At the time, because there was the theme of the Shoah, the theme of the Righteous was there to even it out, to balance it. Because eventually we were attacked by the old Gaullists, "you're doing this against the legacy of de Gaulle . . . ," but well what de Gaulle did can be perfectly understood in the legacy of the postwar period. So with the Righteous it was more well balanced. And even the representatives of the [Jewish] community spoke about it like this. In fact the theme of the Righteous came back in the leaders' discourses. There were speeches on the question, stemming from the leaders of the community, they had the idea of saying that there was the French state but ultimately it was not the same as the French people. Finally everyone recognized and said that 75 percent of the community had not been deported and that is quite different from neighboring countries. And that is thanks to this particular France.[24]

These comments thus reveal the networks present here as well as the cognitive categories of the actors involved in the French state's appropriation of the Israeli term "Righteous among the Nations." In so doing they provide an initial clue as to the relationship with the Israeli origin of the expression as well as to the type of public policy this appropriation fits into.

First, the appropriation of the Israeli expression was not explicit, or even acknowledged, as such. The term was only defined by the apposition of the expression "heroic and fraternal action of numerous French families." Its primary meaning and its initial origin were not specified. On the contrary, the conceivers of this declaration tried to erase the origin of the term, which was only supposed to exist through its official French translation. According to Christine Albanel, the question of the national origin of the expression was "never posed."

In response to my comment that "a national discourse used a foreign title," Pierre Dardenne agreed, stating, "It could not be seen as being part of a bilateral relationship between Israel and France." At no stage of the process the Presidential team considered Israel actually as a member of the network of actors likely to participate in the process of translating the title. On the contrary, and as we will see, the different stages of the process of the public action transfer that would follow consisted in completely evacuating the possible legitimacy of Israel in participating in the construction of the new meanings of the term "Righteous among the Nations" in the French context.

More broadly, and unlike the instrumentalization of the title Righteous in the Israeli context, the use of the expression by the French state was not an instrument of foreign policy. The decision to mobilize this expression was an act of internal policy. The relevant sector—acknowledged as such—was that of memory policy. Per the decree of 1993, which established the national day of commemoration, the organization of the ceremony on 16 July 1995 was itself the result of a service dedicated to this policy, the Delegation for Memory and Historical Information,[25] "a tool for intervention and administration in the area of memory."[26] But the numerous references to the "community" (implying "Jewish") in the words of the main writer of the presidential declaration indicated that this appropriation of the category Righteous is also a part of the state management of ethnic-religious origins. The spokespeople for this so-called community were considered partners in the appropriation of the term, which was in part directed at them.

Thus the term "Righteous among the Nations" was used for two convergent reasons, having an impact on two distinct but intricately connected areas. From the point of view of remembrance policy, the use of this term enabled the resolution of the controversy that began in 1992, while saving France's honor. It thus met the expectations of the French people, or at least the expectations that were anticipated by the public actors of the day. From the political perspective of managing ethnic-religious belongings, not acknowledged here, the reference to the "Righteous" was perceived as a way of ensuring the support of the Jewish community. It was this community that was considered the main users of the term and that had brought it to the attention of the presidential team. This second concern can be clearly seen in the mention of Serge Klarsfeld, the president of the organization Fils et Filles de Déportés Juifs de France (Sons and Daughters of Jews Deported from France), who had for many years publically believed that the "French people had assisted in the rescue of three-quarters of French Jews."[27]

In translating the term "Righteous" and undertaking a change in public policy, the words of the president clearly made reference to the support—apparently considered necessary—of one of the main figures of the French Jewish community in the area of the memory of World War II. Once again, the prior socialization of the president and the network of actors thus constructed played an important role. Prior to this, in July 1986 during his speech as the mayor of Paris for the commemoration of the Vel d'Hiv Roundup, Chirac had already made reference to Klarsfeld in justifying his interpretation of the Jewish survival statistics. In 1998, at the end of the first phase of the process of appropriation carried out by the president, Klarsfeld's organization published a celebratory collection of all the presidential speeches on the question and, in so doing, associated his organization with the president's approach.[28]

These citations from Chirac and Klarsfeld suggest that the appropriation of the term by the French state on 16 July 1995 was part of a process to translate this concept into the French context. This translation process was founded on an agreement between a number of heterogeneous actors concerning the meaning this category was to be given in the French public action context.

Presidential discourse and institutionalization

The appropriation of the Israeli expression "Righteous among the Nations" in the presidential discourse of 16 July 1995 did not provoke any public reaction. If the declaration in itself, and particularly the recognition of a collective "fault," was the objective of numerous critical comments,[29] this was not the case of the comments about the Righteous. It seems that the translation of the term was consensual—at that stage. This support came from both the public authorities and the other social actors involved. It thus led to initiatives liable to develop into a coherent public policy. However, we still need to determine which mechanisms enabled this translation to launch a process of institutionalization that progressively emerged as a genuine public policy transfer.

The legitimation of the commemoration of the Righteous of France by the state

By 16 July 1995, national institutions of the utmost importance—the Senate and the National Assembly—had on two occasions held medal-giving ceremonies to award the French Righteous with recognition by Israel. On 21 January 1996, only six months after the Israeli term was taken up by the

French president, a similar event was held at the Museum of the National Resistance Movement in Champigny. Unlike those that had preceded it, the event had the traits of national commemoration and was the object of hitherto unprecedented investment by the French state. This participation was no longer limited to simply making the premises available but added a symbolic element—although it remained secondary to the role of the Israeli ambassador, the only one authorized to award the title of Righteous. This time the participation of France as a whole was amplified and acknowledged. The state, represented by the executive branch rather than by MPs for the first time, took control of the event.

It was therefore not the Museum of the National Resistance Movement that was presented as being the instigator of the ceremony but the French government, through the intermediary of the minister for education, François Bayrou. Bayrou wanted to make this event as widely publicized as possible in order to present a major press release and a presentation brochure.

The French state appropriated the organization of the ceremony and then cast itself in the role of the ultimate recipient of the honor awarded to the Righteous. The invitation to the ceremony also emphasized the fact that one of the posthumously awarded medals would be presented at the museum. Similarly and equally unprecedented, a member of the government, Xavier Emmanuelli, then secretary of state for humanitarian action, also received a medal on behalf of his deceased father.[30]

This appropriation of the event by the French executive body is in keeping with the president's evocation of the Righteous among the Nations in the previous July. The discourse of the minister for education also assumed the new meaning that the president had instigated earlier: "The Medal of the Righteous . . . must have a clear meaning: the greatness and the honor of a few allow us to save the honor of all."

The convergence between the presidential appropriation on 16 July 1995 and the shape of the medal-giving ceremony on 21 January 1996 suggests that the former had clear social effects. It led to the beginning of the operationalization of the public action for the commemoration of the French people awarded the title of Righteous among the Nations. Consequently we may ask what the vectors and the nature of this influence were.

The investment of the government and particularly the services of the minister for education at this ceremony might suggest the existence of a dialogue between the different protagonists in this burgeoning public action. Aspiring to provide the translation of the term with a social foundation, it seemed like the French president and his advisors gave instructions to organize commemorative events at the national level, thus promoting the new historical memory brought about by the change in policy begun in July 1995.

Yet such instructions never actually existed. On the contrary, it appears that the simple evocation and reinterpretation of the term "Righteous" in the presidential declaration was enough to create a new space of legitimacy for the commemoration of these individuals and thus to incite the actors of the event (both those from the politico-administrative sphere and those from so-called civil society) to mobilize around it. Once again the interaction between these two categories of actors played an important role in the operationalization of this specific public action. If the executive appropriated the event, it was the French Committee for Yad Vashem that initially submitted the idea for the organization of a ceremony in that place and at that time. Moreover, this project was itself suggested by a resident of Champigny who, as a witness in an application for the title of Righteous, wanted the medal for "his" Righteous to be symbolically awarded at the Museum for the National Resistance Movement.[31]

Like the protocol for the services held at the National Assembly and the Senate (respectively two and one previous ceremonies), the involvement of the museum stemmed first from the request of the French Committee, encouraged by the proposal of a particular individual. The inclusion of Emmanuelli's father in the list of recipients for this particular ceremony was also suggested by the association.

The translation of the Israeli expression initiated by the French president amplified the process of socializing state representatives to the Righteous category that was already underway. Conversely, it also opened a new space for the legitimate evocation of the Righteous by the administration, on one hand, and by social actors, on the other. At this stage, on the basis of just the instruments of discourses and commemoration, an agreement on the new meaning given to the title of Righteous appeared to exist between actors, even though they were quite heterogeneous in both their levels of action and their resources.

These conclusions reflect those made by Bruno Jobert concerning socio-economic policy:

> The effect of a program [the declaration of 16 July 1995] cannot be measured simply by the impact of the specific measures adopted. What is sometimes more important is the transformation of the norms and representations of the most important actors—public and private—in that sector.[32]

In this respect it seems like the members of the French Committee for Yad Vashem agree with the proposed translation of the term, or at least recognize themselves in it enough to see it as a source of legitimacy for their own action. In return they then legitimize this translation through their participation and support for the development of public action dedicated to this issue.

Creation of a space for legitimacy and investment by social actors

The appropriation and translation of the expression "Righteous among the Nations" by the French president legitimized the initiatives of the state services and the actions of preexisting associations. It also produced mutual interest that ultimately modified the structure and shape of the sector concerned and, therefore, the configuration that brought these people together to participate in the process of translation underway. From 1995 on, new actors became increasingly mobilized in transforming the Israeli term to a French category. They therefore influenced the public action underway by providing it with social support.

As a result, the Righteous themselves, or at least some of them, felt as though they had been given a social status in the French political context. Thus, on 21 February 1997, during the parliamentary debates about toughening up immigration law, several of them and/or their descendants signed a public declaration published in the newspaper *Liberation*. A public stand by the Righteous was previously unheard of. These comments revealed the way in which, because the term "Righteous" had been given a meaning in the French context, it was now possible to use it to describe oneself according to the values its presidential translation had emphasized—even if this was done in order to oppose measures taken by the government of that very same president. Their declaration read:

> A little over fifty years ago, we, our parents, and our grandparents realized our obligation to help the Jewish men, women, and children who the French laws and the German army considered responsible for all evil. Their lives were at stake. For this, ourselves, our parents, our grandparents, received the title of Righteous among the Nations. Some are still with us. Over time, these acts have become engraved in the memories of their descendants as a model of behavior that we must transmit from generation to generation. . . . That is why the Righteous, their children, and grandchildren, undersigned, affirm that they will continue to shelter whoever they wish. . . . They remind others that the principal elements of the French Republic are liberty, equality, and fraternity.[33]

Although this collective mobilization reveals an acceptance of the translation initiated by Chirac—through the terms that it employs—this association remained temporary and did not become institutionalized.

From 1995 on,[34] and shortly after Chirac's speech, the Central Consistory of France created an association that aimed to pay public homage to the French Righteous among the Nations and to have this homage inscribed in the national space. In so doing, the cultural representation of French

Judaism disrupted the organization of roles between community institutions. Indeed, since the liberation, the CRIF had traditionally been in charge of the management of questions relating to the memory of World War II. In this respect the Consistory's agreement, in 1987, to diffuse calls for witnesses produced by the Volunteers, constituted the first infringement of this principle.

This new involvement of the Consistory was directly attributable to the personality of Jean Kahn, then president of the Consistory, former president of the CRIF, and closely connected to Chirac.[35] More fundamentally, as was the case for Serge Klarsfeld, it was based on Kahn's association (and that of all the other various actors who ultimately joined this initiative) with the new meaning of the title Righteous constructed by Chirac in July 1995.

The statutes of the French Association of Righteous among the Nations were registered in October 1996 by the Consistory.[36] They had two objectives. The Association sought to encourage French citizens to be nominated as Righteous. In this, it was similar to the goal of the Francophone Volunteers and their successors in the French Committee for Yad Vashem. However, they considered themselves complementary to the latter because they sought to establish a form of national recognition for those who had helped Jews during the war but were unable to obtain the Israeli title, because the procedure was too complex and demanding. Anxious to explain its raison d'être, the Association rapidly gave itself a new name, the French Association in Honor of the Righteous among the Nations.[37]

This new title shows just how similar the objectives of this Association were to those of the Department of the Righteous in the French Committee for Yad Vashem. They differ in one important aspect, however. The French Association in Honor of the Righteous explicitly expressed a desire to make the expression "Righteous among the Nations" into a French term. Pursuing the process begun by Chirac on 16 July 1995, this group sought to complete the appropriation and translation of the Israeli title into French space.

For a time the possibility of awarding all of the French Righteous (and those who might be eligible for the title) with a collective Legion of Honor (Légion d'honneur) medal as well as a specifically French version of the award was envisaged. However, this project mobilized instruments that were quite different from simple speeches and commemorations. Awarding a particular status requires defining its criteria and implies reducing the polysemy involved in every translation process. This proposal effectively destroyed the consensus among French actors regarding Chirac's translation of the Israeli title. For the first time, divisions emerged between the different Jewish associations involved. Both the French Committee for Yad Vashem and the CRIF were opposed to the project to create a new French honorific title. Once again a tool that allowed the term and its translation to be more open to interpretation was preferred.

Finally, the establishment of a commemorative monument on French soil was chosen as the means by which to anchor the title of Righteous among the Nations in France. This memorial had to geographically symbolize the French appropriation of the title. In my interviews with the leaders of the Association, they reacted strongly to my (deliberate) comment that such a monument already existed in Israel:

> It was the Consistory that carried out the operation [building the monument]. With the cooperation of Yad Vashem of course. But it wasn't Yad Vashem that initiated it or made it concrete. Because for them it wasn't in the order of things ... [silence]. They had a memorial at Yad Vashem, the Avenue of the Righteous. But for us, especially Jean Kahn, it was important to create that in France.[38]

Some months later, in response to the question of what purpose this monument served compared to the Avenue of the Righteous in Jerusalem, the respondent again answered hotly: "Listen, not everyone goes to Israel. I think there are lots of French people who supported the creation of this monument in France."[39]

This desire for the national appropriation of the Righteous category, both physically and symbolically, occurred alongside the revival of the exact meaning of the word proposed by Chirac in 1995. The first public event organized by the Association was thus held in the Senate on 21 May 1997. It took the form of a conference, compellingly titled "France of the Camps: Vichy's Shame and the Solidarity of the Righteous." Orally as well as in their writings, the leaders of the Association and the president of the Consistory repeatedly described these Righteous French citizens as representing the honor of France. They systematically held up the statistics on the nondeportation of three-quarters of French Jews as being the direct result of the mobilization of the French citizens who stood in solidarity with them. Chirac had used these exact terms in 1986 and in 1995.

This acceptance of the reinterpretation of the Israeli expression by the president as making the Righteous representatives of the national community can also be seen in the initial choice for the town where the monument was to be erected. The only French entity to have been collectively awarded the title of Righteous, the town of Le Chambon-sur-Ligon, was approached first.[40] When the town council in Le Chambon refused, a Memorial to Honor the French Righteous was finally inaugurated by the Central Consistory of France in Thonon-les-Bains on 2 November 1997.

Public action, memory, and governance

This inauguration, given as much publicity as possible by the organizers, was the first media occurrence of the expression "Righteous of France." It simultaneously represented an additional step in the appropriation of the Israeli title by the French state. Formally initiated by a nonprofit organization, this inauguration in fact signaled the institutionalization of the transfer of public action for the commemoration of the Righteous to France. The intervention of the president of the Republic thus gave rise to a space of legitimacy and resources. The fact that this space was then invested by social actors, who also provided legitimation, enabled the development of a public policy that revealed the existence of clear reciprocal interests.

The main representatives for the Jewish institutions also supported the initiative, as did the other actors involved. Thus the Israeli ambassador in France, the chairman of Yad Vashem, and the president of the French Committee for Yad Vashem were all in the Honorary Committee organized for the occasion. Although their participation was not without tensions, the object of the public action instrument (the erecting of the monument) seemed to permit a temporary (re)conciliation.

Alongside these representatives of the Jewish community and the activities of Yad Vashem, representatives from various echelons of the French state (from both political sides of the cohabitation) were omnipresent both before and during the event. They were first visible within the Honorary Committee, which was presided over by Laurent Fabius (then president of the National Assembly). Other members were Jean Denais, mayor of Thonon-les-Bains; Pierre Mazeaud, MP (RPR) and vice-president of the National Assembly; Philippe Seguin, MP (RPR) and former minister; and Jean Mattéoli, president of the Social and Economic Council.

The event itself was placed under the "patronage of Mr. Jacques Chirac, president of the Republic," and four of the seven key figures hosting the event were important politicians. Finally, three representatives of the state were physically present on the day: the prefect of Haut-Savoie, representing the president; Catherine Trautmann, minister for culture and spokeswoman for the Socialist government; and the secretary of state at the Ministry of Defense, responsible for Veterans' Affairs, indicating which sector the appropriation of the Israeli term was part of. At the same time, the cultural status of the organizers of the event clearly emphasized the close relations between remembrance policy and the issue of the management of religious and ethnoreligious identities.

Representatives of the French nation were at the center of this inauguration ceremony and dominated much of the speaking time. In his speech, read by the prefect of the region, President Chirac first intensified the appropriation and translation of the Righteous title by the French state. He emphasized the equivalence between the Righteous and the French population even further, to the point where they incarnated all civil society. He declared, "These men and women from all walks of life, all religions, these Righteous among the Nations, we will never forget them. They are the honor and pride of our country. In a dark time marked by defeat, deprivation, and disarray, they incarnated the best of France: its values of fraternity, justice, and tolerance."[41]

This incarnation of the nation through the figures of the Righteous was endorsed by Serge Klarsfeld:

> In the darkest hours, nobility and hope . . . were in the hearts of those who fought for Free France, the Resistance members, of whom there were so many in this beautiful area. In the hearts above all of those anonymous French citizens, those Righteous among the Nations, who at the darkest point of the turmoil, would save three-quarters of the Jewish community in France.

Although the expression "Righteous of France" was not yet used by the president, his reference to the "Righteous among the Nations" was once again independent of any foreign origin and also here of any internal community association. The event thus served to further legitimize the president's move to translate the title into the French context.

Finally, this appropriation was reinforced by the fact that the spokesperson for the Socialist government in turn proposed an identical translation of the Israeli title. The "Righteous among the Nations" once again referred to the majority of the French population, which they ended up incarnating, in a literal and a figurative sense. Catherine Trautmann addressed those present for the ceremony in these terms: "It is in your name that we want to celebrate the Republic. . . . [This France] that we love and defend, it has your faces, it has your hands." [42]

Finally, the monument was unveiled jointly by Trautmann and one of the Righteous in attendance. This gesture incarnates—physically this time—the transfer of the prestige from the individual Righteous to France, symbolized by the people's representative. Indeed, the choice of the Righteous individual, who was also a volunteer fighter for the Resistance, further pursued the hybridization between the Israeli category and the French honorific status.

The evolution and evocation of the Righteous by the representatives of the French state since July 1995 therefore occurred through interactions with events organized by members of civil society and a progressive and reciprocal familiarization of each of these actors with the meaning given to the title of Righteous in the new presidential narrative. Through a circular mechanism, the mobilization of social actors (including the Francophone Volunteers or Serge Klarsfeld and his organization) socialized Chirac's team to the term "Righteous among the Nations."

Fortified by this legitimacy, the head of state then implemented a translation of the Israeli title. This presidential initiative in turn had effects on legitimacy, opportunity, and mutual interests that lead other social actors to become mobilized. In return, this new engagement increased the legitimacy of the introduction of a policy for commemorating the French Righteous. This reveals not only the importance of the co-production of policies as well as the references they mobilize but also the importance of time in the development, and particularly in the change, of public action.

The social effects of the commemoration of the Righteous of France

By November 1997 the president was strengthened in his approach to the translation of this title. Having held two successive ceremonies, it was once again the words of the president that were at the heart of these events, enabling the appropriation of the Israeli category to be pursued. His final speech completed the changes to the configuration of the commemoration of the Righteous, but the social effects of this translation were felt beyond this sphere. In 1998, it became clear during the trial of Maurice Papon that the term "Righteous" had become a reference for discussing the past.

From the "Righteous among the Nations" to the "Righteous"

In December 1997, on the occasion of the submission of the "Jewish File"[43] to the Shoah Memorial, the president again evoked these characters from the past who were constantly present and occupying an increasing amount of space alongside the Resistance members:

> Of course there was a France that resisted and fought for our honor. There were the fishermen of the Ile de Sein who answered the call of General de Gaulle. There were all the units engaged alongside the Allies on the Freedom front. There was the daily discreet heroism of all the "Righteous," who were recently honored in Thonon; these anonymous people from all walks of life, all religions, who saved, often at risk to their lives, three-quarters of the French Jewish population. Yes, happily there was the best, a France that was generous, courageous, and proud, a France of hope. And it was this France, this France of light, General de Gaulle, the Free French, the Resistance, and the Righteous that finally won the day.[44]

Scarcely more than a year after the Israeli term was first used, the president dropped its extension "among the Nations," which still associated it with its foreign origin. He even ultimately abandoned the endorsement of Klarsfeld in the evocation and interpretation of the survival statistics for French Jews. In this, French national appropriation of this memorial category appeared complete.

The modification of the initial configuration of actors

By autumn 1995, without providing anything other than a "pragmatic" justification, the French Committee for Yad Vashem decided to specify on the brochure given to potential witnesses wanting to have "their" rescuers recognized that it was possible to give one's testimony before a French municipal employee. From this point on, even Israel considered these representatives of the French state as legitimate in participating in the procedure of nominating the Righteous. But the presidential appropriation and its initial implications ultimately lead to more profound changes in the activity and structure of the organization.

In 1998, at the end of this first phase of translation, the French Committee for Yad Vashem changed its internal organization along with its official name. The mutual interests produced by the involvement of the state in the French context around the commemoration of the Righteous led it to make this mission central. In addition to his role as the director of the Department of the Righteous, or rather because if it, Louis Grobart was appointed vice-president of the organization.[45] The Committee also changed its name. From this point on, its letterhead specified the Association for the Memory and Teaching of the Shoah and the Nomination of the Righteous among the Nations. Although it hadn't been one of its original tasks, this nomination henceforth appeared as one of its founding functions.

The benefit-sharing effects generated by the development of public action on the commemoration of the Righteous also led the French Committee to delimit its jurisdiction regarding a category that had become a public issue. In 1995, it had already asked the organization of the Righteous to change its name in order to avoid confusion. In 1998 it demanded that the Association of the Righteous of France for Yad Vashem explicitly state its distinction from the Committee in all its correspondence, particularly with the public authorities. From 1 January 1999, this Association explicitly mentioned on all its correspondence, "Our French Association has no connection with the French Committee for Yad Vashem and the Yad Vashem Institute in Jerusalem."[46]

Between 16 July 1995 and 1 January 1999, references to the term "Righteous among the Nations" thus became a resource that led to a form of competition between actors. This evolution went beyond the simple forum of associations, institutions, and actors initially involved in the public commemoration of the French Righteous.

Beyond public action: the spread of the Righteous of France title

The study of the place of the references to the "Righteous among Nations" in the trials linked to World War II—which came in quick succession after the Francophone Volunteers' activities began in the mid-1980s—is a focal point through which we can see the possible spread of the translation of the term "Righteous" outside this specific context.

In 1987, the trial of Klaus Barbie[47] provided the opportunity for two of the prosecution witnesses to refer to these "French families who risked so much to hide [them]" and "these French neighbors who 'lost' their identity cards and gave them to Jews."[48] This reference was only marginal, however, and it was taken up by neither the defense nor by the prosecution; the Volunteers' activities had only just begun.

By 1994, these activities had fully developed, but the state had not yet begun the process of appropriating the title Righteous among the Nations. In that year, Paul Touvier appeared before the judges. This time, the question of whether the accused had been involved in rescuing Jews was considered an important issue by the defense. In his plea, one of the lawyers for the civil claimants took the time to deconstruct the argument, "France, true France, is made up of countless anonymous citizens who rescued thousands of Jews."[49] Although "rescue" actions became a norm against which the accused had to be judged, the term "Righteous" was not explicitly used in the courtroom. Nor was it used in the comments about the trial. Only the *Arche,* the "monthly journal on French Judaism," used the category to summarize the event: "Touvier against the Righteous."[50] This usage of the Israeli expression solely by the main journal on French Judaism reveals the weakness and the segmentation of French society's socialization to the Israeli title at that time.

Maurice Papon's trial, held in Bordeaux between October 1997 and April 1998 (the exact period when the French translation of the Israeli title was being consolidated), marked a clear evolution in this respect. The term "Righteous" was used both inside and outside the courtroom. The comparison with the previous trials suggests that the progressive introduction of public action in this area had led to the gradual institutionalization of legitimate linguistic use.

The prosecution first provided a list of these "Righteous," whose attitudes show not only that "we" knew but that it was possible to attempt to oppose these directives. Moreover, given that Papon claimed to have saved 130 Jews, the prosecution took the time to dismantle the arguments of the defense, case by case.[51] It then provided the portraits of numerous French Righteous who were indeed responsible for the rescues that Papon claimed to have carried out. Finally the title Righteous among the Nations was explicitly evoked at the bar in reason of the attitude, considered exemplary, of those awarded this title.

On 3 March 1998, Samuel Pisar paid homage to the Righteous of France.[52] He depicted three Righteous among the Nations, senior civil servants of the state, who showed that it was possible to serve without compromise and without disgrace.[53] As a former Auschwitz inmate, Pisar spoke as a witness but also as an international lawyer. He addressed the court two days before the end of the hearings. He concluded with the wish to see Papon judged against these models, saying, "You will consider the guilt or innocence of the accused. I believe I am allowed to suggest that you consider the acts of the Righteous of France."

The quasisummons of the Righteous was a legal tactic here. As the president and founder of the French Committee for Yad Vashem, Samuel Pisar was cited by Mr. Zaoui, one of the lawyers for the civil claimants who was also an honorary member of the French Committee. At his request, Louis Grobart and the Volunteers prepared a detailed brochure for the event, providing the factual elements of the prosecution. Titled *Six "Righteous" Senior Civil Servants: Testimony by Yad Vashem France at the Papon Trial*, this document describes in detail the actions of the three civil servants referred to by the prosecution. As part of the trial, the reference to the Righteous was instrumental to the prosecution of Maurice Papon.

However, the commentators in the audience did not wait for the intervention of these memory entrepreneurs to describe Papon's counterexamples as Righteous. These civil servants were precisely those who were regularly referred to in the coverage of the trial. Unlike in 1994 and the coverage of the Touvier trial, this time the Jewish journals were not the only ones to use this term in describing the event.[54] The whole spectrum of the press was concerned, including the journals of the National Front, the French far-right political party.

The newspaper *Le Monde* was the first to make the parallel between the accused in Bordeaux and the Righteous among the Nations. On 31 October 1997 it published a large article on Aristide de Sousa Mendes, the consul of Portugal in Bordeaux, who had enabled the rescue of some 30,000 Jewish people. The journalist emphasized that Mendes was named "Righteous among the Nations" in 1966.[55]

In June 1998, following the process and the inauguration of the Memorial to Honor the Righteous in France, *Français d'abord* (French First), a publication of the National Front, also referred to Papon's trial. For the first time, it published an article on a Righteous among the Nations, Rolande Birgy, who had been an activist in the far-right party since its creation and was awarded Righteous status in 1983.[56] This use of the term "Righteous" by a branch of the National Front leads to two conclusions.

First, between the Touvier trial in 1994 and the Papon trial in 1998, the French state's appropriation of the Israeli expression had produced profitable effects beyond the initial configuration. It thus allowed the development of the use of the Righteous title outside the forum involved in developing public action. Secondly, but not unrelated, was the extreme heterogeneity of those who referred to the Righteous during the Papon trial—from the *Arche* to *Français d'abord*. This seems to suggest that the effects of the appropriation of the term "Righteous" were accompanied by highly polysemous interpretations of the title.

Several questions remain. What kind of relationship existed between the terms "Resistance members" and "Righteous"—inclusion, exclusion, or hybridization? To what extent does the term "Righteous" retain its religious origin? Or is it now part of a secular vocabulary? Similarly, does the expression "Righteous of France" imply that the term is now a French one, or does it remains an Israeli term?

The translation process is by definition based on a mechanism of agreement between heterogeneous actors. However, we can hypothesize that the meaning of the differences that oppose these actors here suggests that the dynamic of institutionalization is dependent on the use of public action instruments that, for the moment, remain purely discursive.

Notes

1. Speech by Jacques Chirac, president of the French Republic, delivered during the ceremony commemorating the roundup of Jews on 16 and 17 July 1942.
2. Interview with Marek Halter, director of the film *Tzedek. Les Justes*, 29 April 1998, Paris, and consultation of documents in situ.
3. This term refers to the roundups of 16 July 1942 that led to the arrest of 12,884 Jews in Paris. The name "Vel d'Hiv" comes from the fact that 8,160 of them were initially held in the *Velodrome d'Hiver* cycling stadium in Paris. The reader will find more details on this event, along with others that are mentioned here, in Serge Klarsfeld, *Le Calendrier de la persécution des Juifs de France* (Paris: Fayard, 2003).
4. Speech by the mayor of Paris, 18 July 1986, Vel d'Hiv Ceremony, republished in *Discours et Messages de Jacques Chirac*, FFDJF, 1998.
5. Speech by Jacques Chirac during the "Reception at the Ceremony for the Award of 'Medals for the Righteous' of Yad Vashem, Monday, 29 May 1989 at 5 pm," Wertheimer Archives.
6. Olivier Wieviorka, *Divided Memory: French Recollections of World War II from Liberation to the Present* (Stanford: Stanford University Press, 2012).
7. Ruling "Gonzalez vs the Secretary for Veterans' Affairs," 6 December 1988, Administrative Tribunal of Bordeaux, Second Chamber.

8. This definition of historical memory is taken from Marie-Claire Lavabre, *Le Fil rouge. Sociologie de la mémoire communiste* (Paris: FNSP, 1994).
9. This decline can be seen in the controversies that emerged regularly in the public space. E.g., Eric Conan and Daniel Lindenberg, "Pourquoi y-a-t-il une affaire Jean-Moulin?" *Esprit*, no. 198 (January 1994): 5–18.
10. The analysis of this controversy is based on the description given by Eric Conan and Henry Rousso in *Vichy, un passé qui ne passe pas* (Paris: Gallimard, 1996), 47–96 (1st ed. 1994).
11. *Le Monde*, 17 June 1992.
12. Decree of 3 February 1993, *Journal Officiel de la République française, Lois et Décrets*, 29 February 1993.
13. Serge Klarsfled, "Nous avons une condamnation explicite et solennelle des crimes de Vichy. Nous ne pouvons pas demander beaucoup plus," *Le Monde*, 5 February 1993.
14. Recorded 25 November 1992, Document no. 3071, first regular session of 1992–1993.
15. Interview with Jean Le Garrec, 13 November 2002, Paris; and Le Garrec Archives.
16. On a comparable mechanism, see Kathleen Thelen, "How Institutions Evolve. Insights from Comparative Historical Analysis," in *Comparative Historical Analysis in the Social Sciences*, ed. James Mahoney and Dietrich Rueschemeyer, 208–40 (Cambridge: Cambridge University Press, 2003).
17. Interview with Pierre Dardenne, 28 September 2002, Elysée Palace, Paris.
18. Speech by Jacques Chirac, president of the French Republic, delivered during the ceremonies to commemorate the major roundups of 16–17 July 1942.
19. As we saw in the introduction, the objective of this book is not to establish the political nature of the use of references to the past, in light of the distance taken with the facts—as professional historians have established them. However, for readers interested in a historical interpretation of the statistics of the survival of Jews in France, see Robert O. Paxton, "La Spécificité de la persécution des Juifs en France," *Annales*, no. 3 (May–June 1993): 605–19. See also Renée Poznanski, "Comment les trois quarts de Juifs de France ont-ils survécu?" in *Les Juifs en France pendant la Seconde Guerre mondiale*, by Poznanski (Paris: Hachette, 1997), 579–83 (1st ed. 1994); and Claire Andrieu, Sarah Gensburger, and Jacques Sémelin, *Resisting Genocides. The Multiple Forms of Rescue* (New York: Columbia University Press, 2011).
20. These quotations are from Pierre Dardenne and Christine Albanel, respectively.
21. Lucien Nizard, *Planification et société* (Grenoble: Grenoble University Press, 1974).
22. Florian Charvolin, *L'Invention de l'environnement en France* (Paris: La Découverte, 2003).
23. Christine Albanel wrote all Jacques Chirac's speeches on the question. In 1986 she was an advisor to the director of information and communication at the Town Council in Paris. The same year, she became an advisor to the prime minister's cabinet (Chirac was then prime minister) before becoming associate director to the cabinet of the mayor of Paris between 1988 and 1995. In 1995 she became technical advisor to the Elysée Palace before being made responsible for questions of education and culture in the presidency in 1997. See, "Notice biographique de Christine Albanel," in *Who's Who in France*, internet edition, consulted 23 August 2005.
24. Interview with Christine Albanel, 12 February 2003, Elysée Palace, Paris.
25. Decree no. 92–231 of 12 March 1992 relating to the organization of the central administration of the state secretary for Veterans Affairs, *Journal Officiel*, 14 March 1992.
26. In the words of Serge Barcellini, quoted in "Création d'une délégation à la mémoire et à l'information historique," *Le Monde*, 6 March 1992.

27. In 1985, Serge Klarsfeld concluded the second volume of his pioneering work with a paragraph beginning, "The French people provided powerful assistance to the rescue of three quarters of French Jews." He concluded with these words, "French Jews will always remember that although the Vichy regime led to moral failure and dishonor resulting in the loss of one quarter of the Jewish population of the country, the remaining three quarters essentially owed their survival to the sincere sympathy of all the French people, as well as their active solidarity from the moment they understood that the Jewish families that fell into the hands of the Germans were destined for death." Serge Klarsfeld, *Vichy-Auschwitz. La 'Solution finale' de la question juive* (Paris: Fayard, 2001), 369.
28. Speech and messages of Jacques Chirac, mayor of Paris, prime minister, president of the French Republic. *En hommage aux Juifs de France victimes de la collaboration de l'etat français de Vichy avec l'occupant allemand,* FFDJF, 1998.
29. See in particular the passionate debate between Henry Rousso and Nathalie Heinich in *Le débat,* no. 89 (March–April 1996): 198–207.
30. Archives of the French Committee for Yad Vashem, FCYV, File François and Yvonne Emmanuelli, no. 6876, title awarded 2 November 1995.
31. Suzanne Ponnay's medal was awarded at the museum, FCYV, File Suzanne Ponnay, no. 6398, title awarded 11 January 1995.
32. Bruno Jobert, "Représentations sociales, controverses et débats dans la conduite des politiques publiques," *Revue française de science politique* 42, no. 2 (1992): 227.
33. "Les 'Justes parmi les nations', leurs enfants et petits-enfants lancent un appel contre la xénophobie: 'Nous, qui avons hébergé des juifs . . . ,'" *Libération,* 21 February 1997.
34. The first correspondence found in the archives of the association preserved at the Consistory and the archives of the French Committee for Yad Vashem are dated March 1996, but they present an initial project formulated in autumn 1995. Moreover, in 1998 the leaders of the association said they had been working on this project for two and a half years. Interview with Gérard Blum and Jules Bloch, 25 February 1998, Paris.
35. Jean Kahn, *L'Obstination du témoignage* (Paris: Plon, 2003).
36. Statutes of the "French Association of Righteous among the Nations," no. 127392P, registered 16 October 1996, Prefecture of Police Paris, Office of Associations.
37. Statutory brochure published by the association in 1997, Marcovitch Archives.
38. Interview with Gérard Blum and Jules Bloch, 25 February 1998, Paris.
39. Interview with Jules Bloch, 25 May 1998, Paris.
40. The first version of the statutes of the French Association of Righteous among the Nations indeed included a member of the office responsible for "relations with Chambon/Lignon," Statue no. 127392P, 16 October 1996.
41. Message from Jacques Chirac, president of the French Republic, for the inauguration of the "Clearing of the Righteous," in Thonon-les-Bains, Haute-Savoie, 2 November 1997.
42. Extract from Catherine Trautmann's speech, transcribed from the program *La Source de vie,* broadcast 7 November 1997 on France 2. Although the presidential discourse remained predominant on this subject, Lionel Jospin, the prime minister under cohabitation, also used the term "Righteous" (and the translation proposed by Chirac) at the Fifty-Fifth Anniversary of the Vel d'Hiv Roundup on 20 July 1997, http://www.discours.vie-publique.fr. See also the Papon trial intervention of Lionel Jospin, prime minister, at the National Assembly, 21 October 1997, on the subject of the debate about France's responsibility.
43. René Rémond, *Un Fichier juif: rapport de la commission présidée par René Rémond au premier ministre* (Paris: Plon, 1996).

44. Speech by Jacques Chirac, president of the French Republic, on the occasion of the official transfer of the police census files concerning Jews in Occupied France, to the national archives into the Memorial to the Unknown Jewish Martyr, which has since become the Shoah Memorial, Paris, 5 December 1997.
45. Modification of the statutes communicated to the Office of Associations of the Prefecture of Police in Paris, 5 October 1998, statute no. 89249. Dated 22 February 1995, the previous version did not refer at all to the Righteous among the Nations.
46. Circular no. 7/99, Beltrami Archives.
47. Immediately after the war, the question of assistance provided to Jews was not totally absent from the trial, but it occupied a very marginal place. Henry Rousso, "Une Justice impossible. L'Épuration et la Politique antijuive de Vichy," *Annales. Histoire, Sciences Sociales,* no. 3 (May–June 1993): 745–70.
48. Sorj Chalandon and Pascale Nivelle, *Crimes contre l'humanité. Barbie Touvier Bousquet et Papon* (Paris: Plon, 1998), 52–53.
49. Ibid., 222.
50. Meïr Waintrater, "Touvier contre les Justes," *L'Arche,* May 1994.
51. Chalandon and Nivelle, *Crimes contre l'humanité,* 322–25.
52. *Le Monde,* 5 March 1998; *Libération,* 3 March 1998.
53. They were Edmond Dauphin, DRYV, no. 1234, title awarded 12 September 1978; Camille Ernst, DRYV, no. 709, title awarded 30 November 1971; and Paul Corazzi, DRYV, no. 4339, title awarded 13 December 1989.
54. Ariel Goldman, "Lettre ouverte aux Justes qui ont sauvé mes frères," *Tribune Juive,* no. 1423, 24 November 1997; Pierre Birnbaum, "Etre Juste et fonctionnaire? Oui, c'était possible," *L'Arche,* no. 482, March 1998.
55. *Le Monde,* 31 October 1997. Finally José-Alain Fralon published *Aristide de Sousa Mendès. Le Juste de Bordeaux* (Bordeaux: Mollat, 1998).
56. "Rolande Birgy 'Frontiste et honorée à Jérusalem,'" *Français d'abord,* second fortnight in June 1998.

Chapter 4

The National Day as a Public Policy Instrument

The codification of the Righteous of France

In 1998, the process of translation described in the previous chapter took a new turn. The use of a new type of instrument was envisaged. Two members for Parliament (MPs) wrote a bill destined to provide the French Righteous with a specifically French honorific title, and two years later, the French Parliament finally established the "homage to the Righteous of France." However, although this category was henceforth officially inscribed in law, it remained symbolic. Contrary to its initial objective, it did not constitute a legal status that would have implied norms and budgetary constraints.

Understanding the birth of the Righteous of France category thus requires an interrogation of its corollary, which is the fact that France had not created a specific codified recognition of its citizens that was comparable to the Israeli title. This nonact is an important element of the establishment of French public action in commemorating the Righteous. The lack of a formal French title and the establishment of the symbolic qualification of the Righteous of France by way of compensation indeed represent the completion of the translation dynamic initiated by the French president in 1995.

The study of the legislative activity begun in 1998 also allows us to see both the processes of interpretation and of conflict that are at the heart of any public policy implementation.[1] By what mechanisms and in what conditions did these heterogeneous and conflicting actors manage to agree on the forms of the French legislative appropriation of the Israeli expression "Righteous among the Nations?" Providing an answer to this question allows us to use a concrete case study through which to explore the contemporary analysis of the relations between law and memory, on one hand, and the multiplication of national commemorative days, on the other.

A change in public action management

Up until early 1998 the term "Righteous" was used only by the executive body of government. Although the French state had been in a situation of cohabitation since 1997, the right-wing president of the Republic continued to occupy the primary role in establishing memory policy. To do this, he continued to essentially rely on the performative function of public speeches.

From 1998 onward, the Socialist MPs also became involved in the dynamic around the appropriation of the Israeli expression. This new evolution can be seen as part of the exact prolongation of the translation initiated by the president. While it is important to explain that there was a continuity of public action in spite of the discontinuity of actors, it is also important to question the meaning of this political consensus as well as the legislative branch's possible specificity in this area.

The legislative branch's involvement in the translation dynamic

In December 1997, Jean Le Garrec and Daniel Marcovitch, both Socialist MPs, began to write a bill destined to "honor the Righteous of France."[2] Jean Le Garrec was thus continuing the project that he had started, unsuccessfully, in 1992. This time he grounded the legitimacy of his approach in the presidential discourse. While the text explicitly referred to Jacques Chirac's speeches on 16 July 1995 and on 2 November 1997, he justified the use of the Israeli term by emphasizing that "the highest authorities in the French state have used the name 'Righteous.'"[3]

However, there was no contact between Jean Le Garrec and Daniel Marcovitch and the French presidency. Nor was the impetus for their actions provided by the Socialist government; neither the prime minister nor the secretary of state for Veterans' Affairs was associated with the initiative. The decision to develop a bill to "honor the Righteous of France" was purely a product of the legislative branch. The appropriation of the term "Righteous," up until then used only by the president, was not without consequences, however. It led to the creation of a small space of legitimacy, providing a window of opportunity that was also open for MPs on the other side of the political spectrum from the president. It enabled the expression of a preexisting vision of the past, but with the help of an unprecedented term.

Therefore, Jean Le Garrec's decision cannot be explained simply by supposed vote-catching motivations—any more than it could in 1992. His constituency in the north had a particularly high concentration neither of Jews[4] nor of Righteous individuals, if these two categories can be considered the final recipients of the proposed text. Here, Jean Le Garrec's involvement was the direct product of the bill he had written six years earlier. This earlier initiative strongly influenced his later activity.

In 1998 Jean Le Garrec was not the sole defender of the text, as he had been in 1992. He was approached by Daniel Marcovitch because of his previous engagement on the question. Aside from their common membership in the Socialist Party, the political trajectories of these two men were very different. As MP for the north, Jean Le Garrec was a regular in the Assembly, to which he had been consistently elected since 1981. Daniel Marcovitch, on the other hand, was a member of the Council of Paris and an MP only since 1997. How can we understand the engagement of a second MP alongside Jean Le Garrec? What does this tell us about the process at work here?

During the interview with Daniel Marcovitch, he linked "his idea" to a discussion with a friend who was a plenipotentiary minister at the Israeli embassy in Paris, during a Socialist Party Congress in November 1997. Marcovitch's friend apparently asked him to organize a meeting with Jean Le Garrec on the grounds that Le Garrec was responsible for the 1993 bill. Marcovitch "thought that it was a good idea that France make a law on the Righteous."[5] Beyond the effectiveness of this sequence of events and the effect of mutual interests that the French appropriation would have, the account given by Marcovitch first and foremost reveals the cognitive categories he uses that play a central role in his engagement for the adoption of a bill aiming to "honor the Righteous of France."

Daniel Marcovitch is both French and Jewish; at the time he was also a Socialist MP. His father was born in the Yishuv and a large portion of his family still lives in Israel.[6] Through his commitment to this project, he thus incorporated a specific translation of the past by virtue of his social position at the geographical and social intersections of France and Israel, on one hand, and of Jews and non-Jews, on the other.[7] In autumn 2003, in a text published in the *Lettre du Cercle Leon Blum*[8] he made the Righteous themselves the connection between his different identities. Like the Francophone Volunteers, Marcovitch was a vector. Unlike the Volunteers, he was engaged in French political life and it was therefore as a French public actor that he became mobilized for the recognition and commemoration of the French Righteous. He relied on the instruments traditionally mobilized to conduct state memory policy.

From the title of Righteous among the Nations to the status of Resistance members

Rather than create a new form of distinction ex nihilo to "honor the Righteous of France," Marcovitch chose to use the status of Resistance member, a veritable institution of the memory public policy put in place at the end of the war. The original bill thus aimed to "grant the status of Resistance member to those who, during World War II, contributed to saving Jewish people." Set up as a model, the existing institutions and the choices that had previously presided over memory policy provided a framework for what the two MPs simultaneously claimed was a public policy transfer.

Although the text used an established instrument, it also proposed an evolution. This was immediately thrown into question by the Research and Information Service of the National Assembly to which the bill was submitted for its judicial opinion.[9] Through this specific service, the institutions that constituted the constitutional rules provided a strong constraint on the projected evolution and led to the rewriting of the bill. The Research Service drew attention to the fact that the notion of "Jews" cannot exist in French law "because it refers to a racial definition rather than a religious one," which is in any case explicitly forbidden by the secular nature of the French state.[10]

Daniel Marcovitch and Jean Le Garrec thus wrote a new version of their bill that consisted in adding a sixth paragraph to Article L.172 of the Military Infirmity and Victims of War Pension Code, which provides a definition of Resistance member. That definition could now recognize as such "any person having, in enemy-occupied territory or under the control of the de facto authority calling itself the government of the French state, taken in, protected or defended, under the conditions described by decree in the Council of State, one or several people threatened with crimes against humanity."[11]

The combination of constitutional rules first, and then those stemming from the memory policy in place since the Liberation, provide a formal framework that must be applied to any legal redefinition of the past to be commemorated. More fundamentally, the MPs' choice to situate their bill in this framework (even if it was to provoke its evolution) shows that the translation of the Israeli term that began in 1995 was situated within the very dichotomy that had governed the public management of the memory of Occupation since 1945. It demonstrates that the change was occurring in a relationship of continuity rather than discontinuity with previous stages. The mention of the Righteous was designed to serve as a counterweight to the collective failing of France. In this dynamic of hybridization, it thus took on the function hitherto exclusively the responsibility of the Resistance members. Ultimately, the status of Resistance member was the instrument that corresponded best to the permanency of the objective.

However, this modification was refused by the Socialist executive on the grounds that it risked adulterating the very notion of resistance. The attribution of this status was the responsibility of the state secretary for Veterans' Affairs. The two MPs (who also belonged to the same political family) had therefore consulted him on the bill. But in April 1998, the cabinet director of the secretary of state, Serge Barcellini, conveyed to them his "most explicit reservations." He felt that "the notion of Resistance would lose its consistence and would disappear as a reference in national memory" by undergoing "an extraordinary devaluation."[12]

He proposed a strict separation into two memorial registers that would involve the creation of a framework that was "totally autonomous from that defined by the legislator in the wake of World War II" and that would be defined as "a new right to compensation, specific to the effects of the anti-Jewish policy of the Vichy state." However, in spite of his proposition, he judged this solution to be undesirable because "the Righteous would [thus] become the hierarchical epitome of heroism."[13] He requested that the project be abandoned.

Faced with opposition from the Socialist government, and the presidency's lack of interest in the debate, Jean Le Garrec and Daniel Marcovitch backed down. The bill was not registered at the National Assembly. In the different interviews conducted with each of the protagonists of this non-proposition, the text was said to have never existed.[14]

At the end of this first stage it appears that both the constitutional rules and the contours of remembrance policy after Liberation were an obstacle to the renewal proposed by these two MPs. The mechanism can be seen all the more clearly because the proponents chose to use a traditional instrument of that very policy.

This effect was not isolated, however. The influence of institutions plays out through the intermediary of written norms, of course, but also through the activity, identity, and trajectory of those who drive them. Serge Barcellini, for example, followed the development and formalization of state memory policy very closely.[15] He was behind the establishment of a specific administration dedicated to this issue within the state body in 1982, and he has been responsible for it ever since. His past experience sets him in close continuous connection with the historic memory in place until now, which he himself had largely contributed to establishing.

However, the weight of existing institutions in remembrance policy is not sufficient to explain the failure of the project to honor the Righteous of France through a modification of the status of Resistance member. First, it appears that generally in matters of commemoration the executive branch indeed tends to be reticent, or even hostile, to parliamentary initiatives.[16] Yet here too this observation does not explain everything. While the executive body initiated the dynamic in which Jean Le Garrec and Daniel Marcovitch set their proposal, it was not the shift from the executive to the legislative branch as such that explains the destiny of this first bill.

The real explanation in fact lies in the change in public policy instruments that accompanied this shift from the Elysée Palace to Parliament. Since 1995, the president's (and to a lesser extent the government's) homage to the French Righteous regularly set Resistance members alongside the Righteous. However, it did not provoke any criticism or opposition on these grounds. But at that stage this homage was only based on speeches and symbolic ceremonies. The instruments used did not entail any specific budgetary constraints for the state and specifically for the secretary of state for Veterans' Affairs. It left open the question of the interpretation and degree of hybridization between the Righteous and Resistance members, along with that of the possible hierarchy between these two categories of people.

On the opposite, the use of law to establish a new status entailed costs for the state, while creating new resources for social actors. Above all, by necessarily outlining specific criteria, it ended the existing balance between the different actors in the configuration who were previously in agreement, based on the presidential words and gestures that were open to polysemous and divergent interpretations. In order to inscribe an imperative commemoration of the Righteous into French law, it became necessary to renegotiate the agreement and relative consensus preceding the appropriation of the Israeli category through the speeches by the French president.

From Resistance members to Righteous of France

Following this first failed attempt, the two Socialist MPs decided to take another approach. In July 1998, Daniel Marcovitch announced to the Research and Information Service of the National Assembly that they would persevere in their "project to gain recognition for the Righteous among the Nations."[17] A bill was finally submitted on 22 June 1999 at the National Assembly.[18] The authors had taken the cabinet director of the secretary of state's recommendations literally, and they decided to create a new status that was completely distinct to that of Resistance member. They therefore specifically acknowledged borrowing the term from the state of Israel.

This new text above all aimed to create a title for the Righteous of France, which was destined to honor those who acted "to take in, protect or defend one or several people threatened with crimes against humanity." The methods envisaged were directly inspired by those used by the Yad Vashem Institute. They also planned for the establishment of a "national commission of the Righteous of France" made up of nine members, including "a representative of the Jewish community," "a representative of the Gypsy community," a magistrate of the Court of Appeals, and a member of the French Committee for Yad Vashem.[19]

The attribution procedure envisaged was in turn modeled on the functioning of the courts. It was based on "witness hearings" and "*audi alteram partem.*" Finally, in accordance with the jurisprudence established in 1963 by the Israeli Commission, the nomination was based on the criteria of "risk taken" and the lack of self-interested "reward," the possibility of posthumous recognition and the impossibility of making a demand in one's own name were also decided. In a second phase, the bill established a "national day in memory of the victims of racist and anti-Semitic crimes by the French state and in homage to the Righteous of France."[20]

This time the two MPs modeled their project exclusively on the Israeli experience. Not only did they use the exact term "Righteous," which was absent from the first text, but in Article 4 of their bill they proposed that "those recognized as Righteous Among the Nations by the Yad Vashem Institute be awarded the title of 'Righteous of France,' in light of the documents examined by the Institute." However, although this second bill used other tools to pay homage to the Righteous (in the words of those who conceived of it), it was clearly still situated within the same dichotomic structure of historical memory established in the wake of the Liberation. Although the text did not mention the Resistance at all, its statement of motives contains a description of the Righteous that occupies all the lexical field characteristic of the Resistance. It thus mentions "heroes in the shadows" who "waged their war with their bare hands, without a shot fired, armed only with their courage" and "at risk of their lives."[21]

Hampered by the unfavorable precedents on the path to the implementation of remembrance policy, under the influence of the secretary of state for Veterans' Affairs and to a lesser extent the Research and Information Services of the National Assembly, the two MPs began to self-censor. They appeared to avoid all mention of the previous register of French memory policy, while still keeping it in mind as the framework within which they wanted to insert their new homage to the Righteous of France.

However, in spite of the intentional omission of any reference to the Resistance, in keeping with what had been established in the memo by the cabinet director of the secretary of state, this new proposition did not find greater favor with the executive. Its two authors had to insist that the text be submitted by the Socialist group in the Assembly,[22] which defended the text only with a certain reticence. Finally, presented in the name of the group at the end of 1999, the proposition was deferred to the Commission of Social and Cultural Affairs at the National Assembly. Daniel Marcovitch was appointed rapporteur.

The text underwent some final modifications before being debated in the Commission. The Research and Information Service at the National Assembly raised some new "legal issues." It once again submitted the legislative change envisaged to the principles of the constitution.[23] This time it was not the term "Jew" that was problematic in light of the Republican principles of secularism and universality but the unprecedented nature of the Righteous category, as well as its religious and foreign origin.

As a result, the rapporteur reformulated his project once again. The order of the instruments to be mobilized was inversed. Article 1 was consequently dedicated to the national day of homage, explicitly set as 16 July. The procedure for the nomination of the Righteous of France as such became secondary. A relative emancipation regarding the Israeli title was affirmed, and the attribution of the French title to French citizens previously recognized by Israel would no longer be automatic. The principle of France's autonomy in this area was established.

Finally, with this new project, the pendulum began to swing the other way. The addition of a sixth article was envisaged. It took the form of a new paragraph in Article L.262 of the Code of Military Invalidity and War Victims' Pensions. It allows for those awarded the title of Righteous of France to be considered "voluntary combatants of the Resistance."[24] This was of course going back to the spirit of the first bill of March 1998. At this point it was difficult to find the balance between universalism and particularism, between Righteous and Resistance member, between Israel and France; yet that balance was needed to achieve the legislative form of the translation begun in 1995.

The presidential appropriation of the term "Righteous" thus brought together heterogeneous actors at different levels and with potentially divergent points of view. The desire to create a new honorific status thus emphasized the constraints on changes to memory policy that had begun in 1995 by other means. In this sense, although the investment by the legislative branch in the dynamic of the translation of the Israeli category signaled a change, it was primarily because it was accompanied by the use of a public policy instrument—a specific legal status—that was unprecedented in the first stages of the process.

Modification of the imported instrument

This change is not only manifest in the interactions between the different components of the state, the government, the Parliament, and the administration. In the context of the Commission's work Daniel Marcovitch held hearings with several social actors involved in the French configuration relating to the commemoration of the Righteous. The different steps involved in the constitution of this configuration since 1986 would, in turn, come to constrain and structure the public action evolutions that concern us here.

The translation dynamic within a conflictual process

On 17 February 2000, a hearing was held with five leaders of Jewish institutions,[25] the president of the Gypsy Confederal Movement, and a "representative of the Resistance," Jean Mattéoli.[26] The French Committee for Yad Vashem, the Central Consistory, and the Memorial to the Jewish Martyr had also been involved in different stages of the presidential appropriation that began in 1995. The presidents of the Representative Council of Jewish Institutions in France (CRIF) and the Former Jewish Deportees from France Friendship Society were also heard.

The final list indicates once again the type of public policy the parliamentary initiative was associated with. It converged on this point with the prior actions of the presidency, which it considered as its precedent. Above all, it was a form of domestic public action, the absence of a representative of the Israeli embassy[27] confirming that the question was not at all one of foreign and bilateral relations. The identity of the participants, and particularly their different social functions, once again reveals the deep embeddedness that seems to exist between memory policy and the regulation of ethnoreligious belongings by the state.

The simultaneous summons of a representative of the "Gypsies"(the spokesperson of an ethnic group) and one of the Resistance (as the spokesperson for memory actors) manifests this permeability between two spheres of public action that appear to be increasingly close. Although they were marginal to the heart of the text under discussion, the two men both expressed their support.[28] The president of the Consistory also gave his approval and, moreover, specified that he considered this parliamentary initiative to be the logical—and necessary—extension of his own work.[29]

His position within the Jewish institutions was isolated, however, which otherwise stood behind the French Committee for Yad Vashem.[30] This association took precedence and thus had a particular legitimacy within the configuration. It refused to allow the Israeli category to be reused by the legislative body as the title for a new French honorific status. Its president and manager of its Department of the Righteous both thought that "the use of the same term of Righteous to express France's recognition will necessarily create confusion."[31] Just as the use of the title of Resistant was refused by the government, the title of Righteous was refused by the social actors responsible for it in France.

As the extension of the mobilization of the Francophone Volunteers, the French Committee for Yad Vashem was the source of the French public actors' socialization to the term "Righteous." Yet the association also constituted the main source of opposition to one of the direct consequences of this socialization, which was the proposed creation of the title "Righteous of France."

This position might seem like an illustration of an analysis in terms of memory "competition" or "wars," which appear self-evident today.[32] The French Committee and the Yad Vashem Institute were defending their turf by refusing any external use of the term. The leaders of the Committee indeed demonstrated that they considered themselves to be the only ones competent—legally but also in terms of ability—to determine who is worthy of the title of Righteous. Like all social actors, those running associations linked to the commemoration of the past were making the most of their resources. Yet, this was even more the case given that for the French Committee these resources suddenly had new social value because of the interest generated by the increasing mobilization of the state regarding these events and the organization of their commemoration.

In this case, speaking about "competition" and thus only looking at the strategies of social actors prevents us from seeing the process as a whole. This leads us to neglect the way in which public action creates and structures the social configuration or, to continue with the economic metaphor, the market in which these competitive relations are likely to exist. According to this analysis, everything occurred as though the state was simply reacting to potentially contradictory demands, which developed entirely independently of its own actions.

Indeed, an approach in terms of "memory wars" does not allow us to fully understand the mechanisms at work here. Although in 1999 the French Committee for Yad Vashem refused the creation of the actual "Righteous of France" title, it had accompanied the previous stages of the appropriation of the Israeli title of which this project was the final step. In 1996, it actively participated in the organization of a medal ceremony at the Museum of the National Resistance. In 1997, it was closely associated with the inauguration of the Memorial in honor of the Righteous of France. It thus did not take a consistent univocal position of opposition to the translation dynamic initiated by the president in 1995.

The nature of instruments mobilized by the state up until now to appropriate the term "Righteous" left open the question of the meaning of this linguistic loan. The use of the Israeli category could previously have been interpreted by some as a sign of an evolution of the notion of the Resistance or by others as a new status likely to replace it. However, the new bill presented to the Committee broke with this polysemous interpretation of the relationship between the Resistance and the Righteous.

There is thus no contradiction as such between the position of the leaders of the association during the hearings and their previous support for the state's initiatives. They have a common origin. The animators of the association all live in and are citizens of France. But they also at least partly recognize themselves in the state of Israel. This particular position is accompanied by a double undertaking relating to memory. In the wake of the commitment of the Francophone Volunteers, the activities of the French Committee sought to valorize the state of Israel. However, in both their discourses and their actions, the volunteers of this association expressed strong support for the symbols that had structured French memory policy since the end of the war, including references to the Resistance and its members. This was less pronounced among the Francophone Volunteers.

The French Committee's criticism of the intention of creating the French title of the "Righteous" was thus also accompanied by unwavering support for the idea that the state should honor these citizens who had helped the Jews. However, just as Daniel Marcovitch and Jean Le Garrec had initially planned, the leaders of the French Committee wanted the Righteous to be recognized as members of the Resistance and proposed that this status evolve to reflect this.

In November 1997, before any bill had been proposed, Lucien Lazare, former Francophone Volunteer and rapporteur for the Commission for the Designation of the Righteous among the Nations, wrote to the secretary of state for Veterans' Affairs. He expressed his wish to see the Righteous among the Nations benefit from "a status defined by the Nation, inspired by the status of the heroes of the Resistance, along with the rights pertaining to it."[33]

In 1999, this time following the text being registered at the presidency of the National Assembly, the representative of the Department of the Righteous in the French Committee for Yad Vashem adopted a similar discourse. He began by thanking "the initiators of this bill who recognized the merit of these heroes of the civilian Resistance who risked their lives, those of their families or members of their institutions, and who fought bare-handed to save these victims of Nazi barbarity and their accomplices." He also suggested that the term "Righteous" be replaced with another, such as "hero of the civilian Resistance."[34]

This linguistic proposal and the aspiration that it expressed were not the result of circumstance. In 1994, when the configuration was quite different (in that the state was not yet fully committed), Louis Grobart was already publically referring to the Righteous as these "heroes of the civilian Resistance."[35] In the eyes of the Committee leaders, the recognition of the Righteous among the Nations by the French state had to necessarily pass through the use of the national insignia of honor represented by the status of Resistance member. Obtaining Israel's official recognition of French citizens as Righteous and obtaining France's official recognition of the Righteous as Resistance members is a way of expressing and reconciling two feelings of belonging—or, rather, a joint symbolic belonging to both Israel and France.

The mechanism at work here refers to what Pierre Birnbaum qualifies as "subtle play" in his reflection on the situation of Jews in France. "If the real or imaginary links with Israel give more substance to the idea of exile, the conditions are all the more united for the Jews of France to see France as their home. To what extent, for them, and for others, is this subtle play between belonging to the nation-state, home and exile, fully conceivable in today's France?"[36] In this instance, the failure of the first bill written by Le Garrec and Marcovitch seems to indicate the government's inability to conceive of, or at least to allow, the expression of this "subtle play."

Caught between the creation of a new title of Righteous of France and the enlargement of the status of Resistance member, between the position of the executive and most of the Jewish institutions consulted, Marcovitch had to backpedal once again.[37] The path of the different proposals written by the two Socialist MPs shows the proceduralization of public action that alone enables the production of a consensus based on the "adjustments of contradictory interests."[38] The construction of this agreement entailed the abandonment of the project to create a legal status to "honor the Righteous of France."

The translation dynamic and the construction of an agreement

The work of the Commission led to the writing of a new text that included only one article:

> A national day will be instituted in the memory of the victims of racist and anti-Semitic crimes committed by the French state, and to pay homage to the "Righteous of France" who sheltered, protected, and defended one or several people from the threat of genocide at the risk of their own lives and without any recompense. This day will be 16 July, the date of the Velodrome d'Hiver Roundup in Paris, if this day falls on a Sunday; if not, it will take place the following Sunday.[39]

The law "establishing a national day in memory of the victims of racist and anti-Semitic crimes by the French state and in homage to the 'Righteous of France'" was passed in the Senate without modification on 10 July 2000.[40]

Back in 1993, the creation of a national day by decree had already been considered as a way of appeasing the controversy. In 2000, and at the end of nearly two years of consultations and contradictory positions, but in a relatively calm context this time, the addition of a date on the official calendar of historic memory once again became the only public policy instrument able to produce a consensus.

The use of such an instrument can be explained by the fact that, like the presidential discourse, this has the particularity of leaving room for different interpretations. Indeed, the nature of the relations (hybridized, inclusive, exclusive) between the category "Righteous of France" and the category "Resistance member" remains unspecified. Similarly, given that the "Righteous of France" category does not refer to an operational honorific title, it can be associated with different national origins and belongings, depending on one's perspective. It can be seen in light of its Israeli origin, which is signified by the use of quotation marks. It can also be seen as a strictly national designation, symbolized of course by the addition of the expression "of France." Faced with two simultaneous and contradictory demands for continuity and change in memory policy, the two MPs used the creation of a national day as an instrument for action without decision.

Following the vote in Parliament, each actor of the legislative process thus supported the final form that the transfer of the Israeli expression took in French law. The government paid homage to the Righteous on 16 July that very year, even before the decrees for implementation were made—in recognition and support of the recently voted on law.[41] In March 2000, just days after the law was adopted by the National Assembly, the representative of the Department of the Righteous of the French Committee, expressed his pleasure that "the Righteous have entered French history." On 2 May of the same year, he thus organized a new award ceremony for the Israeli title within the National Assembly itself.

Similarly, the CRIF, which had been opposed to the project of creating a French honorific status, rapidly adopted the category created by the law of 10 July 2000. It organized several events in homage to the Righteous of France in regional areas. The national day thus allowed the Parliament to deal with issues of memory while still leaving them open to interpretation. It thus primarily constituted a state response to the expression of a wide diversity of perspectives on the past by an increasing number of heterogeneous actors at different levels.

At this stage of our analysis it is possible to draw some conclusions, or at least to formulate questions relating to the contemporary approach toward the relationship between memory and politics.

This case study shows how the mechanisms at work here are not only more complex but also quite different from those generally analyzed in the relations between law and memory, on one hand, and the multiplication of national commemorative days, on the other. It seems to suggest that, when they exist, demands made to the state in terms of memory do not necessarily reflect a "communitarian atomization," or "identity fragmentation," or a mobilization of "competing" actors. On the contrary, they can be an expression of identification, albeit partial and polysemous, by social actors (who hitherto remained essentially silent in the political arena) with the institutions that structure state-controlled memory policy in the long term.

The proceduralization of public action that has been presented here suggests that in this instance the social actors involved did not primarily demand the creation of a new commemoration. Instead they were more focused on the recognition of their experiences, their memories, and their multiple belongings through categories that were created during the period in which memory policy regarding the Occupation was developed. Here the "fragmentation of memories" that marked the establishment of an additional national day is not due to the social actors involved. It is primarily the product of the state's specific treatment of issues of memory. This instrument of public action enables discussion of the past while leaving the different actors room for their interpretations.[42]

In a word, the use of the national day as a policy instrument seems to be a way for the state to manage the tension between developing memory policy and operating state propaganda. In this respect, limiting the analysis of these links between memory and public action and the denunciation of "memory public policy" primarily defined as political utilization of the past, thus assimilating it to propaganda, leads to a possible misinterpretation that would prevent us from seeing the complexity of the processes at work here. It is therefore possible to envisage that increasing the number of public actions relating to memory might, on the contrary, be a sign of the increasing democratization of French society.

It would thus be seen as a specific way of regulating the tension between increasing pluralism and the diversity of perspectives resulting from wider access to political action, on one hand, and the continued permanence of political institutions conveying the constitutional rules and legal norms that affirm the principles of secularism and universalism, on the other. Therefore, according to this interpretation, it is paradoxically not the rise of communitarianism but the refusal of the state to reform the rules governing multiple belongings and, above all, their possible embeddedness within the idea of citizenship itself that has led to the increase in the number of national commemorative days.

Confronted with this democratization and thus with the expression of partially differing perspectives, it was therefore the state that, through its action, gave rise to competitive relations that did not necessarily exist before it intervened. It is striking to observe here that although the secretary of state criticized the principle of national recognition for the Righteous on the grounds that this would reduce the prestige associated with the Resistance as the epitome of heroism, Jean Mattéoli did not object to establishing a French honorific distinction when he spoke at the parliamentary hearing as the "representative of the Resistance."[43]

This mechanism can be found in identical form in other areas of the state. There is in fact no real difference between the executive and the legislative branch in this regard. Contrary to what several other studies have suggested,[44] the increasing number of laws relating to memory is not a compensation for limits to parliamentary power in favor of the national government or European institutions (which also set up actions relating to the evocation of the past around the same time). The comparison between the two poles of the public policy transfer studied here show that the first initiative was a matter of power, the backbone of the state.

In the 1950s, Israel (as a purely parliamentary regime) made the first official decision in this area, through the Knesset. In the second half of the 1990s, in France (where the regime strongly resembles a presidential system) it was the action of the president of the Republic that opened the door for the parliamentarians' actions. The use of the national commemorative day as a policy instrument by the state (in its various forms) thus constitutes a specific way of managing the question of how public policy can be changed in the realm of memory.

The creation of the Righteous of France category and the manifestation of a paradigm

Although the establishment of a commemoration of the Righteous of France was the result of the state's treatment of conflictual interactions, contradictory interpretations, and various social positions and belongings of the heterogeneous actors involved, it cannot be reduced to this. As was the case for the 1953 vote in the Knesset, paying homage to the Righteous of France provoked the crystallization of a paradigm that went beyond the strategies at work here—such as the simple question of evoking the past.

From the individual to the collective: from the Righteous among the Nations to the Righteous of France

In establishing a commemorative day, the law of 10 July 2000 was careful to avoid providing a definitive answer to the question of the relations between the categories the Righteous of France and the Resistance. It was also careful not to define the nature of the connection between the French expression and its Israeli model. Nor was the symbolic meaning of this national homage further explained. Unlike previous questions, this one had not been the subject of discussions and divergences over the course of the different stages that had preceded the final vote on the text.

This time, the lack of explanation did not lead to the need to maintain the possibility of multiple interpretations through cultivating the polysemy of the terms used. On the contrary it expressed a convergence of perspectives that was sufficient in itself and was able to remain implicit. As the result of a negotiated agreement, the text—which was ultimately reduced to its single article—brought together the different parties in a consensual interpretation. It provided a collective meaning to the Righteous of France in order to make them the incarnation of "the honor of France."

In the presentation of his motives for the bill, Daniel Marcovitch explained his decision to shift the recognition from an individual to a collective register: "The solution we have chosen is the most honorable because it reflects the collective recognition by France of its heroes, who are for the most part already dead and sometimes unknown." He continued, "Rather than paying them homage individually . . . it is preferable to remember their actions in a collective way." The collective redefinition of the homage to the Righteous resulted from the reactions and obstacles encountered over the course of negotiations that preceded the vote on the law. However, at the same time, it existed before and remained largely independent of the legislative process.

First, this collective recognition was already present in the presidential discourse in July 1995 and November 1997. It was also visible in the speeches of the presidents of the National Assembly and the Senate in January 1994 and March 1995, respectively. Finally, when a legislative project was first considered on an individual level, it rapidly gained collective significance. The work of the Commission reflected a disembodied vision of what the title of Righteous refers to in France. The fact that none of their possible spokesmen or representatives was consulted confirms that these new heroes of historic memory were only superficially taken into account. Not only did the members of the Association of the Righteous of France theoretically constitute the primary beneficiaries of the proposed title (which they themselves had called for), but they were also the first to have registered (so to speak) the expression "Righteous of France" during the name change in 1995. Yet their representatives were never consulted, even though the initiators of the bill were aware of the existence of this association.[45]

Omnipresent leading up to the Commission's report, the collective nature of the homage decided on by the law of 10 July 2000 was also emphasized afterward in the speeches by the MPs and senators in the debates on 29 February at the National Assembly and 28 June in the Senate. Once again a strong consensus was seen here.

The speakers thus systematically portrayed the Righteous of France as a kind of village community. The Socialist rapporteur explained first that:

> We can also talk about the Righteous as being those communities such as the villages of the Creuse, Saint-Pierre-de-Fursac (with the Chateau de Chabannes), Grand-Bourg, or Saint-Hilaire-le-Chateau, or the town of Le Chambon-sur-Lignon in the Haute-Loire, which collectively gave refuge to the Jews.[46]

Already present at the heart of the first consistorial project for the memorial in homage to the Righteous of France, the town of Le Chambon-sur-Lignon served as a model for what the parliamentarians appeared to understand by the term "Righteous of France." For François Baroin, conservative MP (Rally for the Republic [RPR]), for example, the epitome of the Righteous was "the heroic village of Le Chambon-sur-Lignon, it was here the pastors, here the teachers, here the farmers, who hid families and who at the risk of their lives, allowed three quarters of French Jews to escape the final solution." Sometimes other towns were mentioned. The centrist MP Rudy Salles referred to the "collective application for the title of 'Righteous' by the village of Braux in the Alpes-de-Haute-Provence, in recognition for the action of the whole population of the town."[47]

Along with slippage in scale from physical persons to collective bodies, the Righteous went from being an individual to a multitude. They came to incarnate "these thousands of French citizens," "these hundreds, these thousands—we will never know how many—of anonymous heroes," "the French people, in its majority." As a multitude, they are described as diverse and probably encompassing the full spectrum of French society. They came from all kinds of professions, from all walks of life. They were "friends," "neighbors," or "strangers."

As we saw in the presidential discourses of summer 1995 and winter 1997, reference to the survival statistics of French Jews was systematically used to support this shift of the Righteous from the individual to the group. As a multitude and a majority, the "Righteous of France" came to represent the collective to which they belonged: the nation. In the speeches by the MPs, as in the comments by the rapporteurs, the shift from the individual to the collective was ultimately shadowed by a parallel between the actions of the Righteous and the "honor of France." Michel Herbillon, Liberal Democrat MP, thus declared, "The denunciation of a dark period in our history must be accompanied by homage paid to these anonymous people who, by their courageous action, saved so many human lives, and by the same movement, the honor of France." Socialist senator Elizabeth Guigou believed that "it was indeed due to the courage of these thousands of anonymous people, like that of the Resistance members, that France was able, in the torment, to conserve its honor."

In 2000, the legislative adoption of the term "Righteous" by the French Parliament thus occurred according to methods and frameworks for interpretation that opposed, point by point, those that had governed the vote in the Knesset. In Israel in 1953, the idea of honoring the memory of the Righteous was first evoked through the example of the USSR and thus a collective entity, but the parliamentary debates ultimately led to the creation of a strictly individual distinction. The "Righteous among the Nations" were thus considered exceptions to the presiding principle of the hostility of non-Jews toward the Jews.

In Paris, almost fifty years later, the intention to create an individual title gave way to a collective recognition in the form of a national day of commemoration. The Righteous of France were thus considered symbols of the benevolent attitude of the whole French population toward the Jews. If the creation of the Righteous of France category constituted a public policy transfer, the translation of the Israeli title was accompanied by a total reversal of the original paradigm in the adaptation of the instrument initially chosen by Israel.

There is, however, a point in common between the establishment of the Israeli title and the legislative creation of the Righteous of France category. In both countries, in 1953 and in 2000, the votes were unanimous. In both cases, this unanimity revealed the existence of a framework of interpretation that was shared between all the MPs in spite of their political affiliations. They all adopted the positive image of the nation, which in spite of the vicissitudes of history and the compromises of its leaders could not be fundamentally challenged.

If the significance of the word "nation" itself might vary depending on the speaker, particularly in relation to the word "Republic," it seems that alongside the negotiation of the agreement that preceded the vote on the law, the existence of this shared framework for interpretation played a major role in the adoption of the text. In this respect, the text did not signal a change of the paradigm that had presided over state memory policy that was in place since the war. At its core, the latter already conveyed the subscription to an identical framework for interpretation. Given this, we might wonder what other transformations the use of the term "Righteous" reflects.

The naturalization of the term "Righteous"

At the end of the study of the concrete sequences that have governed the introduction of the term "Righteous" into French law, the use of the Israeli category appears to be intrinsically paradoxical. Daniel Marcovitch and Jean Le Garrec sought to use the language of the Resistance; the French Committee for Yad Vashem, and with it most of the associations consulted, spoke of "civilian Resistance." The use of the Israeli category finally dominated even though none of the main actors defended its use in principle.

A similar mechanism was also at work over the course of the parliamentary debates. Thus, although several senators conveyed their doubts as to the reuse of the Israeli term, they seemed to think this reappropriation was inevitable. In his report, and even before returning to it in his speech, Senator Jean-Pierre Schosteck made it clear that "several members of the Legal Committee wondered about the possibility of inscribing the term 'Righteous' into French law, given that it is a distinction attributed by the Israeli authorities, and whether it might not be preferable to mention, more generally, 'those' who protected people threatened with genocide."[48] However, he also thought that it was impossible to do otherwise.

Then, during the debates themselves, Senator Michal Charasse in turn criticized the bill for the same reason, before adding "the problem that this bill might represent in terms of the Republic's principle of secularism, because it ultimately introduces a purely religious notion into the laws of the Republic, by referring to an expression evoking the thirty-six Righteous of the Bible, and I could go on." However, before speaking on this question, he seemed to accept the impossibility of not using the term "Righteous." He specified that, whatever the case may be, his vote was guaranteed. The doubts expressed here were only rhetorical. They shed light on the role that global norms appeared to play in this process, beyond the simple strategies and choices of actors.

Of course, this actualization of more general references was only possible because of the long process of socialization of the actors, which began in 1986 with the mobilization of the Francophone Volunteers. It thus appears that, although rhetorical, this critical distance was totally absent for the MPs who were likely to have had a longer and closer familiarization with the term "Righteous."

The centrist MP Rudy Salles was the president of the France-Israel Friendship Group in the National Assembly. During the debates in the House, his discourse contributed to the naturalization of the term "Righteous" that was supposed "to be sufficient in itself." He thus told Marcovitch:

> You were envisaging the creation of an order of the Righteous of France, which would eventually be in competition with the order of the Righteous among the Nations. That is a trap we wanted to avoid. Also, we did not aim to define, in French law, the meaning of the term "Righteous," which is a biblical notion. The word is sufficient in itself.[49]

One month earlier, when Le Garrec was concluding the work of the Commission,[50] he had emphasized the importance of paying "solemn homage to those whom it is impossible to call anything but the Righteous."

The inductive approach based on the observation of actors and the strategies that they implement has reached its limits here:

> This approach is unable to account for the complexity of the relations between the "actor and the system." It does not allow us to understand how the actor is constrained by the whole, while still acting in and on it, which means that there is "something" more to the whole, which somehow transcends the strategies of individual or collective actors and cannot be reduced to the sum of individual behavior.[51]

Exactly what this "something more" might be in the institutionalization of the Righteous of France category remains to be seen, however. What are the global social norms that are at work here? What is their degree of efficiency? Through which mechanisms do they influence the evolution of memory policy that prescribes a narrative of the past whose internal dichotomy remains intact?

Notes

1. Peter A. Hall and Rosemary C.R. Taylor, "Political Science and the Three New Institutionalisms," *Political Studies* 44 (December 1996): 936–57.
2. See Appendix 1 for the detailed composition of the corpus used in this chapter.
3. Statement of reasons, bill, March 1998, Marcovitch Archives.
4. According to the distribution revealed by the study commissioned by the United Jewish Social Fund (Fonds Social Juif Unifié) and the Jewish United Appeal of France (Appel Unifié Juif de France) in collaboration with the Alyah Department of the Jewish Agency for Israel. Conducted by Erik Cohen, this research was carried out according to the patronymic method, based on 1,132 questionnaires completed between 13 and 31 January 2002. Erik Cohen, "Les Résultats de la grande enquête sur les Juifs français," *L'Arche*, no. 538 (December 2002): 52–79; also Erik Cohen, "Une Communauté inscrite dans la socialité. Valeurs et identité des Juifs de France," *L'Observatoire du monde juif*, Bulletin no. 10/11 (May 2004): 7–14.
5. Interview with Daniel Marcovitch, 17 October 2002, Paris.
6. Ibid. and http://www.cercle-leon-blum.org.
7. On the importance of the individual trajectories of those who conceive or implement memory policy, see particularly Valérie Rosoux, *Les Usages de la mémoire dans les relations internationales* (Brussels: Bruylant, 2001).
8. Daniel Marcovicth, "Les Justes," *Lettre du Cercle Léon Blum*, autumn 2003. This review was created the previous May by Socialist party members who wanted to denounce what they considered to be the rise of anti-Semitism among certain movements and parties on the political left.

9. The Research and Information Service (Service des études et de la documentation) of the National Assembly is responsible for overseeing the legal and constitutional coherence of bills proposed in the National Assembly. It is thus called upon to provide legal expertise on how a proposed law may fit (or not) into the French legal framework.
10. Report by the Research and Information Service of the National Assembly, handwritten version, Marcovitch Archives, December, 1997.
11. Mentioned in Section 1 of Book II of the penal code resulting from the law no. 92–1336 of 16 December 1992, modified, bill tabled by Jean Le Garrec and Daniel Marcovitch. Document undated and unnumbered. This bill was not ever tabled in the Assembly. It appears, however, in the list of bills on the minutes of the meeting of Socialist members of the Senate Legal Committee of Wednesday 25 March 1998, dated 18 March 1998, Marcovitch Archives. We have designated it the "bill of March 1998."
12. Note, CAB/CT/AD/BO/NO. 4790, of 28 April 1998, Marcovitch Archives.
13. Note, CAB/CT/AD/BO/NO. 4790, of 28 April 1998, Marcovitch Archives.
14. Interviews with Jean Le Garrec, 13 November 2002, Daniel Marcovitch, Serge Barcellini, 3 October 2002 and Jean-Pierre Masseret (then secretary of state for Veterans' Affairs), 6 May 2003, Paris.
15. Pierre-François Raimond, *Un Exemple de politique de la mémoire: la délégation à la mémoire et à l'information historique* (M.A. dissertation, Paris, Institut d'Etudes Politiques, 1994); and the speech by Serge Barcellini before the Parliamentary Study Group of the French Association of Political Science, 10 April 1992, titled "Le Parlement et la Politique de mémoire des guerres et conflits contemporains." This text was provided by Yves Déloye. See also 1 K 841, Historical Service, Defense Secretary of State (SHD).
16. Claire Andrieu, "La Commemoration des dernières guerres françaises: l'élaboration de politiques symboliques, 1945–2003," in *Politiques du passé. Usages politiques du passé dans la France contemporaine,* ed. Claire Andrieu, Marie-Claire Lavabre, and Danielle Tartakowsky, 39–46 (Aix-en-Provence: Publications de l'Université de Provence, 2006).
17. Letter by François Tchekemian, on behalf of Daniel Marcovitch, to Christian Eude, Research and Information Service of the National Assembly, 17 July 1998, Marcovitch Archives.
18. Bill establishing a National Day in memory of the victims of racist and anti-Semitic crimes by the French state and to honor the Righteous of France, no. 1727, registered at the Presidency of the Assembly, 22 June 1999.
19. Bill establishing a National Day in memory of the victims of racist and anti-Semitic crimes by the French state and to honor the Righteous of France, no. 1727, registered at the Presidency of the Assembly, 22 June 1999.
20. Article 2. Although the date was not specified in the text, and the choice was to be subject to consultation, 16 July was already envisaged by the authors. On 15 July 1999, Marcovitch's office sent out a press statement stating that this bill had been presented. It called on the authorities to evoke the "role of all the Righteous of France" during the ceremonies of the following day. Marcovitch Archives.
21. Article 2. Although the date was not specified in the text, and the choice was to be subject to consultation, 16 July was already envisaged by the authors. On 15 July 1999, Marcovitch's office sent out a press statement stating that this bill had been presented. It called on the authorities to evoke the "role of all the Righteous of France" during the ceremonies of the following day. Marcovitch Archives.
22. Letter from Jean-Marc Ayrault, president of the Socialist Group, to Daniel Marcovitch, 26 May 1999; from Daniel Marcovitch to Jean Marc Ayrault, 7 September 1999, and to Arielle Texier, general secretary of the Socialist Group, 4 November 1999, Marcovitch Archives.

23. This led to a new document titled "text submitted by the rapporteur." It remained a working paper and was never registered. Marcovitch Archives.
24. Article 6 of the "text submitted by the rapporteur," Marcovitch Archives.
25. In their order at the hearing, Jean Kahn for the Central Consistory, Jacques Fredj and Pierre Kauffmann for the Memorial of the Jewish Martyr/Contemporary Jewish Documentation Center, Richard Prasquier and Louis Grobart for the French Committee for Yad Vashem, Henri Hadjenberg and Haïm Musicant for the CRIF, and finally Henri Bulawko for the Former Jewish Deportees of France Friendship society.
26. "Hearings on the 'Righteous of France' bill," Marcovitch Archives. The list of people who spoke at the hearing was reproduced at the end of the report, no. 2195, submitted to the presidency of the National Assembly, 23 February 2000. But these hearings did not lead to any public report. We deduce their content here based on cross-analysis of interviews between the various actors, on one hand, and participant observation and document collection within the French Committee in February 2000, on the other.
27. The position of the Israeli embassy cannot be completely reconstructed largely due to the lack of supporting archives, the embassy having burned down. However, Marc Knobel, who was then responsible for these questions within the embassy declared his support in his interview on 12 February 2004 in Paris. This is confirmed by a memo that he wrote on 30 June 1999. He concluded in these terms: "The title of 'Righteous Among the Nations', awarded to the most deserving of individuals, was already the greatest homage that the Jewish people could pay. The title 'Righteous of France' awarded by the French Republic will thus and rightly complement this title," Marcovitch Archive.
28. Interviews with Daniel Marcovitch and Jean Mattéoli, 15 January 2004, Paris.
29. Interviews with Daniel Marcovitch and Jules Bloch, who were responsible for the Righteous among the Nations Association, 25 May 1998 and Jean-Marie Pouplain, 16 December 2003, Paris.
30. Interviews with Daniel Marcovitch and Jean Le Garrec, 31 December 2002 and Jacques Fredj, 8 July 2004, Paris. Also, participant observation during February 2000 within the French Committee for Yad Vashem.
31. "Regarding the bill presented by Jean Le Garrec and Daniel Marcovitch," memo written by the president of the Department of the Righteous among the Nations at the French Committee for Yad Vashem, FCYV. This memo was dated 27 September 1999 and addressed to the two socialist MPs.
32. These terms were borrowed from Jean-Michel Chaumont, *La Concurrence des victimes. Génocide, identité, reconnaissance* (Paris: La Découverte, 1997) and Daniel Lindenberg, "Guerres de mémoire en France," *Vingtième Siècle. Revue d'Histoire,* no. 42 (April–June 1994): 77–95. On this approach, see the recent publication of Pascal Blanchard and Isabelle Veyrat-Masson, *Les Guerres de mémoires: La France et son histoire, enjeux politiques, controverses historiques, stratégies médiatiques* (Paris: La découverte, 2008).
33. Letter from Lucien Lazare to Jean-Pierre Masseret, secretary of state for Veterans' Affairs, under the care of the French ambassador to Israel, 10 November 1997, FCYV.
34. A near identical note was addressed to Jean Le Garrec, 14 February 2000, Marcovitch Archives.
35. Louis Grobart, "Review of Lucien Lazare, *Le Livre des Justes* (Paris: Lattès, 1993)," *L'Arche,* February 1994.
36. Pierre Birnbaum, *Sur la corde raide. Parcours juif entre exil et citoyenneté* (Paris: Flammarion, 2002), 396.
37. Commission of cultural and social affairs, report no. 31, 23 February 2000. Only the debate that followed the exposé by the rapporteur was published in the report, no. 2195, submitted to the presidency of the National Assembly, 23 February 2000.

38. For a similar conclusion based on another example of the links between public policy and memory, see Francesca Polletta, "Legacies and Liabilities of Insurgent Past: Remembering Martin Luther King, Jr., on the House and Senate Floor," *Social Science History* 22, no. 4 (1998): 479–512.
39. Text adopted by the Committee, report no. 2195 then bill no. 457 (1999–2000).
40. Law no. 2000–644 of 10 July 2000, instituting a national day in memory of the victims of racist and anti-Semitic crimes by the French state and in homage to the Righteous of France. For the sake of readability this text will be referred to simply as the Law of 10 July 2000.
41. Speech by Jean-Luc Mélenchon, minister for professional training, http://www.education.gouv.fr.
42. For a more systematic study, see Sarah Gensburger, "Comprendre la multiplication des 'journées de commémoration nationale': étude d'un instrument d'action publique de nature symbolique," in *L'Instrumentation de l'action publique. Controverses, résistances, effets*, ed. Charlotte Halpern, Pierre Lascoumes, and Patrick Le Galès (Paris: Presses de Sciences Po, 2014), 345–65. For insights regarding the Italian case, see Andrea Cossu, "Memory, Symbolic Conflict and Changes in the National Calendar in the Italian Second Republic," *Modern Italy* 15, no. 1 (2010): 3–19.
43. For several similar hypotheses, see Sarah Gensburger, "L'Émergence progressive d'une politique internationale de la mémoire: l'exemple des actions publiques de 'partage' de la mémoire," in *Traumatisme collectif pour patrimoine. Regards sur un mouvement transnational*, ed. Bogumil Jewsiewicki (Laval: Presses de l'Université Laval, 2008), 25–42.
44. Marc Frangi, "Les 'Lois mémorielles' de l'expression de la volonté générale au législateur historien," *Revue du droit public, de la science politique en France et à l'Etranger*, no. 1 (2005): 241–66; Marc Olivier Baruch, *Des lois indignes? Les Historiens, la politique et le droit* (Paris: Tallandier, 2013).
45. Marcovitch Archives and interviews with Daniel Marcovitch and Ivan Beltrami, 18 March 2003, Marseille.
46. Report no. 2195 (1999–2000). Similarly, the report by Jean-Pierre Schosteck for the Senate's Legal Committee (apparently inspired by the previous report) concluded its enumeration with this phrase: "We also cite whole communities who collectively organized the rescue of Jews, such as the villages of Saint-Pierre de Fursac (Creuse) or Le Chambon-sur-Lignon (Haute-Loire)," report no. 353 (1999–2000). Among other examples, consider the identical formulations by Elisabeth Guigou and Robert Badinter on 28 June 2000 in the Senate.
47. Session of the National Assembly, 29 February 2000, official analytic report.
48. Report by Jean-Pierre Schosteck, no. 353 (1999–2000).
49. Session of the National Assembly, 29 February 2000, official analytic report.
50. Report no. 2195 (1999–2000).
51. Pierre Muller, "Esquisse d'une théorie du changement dans l'action publique. Structures, acteurs et cadres cognitifs," *Revue française de science politique* 55, no. 1 (2005): 193.

Chapter 5

Social Norms and Memorial Categories

The globalization of the term "Righteous"

Contemporary studies of memory have shown little interest in global social norms. They primarily consider the past, as it happened, to be the main horizon from which to evaluate its political uses. This circularity, this "symbolic isolation" as Alon Confino called it, also prevents any kind of perspective on the evolution of memorial categories compared with that of cognitive categories. However, it is possible to envisage that "memory might be thought of as the product of an interaction between a specific representation of the past and the global specter of current representations in a particular culture."[1] It is the same for the relationship between memory and politics.

Trying to explain memory changes by something else that the representations of the past requires to shift the scale of observation. Because the term "Righteous of France" results from a translation, understanding the connection between the term's origin and the possible emergence of new social norms obliges us to put the French case into a global perspective. To what extent are the processes discussed in the previous chapter specific to France? To what extent are they part of a larger evolution that makes the expression "Righteous" an increasingly universal reference? And, conversely, what remains of the "national" in what most protagonists have called "national memory policy?"

Taking up the Israeli term: a worldwide phenomenon

Since the mid-1990s, many European and non-European states as well as international organizations have come together in their systematic use of the Israeli title. This convergence reveals the contours and nature of the paradigm that emerged to participate in the birth of the "Righteous of France" category.

The appropriation of the Israeli title by European states

In 1999, parliamentarians in two other European countries voted on laws to enable a national appropriation of the Israeli category similar to that which was implemented in France. In Belgium, the Chamber of Representatives created the Honorary Award of the Righteous. In Poland, the National Assembly decided to bestow the status of war veteran on the Righteous among the Nations.

In Poland this evolution was a revolution in its own right. The people who had helped the Jews, and particularly those who had been honored for this by Yad Vashem, had until then been regularly subject to discrimination by the Polish state.[2] Although elsewhere in Western Europe the Righteous had only rarely been the recipients of national honors, they had not been subject to persecution as such. Yet in spite of these strong differences in the previous treatment of the Righteous, from the mid-1990s on the actions of most European governments converged in paying homage to those among their citizens who had come to the rescue of the Jews during World War II. They thus overwhelmingly adopted the use of the term "Righteous" to refer to these citizens.

In the year 2000, Greece paid unprecedented attention to its Righteous citizens. The general secretariat for information, for example, developed a traveling exhibition designed to communicate the reality of the Holocaust in Greece, in which a special section presented the "Greek Righteous Among Nations." Like Le Chambon-sur-Lignon in France, a particular town was held up as an example: Zakynthos, the Island of the Righteous. Finally, on 27 January 2004, as part of the first official day of remembrance of the Holocaust in Greece, a medal ceremony was organized for the first time in partnership with the Greek state. The principal state representatives attended and spoke at the event.

Similarly, on 6 November 1998, the Bulgarian National Assembly devoted a session to the memory of one of its former members, Dimitar Peshev, Righteous among the Nations. On 18 February 2001, the president of the Assembly unveiled a commemorative plaque in the street where this Righteous individual had died amid general indifference nearly thirty years earlier.

However, this generalization of state commemoration of the Righteous from the mid-1990s onward does not in itself attest to the existence of a paradigm characterized by the use of the Righteous of France category. The convergence that we have observed was indeed accompanied by an objective situation shared by several of the governments in question. Jews were deported to extermination camps from all the territories of formerly occupied Europe.[3] Confronted with the same structural need to offer a positive counterpoint to real or anticipated accusations of complicity in the Holocaust, which indeed began to spread during the 1990s, the leaders of these states found a solution in promoting the Righteous as the new hero able to embody the nation.

However, this explanation, based on the strategy of the actors, is once again clearly insufficient. On one hand, as we have seen in the French case, although this mechanism enables us to explain why those who saved Jewish people were mentioned, it does not explain why the Israeli expression was used for this. On the other hand, the term "Righteous" was used in a similar way in countries where the Jewish population was not subject to persecution during World War II.

The countries that adopted an officially neutral position between 1939 and 1945 provide the first example.[4] The evolution of the fate of Aristide de Sousa Mendes at the hands of his government is exemplary in this respect. At the end of the war, Mendes was punished for assisting Jews in his role as Portuguese consul in Bordeaux. He died disgraced and destitute in 1954. However, from 1988 onward, the Portuguese state progressively modified its position concerning this Righteous figure, and he gradually came to be seen as an example, rather than as a deviant. Finally, in 1995 his country paid homage to him; the Portuguese president presented one of Mendes's sons with the highest national honor, the Cross of the Order of Christ.

There was a similar turnaround in the policies of federal leaders and local authorities in Switzerland. At the end of the 1980s, in Switzerland as in Portugal, the civil servants who had disobeyed orders in order to help the Jews were still considered criminal offenders.[5] For having helped Jews enter Switzerland, Paul Grüninger was sentenced before the law, lost his status as a civil servant, and found himself permanently unemployed. Although he was recognized as Righteous by Yad Vashem in 1966, he died in 1982 in misery and shame.[6]

The mid-1990s marked a complete reversal of this stigmatization. Paul Grüninger was progressively held up as a model by Swiss political leaders.[7] In 1995, the court of justice of his canton reopened his trial and found him innocent, and a square was renamed in his honor in his hometown. The parliament of the canton finally approved the payment of compensation intended to fund the creation of a foundation in recognition of his status as Righteous.

The end of the social and legal condemnation of the Swiss civil servants who had helped the Jews goes beyond this one case, however. On

7 May 1995, on the fiftieth anniversary of the armistice, the president of the National Council had the Parliament observe one minute of silence in memory of these Righteous men and women "who did not hesitate to listen only to their conscience, to disobey, and save human lives." In 1998, a medal ceremony was—once again for the first time—organized in the federal Parliament.[8] Finally, in 2001, the federal minister of foreign affairs wrote the preface to a book on the Righteous of Switzerland, in which he explained that these men and women were now an integral part of "national history."[9]

Of course the emergence of the Righteous in Swiss historical memory occurred at a time when Switzerland and its bankers were being criticized for their management of unclaimed Jewish accounts.[10] However, aside from the fact that the configuration was not identical in the Portuguese case, the hypothesis of a utilitarian appropriation of the Israeli category still does not explain the whole process.

Setting up the Righteous as a symbol

The existence and shape of what is not explained by actors' strategies can be more clearly seen in the fact that the term "Righteous" was also adopted by states with no particular link to the Holocaust.

The celebration of Raoul Wallenberg[11] and his increasingly systematic portrayal as a Righteous among the Nations reflect the extent to which the Righteous have been established as a global reference. Until the 1980s, Wallenberg was not really the object of public recognition or homage outside of Sweden, his native country. In October 1981, initially in response to a proposition by a member of Congress, who he had rescued during the war, he was named an honorary citizen of the United States; in 1985 he received a similar distinction in Canada. The fight against communism explains this initial phase—and the untimely disappearance of this Swede apparently illustrates its arbitrariness.

At this point, Raoul Wallenberg was not yet recognized by the Yad Vashem Institute; it did not award him Righteous status until 1996, some ten years later. This exceptionally late nomination reflects a cognitive change and opens a new period for the celebration of this man. From this point onward, many monuments or places were dedicated to him, in Sweden and Hungary but also in Argentina, Australia, the United States, Great Britain, and Russia.[12] Although the governments of these states were not responsible for the dedications, they were systematically associated with them. Similarly, several countries issued stamp collections with his image, as was the case in Argentina in 1996 and Uruguay in 2000.

In 2001, Canada, a non-European country not subject to any kind of accusation regarding its possible participation or passivity in connection with the Holocaust, set up a Raoul Wallenberg Commemorative Day. Its instigators intended it to "help Canadians understand that he was an international hero who saved thousands of people."[13] On 17 January every year, the Canadian state thus pays "homage to the courage, the strength of character and the humanity of this exceptional being."

The increase in the number of tributes to Wallenberg since the mid-1990s suggests that the appropriation of the term "Righteous" is not primarily a tool to renew historical memory and to allow the preservation of "national honor." The commemoration of the Righteous is first and foremost a means by which to propose a behavioral model in keeping with the social norms in place.

The mechanism by which the Righteous have come to symbolically constitute an incarnation of contemporary values can be seen especially clearly in the way the term has been used by several international organizations over the same period.

In May 1999, UNESCO also publically paid homage to Wallenberg. Although the actions of this Righteous individual were briefly presented, and several French Righteous were invited to attend the ceremony, the objective was not the reformulation of the WWII narrative:

> With the recent publication of the book *Mahatma Gandhi and Martin Luther King Jr.: The Power of Non-Violent Action*, and with today's homage to Raoul Wallenberg, UNESCO is preparing for the year 2000, proclaimed the International Year of Culture and Peace by the United Nations, emphasizing the exemplary value of non-violent actions that have changed the world.[14]

This was not about talking about the past, or even about anti-Semitism or racism in today's societies, but about providing models that young people can refer to.

In 1998, the European Parliament had already honored Dimitar Peshev and Aristide de Sousa Mendes as Righteous. The discourse of its president did not refer to the concrete acts of these two Europeans, however; only their humanitarian disobedience was cited. Reference to the Righteous had to primarily symbolize a commitment to humanity and human rights.

One final evolution allows us to specify the mechanisms at work here. The use of the Righteous category is not limited to references to World War II. Several states also use it to commemorate other genocides. For several years, the Rwandan state has used the term in relation to the commemoration of the genocide of the Tutsis. In 2004 Claudine Vidal continued to condemn the attitude of the government and the administrations who "do not give these 'Righteous' the place that they should have" and "suspect the projects seeking to recall this truth, of 'negationism.'"[15] However, a change is clearly underway.

From 2002 on, the initiative by Ibuka (the main association for survivors of the Rwandan genocide) to "record all the 'Righteous' who saved lives during the genocide"[16] began to be adopted by the Rwandan state. The state published a register of these figures and awarded them specific funerary rites. Although the president Paul Kagame did not use the term "Righteous" explicitly, in his speech on 7 April 2004 at the Anohoro Stadium he paid "very particular" homage for the first time to these "men and women who showed enormous courage, who risked their lives to save their friends and neighbors."[17] That same year, the organization of the Gacaca was altered.[18]

Among the categories used to classify the information collected, the judges were required to use a new category of "those who had helped the persecuted,"[19] which was presented as a translation of the Israeli category. Finally, bringing together the main administrations and associations involved both in Rwanda and overseas, in 2004, the group Rwanda Genocide 10 henceforth included the promotion and commemoration of the Righteous among its missions. In Rwanda, it particularly focused on the inclusion of the actions of these Righteous in school textbooks. In addition, they held these individuals up as models of behavior for young people to aspire to.

Although such public action only emerged thirty years after the event in the case of the French commemoration of the genocide of the Jews, it was only ten years after the genocide of the Tutsis that the Rwandan government set up several measures to pay homage to those who had helped victims, regularly referring to them as "Righteous." The speed with which the Rwandan government adopted the term cannot be solely explained by the precedent of the Israeli institutionalization of this recognition.

Indeed, the Armenian genocide was carried out nearly fifty years before Israel decided to establish the title of Righteous among the Nations. Yet none of the actors concerned by the memory of the massacres carried out by the Turks took up this memorial category when it was initially created. However, in Erevan, the Armenian capital, there has been a Garden of the Righteous since the end of the 1990s, where those who resisted the massacres are remembered.

The explanation for the precocity of the establishment of this homage to the Righteous by the Rwandan state is a result of the period in which the Tutsi genocide occurred. The dominant paradigm then transmitted values and norms susceptible of generating and reinforcing an evocation of the past with the help of the Righteous category. These few examples thus confirm the need to break the symbolic isolation, which, up until now, has led work on the relationship between memory and politics to restrict itself to considerations of the past, its representations, and its uses. They demonstrate the existence of a link between the emergence of new global norms and the increased use of the term "Righteous" in Western public action.

Global norms and memorial categories

What are, then, the contents and nature of this paradigm? At the National Assembly, during the debates on 29 February 2000, François Baroin finally mobilized it when he explained that the "homage to the 'Righteous of France'" had to help "construct the most beautiful national and international community worthy of humankind." The renewal of the social norms that participated in this globalization of the appropriation of the term "Righteous" in national and international public policy also involves a reduction in the number of references to patriotism and military engagement in favor of the establishment of a paradigm of human rights and humanitarianism.[20]

From the mid-1990s on, there was a challenge to military values and the affirmation of particularistic patriotism in France and other Western countries. While the French Parliament put an end to military service,[21] compulsory conscription progressively lost ground in many Western countries.[22] Homage to victims of war came to replace honoring soldiers; the social status of "victim" emerged,[23] and "victims' rights" were decreed.[24] Henceforth it was a question of "public policy to assist victims" characteristic of a "society of victims."[25] This evolution is not specific to France.

Over the course of the 1990s, the rights and the voices of victims came into the spotlight, to the point where they sometimes brought about a veritable social revolution.[26] In connection with this, "human rights" and "humanitarianism" became central references in this discourse. This evolution is not particular to Europe and the United States. Human rights movements have also become an unavoidable reference within the political arenas of South American countries, for example.

The emergence of this figure of the victim and the systematic reference to human rights leads to a redefinition of exemplary social conduct. The awarding of the Nobel Peace Prize to the organization Médecins Sans Frontières (MSF; Doctors without Borders) in 1999 reveals the social recognition of a new model: the humanitarian actor. While the discourse of the Nobel Committee appeared to be the consecration of this normative change, it echoes the comments made by various public figures using the term "Righteous" since the mid-1990s.

The Nobel Committee explained why they awarded the prize to Médecins Sans Frontières in these terms:

> A characteristic feature of Médecins Sans Frontières is that, more clearly than anyone else, they combine in their work the two criteria we have mentioned,

> humanitarian work and work for human rights. They achieve this by insisting on their right to arouse public opinion and to point to the causes of the manmade catastrophes, namely systematic breaches of the most fundamental rights. The award to Médecins Sans Frontières is first and foremost a humanitarian award. . . . By showing each victim a human face, by showing respect for his or her human dignity, the fearless and selfless aid worker creates hope for peace and reconciliation.[27]

At the French level, this statutory development appeared once more in the discourses of the French president. In November 2003, Medals of Honor for courage and devotion were awarded for the first time at the Elysée Palace:

> In a society that we deplore as having become too individualist and egoistic, the acts rewarded by this medal speak for themselves. They are a spontaneous refusal of indifference, cowardliness. They reflect an attention to the Other, and a feeling of solidarity that are at the foundation of our social and national cohesion. These acts, accomplished without regard for danger, required clearheadedness, courage, and devotion, and sometimes a veritable abnegation. They all express the generosity without calculation, of a man or a woman who, faced with an unforeseen event, only listened to their heart to react in an emergency and to help their fellowmen.[28]

This speech remobilizes many elements ordinarily used by the head of state to evoke the Righteous and their "active solidarity."

The paradigm that emerged during the study of memory public policies can be found almost word for word in a presidential discourse that in no way deals with the evocation of the past. During the 1990s, the increasing legitimacy awarded to humanitarian actors led to the (re)discovery of the Righteous as exemplary figures for talking about World War II. Instead of an analysis that would situate the representation and uses of the past at the heart of the changes in memory policy, the evolution of global social norms allows us to undertake more complex analysis.

The constitution and actualization of the paradigm we have documented here is an integral part of the birth of the legal category the Righteous of France, as is the formation of the French configuration dedicated to its commemoration. From a dynamic point of view, the state's use of the Israeli title encourages the development of this configuration because it crystallizes the global paradigm and gives it additional legitimacy and visibility. On the other hand, this appropriation was only possible because of the prior establishment of an embryonic configuration that enabled French political leaders to be socialized to the term "Righteous."

Therefore, just as was true in the French case, the influence of global social norms on the international use of the term "Righteous" was not an isolated process. It combined strategic issues and symbolic operations. This generalized appropriation of the Israeli category was based on the existence of several transnational actors. Thus the Raoul Wallenberg International Movement for Humanity played a driving role in the multiplication of state initiatives in honoring this Righteous individual. Similarly, Pietro Kucukian, an Italian doctor of Armenian origin very involved today in the events organized by the Garden of the Righteous Worldwide organization, was behind the creation of such a garden in Armenia.

However, the constitution of such transnational collectives that specifically aim to promote the Righteous are in fact a result rather than a cause of this new paradigm, even though they have also helped reinforce it. Moreover, the adoption of the term by so many states has had profit sharing and opportunity effects that are liable to encourage the exponential development of these collective actors.

The chronology is instructive in this respect. The association Garden of the Righteous Worldwide was only officially created in 2000. Its founders then became the spokespeople for the paradigm that had just emerged. Through their actions, they intend to promote "the universal value of the concept of the Righteous as far as the genocides of the twentieth century are concerned." Over the years they have increased the number of initiatives and installation of gardens in towns and countries that were themselves involved in the commemoration of the Righteous.

As in the French case, Israel was not an actor in the globalization of the term "Righteous"; it was sometimes even reticent about it. The paradigm that was a part of this process from the mid-1990s on was in fact radically different from that which had led to Israel's instauration of the term "Righteous among the Nations" in the 1950s and 1960s. It was not any closer to the paradigm that emerged during the early 1970s and the Yom Kippur War either. The generalization of the transfer of the Israeli expression has thus been accompanied by a translation of the term. While this has substantially modified the original paradigm, it is also subject to polysemous interpretations on the part of the actors involved and even within the shared cognitive framework that we have seen operating here.

The extent of the disparity between the original meaning and the translation of the term "Righteous" also enables us to see how this term became necessary. Even as the figure of the humanitarian hero as the savior of innocent victims became a social model, a certain number of states (particularly European states) had become familiar with the Israeli category through the local organization of medal ceremonies. It was in this way that the term appeared for some, and then for most, as the legitimate and established term to describe those who helped Jews during World War II, and more broadly any person threatened with persecution and genocide, both before 1939 and since 1945. In this respect, the fact that the Rwandan state used the expression less systematically than Western governments to refer to "these men and women who showed enormous courage, risking their lives to save their neighbors and friends" reveals the close interconnectedness between a new paradigm and the process of socialization and interaction between actors.

These intermediary conclusions raise new questions. On one hand, once public actions for remembrance experience the same influences as the rest of state policy, the question of whether a specific sector of memory public policy actually exists arises once again. On the other hand, while memory public policy is ordinarily dealt with in its relationship with so-called national memory, the globalization of the use of the term "Righteous" leads us to evaluate the relevance of using a state and national focus through which to deal with contemporary relations between memory and politics

Paradigm, memory policy, and institutions: the case of Belgium

To respond to these questions, we must first focus more closely on one of the examples mentioned above. A comparison will shed light on how the Righteous of France category became institutionalized:

> If we suppose, for example, that a nation can be considered a subsystem, and by estimating that each country can be subject to a comparable metanorm . . . , it seems indeed possible to recognize those that do not conform in terms of the diffusion of societal paradigms.[29]

To make this comparison we have chosen to focus first on the legislative use of the term "Righteous" by the Belgian Parliament. It seems relevant to choose an example where, as in France, it was through the law that the Israeli term emerged into historic memory.

A partly Francophone founding member of the European Community, and an established pluralist democracy with a well-developed economy, Belgium shares many structural characteristics with France. Although this linguistic reinvestment occurred at the same period, it took place according to very different modalities from those at work in the French case.

A different proceduralization for a similar public action

Unlike in France, Belgium's creation of an Award for the Righteous was not the result of a need to provide a positive counterpoint to the public recognition of the state's responsibility in deportation. The transformation of this question into a public issue did occur, but its emergence was not connected to the use of the Israeli category. The two questions followed paths that were parallel and disconnected in time.

Of course in Belgium as elsewhere, the 1990s were marked by the establishment of public action relating to the heritage of World War II. In the first instance, these measures did not deal with the question of the state's possible responsibility in the racial deportations. Thus, just as the president of the French Republic had done three years earlier, in 1996 the Belgian government decided to institute a specific new national day. It was to be called the day "Commemorating the Holocaust perpetrated by Nazi Germany."[30] But while its title did not raise the question of the Belgian state's possible responsibility in the extermination, the date chosen was that of armistice, 8 May, and not the date of an event with a connection to persecution of Jews on Belgian national soil.

As in most countries of formerly occupied Europe, the second half of the 1990s also saw the establishment of inquiry commissions relating to how the Holocaust was carried out on national territory. In 1997, a study commission was set up to examine the fate of the assets of the Belgian Jewish community that were plundered or abandoned during the war.[31] Its official purpose did not deal with the question of possible complicity between the Belgian administration and the Germans, nor with the attitude of the civilian population. Neither were these issues part of the twelve points dealt with by Maxime Steinberg, in the name of the Belgian state, in the report to the delegation at the Stockholm forum in January 2000. From that date onward, however, the question of Belgium's responsibility in the deportation of its Jewish population progressively became a public issue.[32] Several publications of historical monographs[33] and various demands by associations[34] converged to demand that a full study be conducted on this theme.

On 30 January 2003, the senators Alain Destexhe and Philippe Mahoux finally submitted a "bill relating to the need for a scientific study on the persecution and deportation of Belgian Jews during World War II" to the Senate Committee for Institutional Affairs. The text was adopted on 8 May 2003.[35] In their presentation of the motivations for this bill, the authors focused on the question of responsibilities. They thus continually refer to the policies of their French neighbor:

> In France, the final report by the Mattéoli Commission, which appeared in April 2002 indicated that, "the French state chose to collaborate with the Nazi occupier." In Belgium there was manifestly never the same kind of collaboration. The government was in London with the Allies, but the administration, led by

> the general secretaries, remained in place to liaise with the German authorities. The different attitudes of the national or local Belgian authorities regarding the Holocaust have never been the object of either an official report or a parliamentary debate. Yet the history of this period is far from being straightforward and well-known. . . . On the political level, official apologies have never been made by Belgium to the deported Jews for the acts of collaboration that led to their deportation. One of the reasons is most likely because the work establishing the facts and the responsibilities has not yet been done. However, the representatives of Jewish organizations have often deplored this lack of an official solemn gesture, comparable to that by Jacques Chirac on Vichy. Belgium has apologized in regards to the Lumumba affair and in relation to the Tutsis genocide in Rwanda.[36] The deportation of Belgian Jews undoubtedly also deserves a powerful and solemn gesture.

In 2003, in spite of the explicit use of French policy as a model for the establishment of Belgian public action in this area, and even though the category the Righteous of France had already been legally established in France, there was no mention of the Righteous in these texts. There was not even any mention of saviors or other Belgians "in active solidarity with the Jews." Whereas the term "Righteous" integrated historical memory in France simultaneously with the recognition of national faults and was intricately connected with this recognition, in the Belgian case it was appropriated by different means and disconnected from any rhetoric of collective cleansing of guilt.

The term "Righteous" had in fact become a legal term during the vote on a general law relating to the range of statuses of national recognition, finalized at the end of 1999—some four years earlier. This text led to an exchange between the government and patriotic groups and, secondarily, Jewish associations. The goal of the commission that was created as a result was to "examine and realize the unsatisfied demands brought together by the patriotic associations for the fiftieth anniversary of the end of the War in Europe and, as a result, to envisage, for motives of justice and equity, reopening deadlines for applications for all veterans' statuses 1940–1945 and for the Korean campaign."[37]

The law that resulted from this process organized the reopening—on a strictly honorific level—of nineteen statuses established between 1945 and 1983. From the very first version of the text, the third and last chapter listed the "dispositions relating to the members of the Jewish community." These measures were marginal in the basic structure of the text. The opinion of the State Council on the preliminary project therefore only concerned the statutory provisions on combatants.

Two new honorific statuses were created from scratch: the status of children hidden during World War II and another, eligible for an Honorary

Award for the Righteous.[38] Finally adopted on 26 January 1999,[39] the law establishing new measures for war victims explained the second status in these terms: "On the condition that the acts, resulting in recognition as a civilian Resistance member, were performed for the benefit of members of the Jewish community, the beneficiary of this status can apply for an Honorary Award for the Righteous."[40]

The use of a different public policy instrument

In France, the option of modifying existing statues was set aside to allow the integration of the term "Righteous" into the legislation. This appropriation took place through the renewal of the narrative proposed by the state. Within this, the homage to the Righteous was a counterweight to the simultaneous recognition of the state's collaboration.

In the Belgian case, the Righteous category is defined as a side effect of the traditional statuses that it directly depends on. It is not a part of the more general reconstruction of the forms of recognition of war victims, independent of any discussion of Belgium as implicated in the deportations. Confronted with the emergence of a similar paradigm, political leaders in France and Belgium used different public policy instruments.

Even though it had remained in the tradition of a strictly military honorary status since 1945, and consequently did not recognize civilian action, the French legislation eventually incorporated the Righteous in a completely new way that was parallel and distinct from the existing order. Inversely, the Belgian Parliament, strengthened by the long-established recognition of civilian resistance and assistance to Jews during the Occupation, drew from this its own structure with which to recognize these new heroes of national historic memory.

Indeed, the attribution of this Honorary Award for the Righteous was defined consecutive to the reopening of the status of civilian resistance.[41] The civilian resistance has in fact been recognized in Belgium since 1946. It is legally defined as "active participation in clandestine struggles against the enemy, deploying an activity involving genuine risk."[42] Because of the risks they had taken, those who had provided help to Jews found a form of state recognition in this status from the very beginning.

From 1946 on, the Belgians who had helped the Jews had a prestigious national form of recognition and commemoration at their disposition (and at the disposition of those they helped). Partly the result of a specific political conjuncture, specifically the arrival of the communists in government, which on top of the armed struggle played an important role in civilian resistance, this measure established durable legal recognition. But the government's honoring of the Belgians who came to the aid of the Jews did not stop at the attribution of a simple administrative status. Even as, on this very theme, the French state only adopted it in the mid-1990s, Belgian political leaders were involved from as early as 1945 in the tributes regularly organized by representatives of Jewish organizations.

Indeed, after liberation, the Council of Jewish Associations of Belgium, which included nearly all the Jewish organizations in the country, publicly paid homage to the "generous Belgians who gave their lives for Jews throughout the war." They organized an important ceremony on 5 May 1946, two thousand "awards of recognition" were finally "given to those who were reported to have saved or helped Jews during the war." The event was placed under the patronage of Queen Elizabeth, who, like the principal members of government, attended and spoke at the ceremony.[43]

In 1978, the Vigilance Committee of the Jewish Central Consistory of Belgium sought to honor those who had helped Jews during the Holocaust. They created the Committee for the Jews of Belgium to Pay Homage to Their Heroes and Saviors particularly in order to "express [their] recognition to all those non-Jewish Belgians who helped [Jews] under the Occupation."[44] On 12 October 1980, in the National Forest in Brussels, 1,800 individuals were finally given awards, before some 600 spectators. The event was once again placed under the patronage of the king of Belgium, and several political leaders participated.

In 1999, the appropriation of the Israeli term by Belgian law had become a part of the continuity of state memory policy carried out since the end of World War II. It was most notably based on the instruments already mobilized to honor the Belgians who had saved Jews. On one hand, the Award for the Righteous was complementary with the honorary status already in place. On the other, the participation of national representatives in ceremonies organized by representatives of Jewish institutions lasted beyond 1999. In 2003 again, Prince Philippe and Prime Minister Guy Verhostadt attended a ceremony to honor the "saviors of the Jews," henceforth regularly referred to as the "Righteous." This was still organized by the "main Jewish organizations in Belgium."[45]

As in the process that led to the French vote, the prior application of preexisting public policy also played a fundamental role here. However, unlike in France, it was not an obstacle to the state's use of the term "Righteous." In fact it was its main support. In Belgium, this appropriation through the modification of the preexisting honorary status did not lead to the expression of divergent points of view among the actors involved. Instead it raised only a relative consensus. Although, since the vote on the law, many negative reactions have emerged regarding the definition of the status of hidden children, this was not the case concerning the Award for the Righteous. On the contrary, the public reaction was extremely positive. David Süsskind, the president of the influential Jewish Secular Community Center, expressed his delight at its adoption.[46]

Memory policy and institutions

Whether the modes of previous memory policy help or hinder the appropriation of the term "Righteous," the strength of their impact raises a new question. To what extent does the difference in instrumentation we have observed primarily reflect a difference between the political institutions that structure the two national subsystems considered here?

Of course, just as in the French case, the appropriation of the term "Righteous" in Belgium is a part of memory policy that is associated with internal affairs. Belgian members of Parliament (MPs) mark even more clearly their independence from Yad Vashem than their French counterparts.[47] It is therefore not on this point that the divergence between the institutions structuring these national subsystems is most apparent. However, it is striking to observe the size of the disparity on another issue.

In 1999, the Research and Information Service of the National Assembly considered it impossible to award a distinction for help given to a Jew or any given community, because the two categories are not recognized by the French Republic. At the same time in Belgium, the Chamber voted in a law that included dispositions explicitly directed at the Jewish community, according to which a person is honored not because of assistance given to an individual threatened under specific rules but because she or he is a member of the aforementioned community. Beyond the forms of public action, the proceduralization and instrumentation observed reveal more fundamental differences in these political institutions.

From the very birth of the nation, and even at the end of the war, Belgium was different on this point from republican France, with the latter constructed on the affirmation of the principles of laicity and universalism. In 1946, as in 1999, Belgium was characterized by an established cultural identification. There are several state religions organized in a system of "pillarization."[48] This refers to an "organization of collective life around two or three groups marked by a particular ideology."[49] Catholicism and, by extension, religion have an important place in this. Although Belgian pillarization is less clear-cut than that of its neighbor the Netherlands,[50] it is nevertheless an old political institution, which explains why it is so different from the French in the actualization of this shared paradigm.

The form of political institutions has a direct impact on the specific ways that each state accommodates the individual belongings and identities of its citizens. At this stage of our analysis, this element must be added to the strategic logic of the actors and the symbolic operativity of a new paradigm in order to understand the birth of the Righteous of France category.

In the Belgian case, from the end of the war, the political institutions allowed for differentiation between groups—between Jews and non-Jews—which, to different extents and degrees, constitutes an implicit use of the term "Righteous." In France, at the same time, the recently restored republican institutions left no room for this kind of social categorization. Inversely, the appropriation of the term "Righteous" by French law, like the conflicts and negotiations that preceded it, was liable to reveal an evolution in the political institutions that (in France) govern the state's management of individual belongings and their articulation with citizenship. A close link has already emerged in the previous chapter between a possible change in the constitutional rules in this area and the possible democratization of French society.

Paradigm, memory policy, and institutions: the Polish case

The analysis of a third case enables us to move forward on this path.[51] In 1999, Poland also used a law to seal the national appropriation of the Israeli category. However, the nature and history of Polish institutions is clearly different from those of France and Belgium. Whereas these two countries are relatively old nation-states,[52] the birth of modern Poland and the introduction of representative institutions only date from 1918. Indeed, a popular democracy only since liberation, Poland held its first free elections in 1990.[53]

This late introduction of democracy enables us to refine our analysis by identifying the influences of the different components of the political institutions—constitutional rules and citizenship regimes in their attitudes toward minority belongings, on one hand, and the political regime that oversees the organization of power and government, on the other.

Changes in the political regime and public policy implementation

Immediately following the war, in a context where strong popular hostility fed on anti-Semitism and was expressed against the survivors of the Holocaust, the Poles who had helped Jews were not rewarded or recognized by the new Communist regime. However, from 1968 on, the rescuers of Jews in general, and the Righteous in particular, were regularly evoked by state leaders. In this respect Poland took an intermediary stance. Like Belgium, Polish state action referred to those who had saved Jews well before the 1990s. Like France, it did so in close (but inverse) relation to the question of responsibility in the Holocaust. Here, references to the Righteous were not used to recognize responsibility but rather to shrug off the issue.

In 1968, the Polish government began an anti-Semitic battle against "hostile foreign groups," both inside and outside Poland; the most prominent among them were the Zionists. Paradoxically, their representatives paid homage to the Polish Righteous in the same breath. The inclusion of these figures in national historic memory served to illustrate the "moral greatness" of the nation, judged "unjustly" by the rest of the world. It simultaneously provided "proof" of the "ingratitude" of the Jews toward those who helped them. In the campaign orchestrated by those in power, this use of the "savior figure" was intensive.[54] The rare references to the memory of the Righteous were used by the administration and the government to support the anti-Semitic purge and to justify the expulsions it gave rise to.

In order to defend Poland's honor, members of the government and leaders of state institutions used and distorted the book by Wladyslaw Bartoszewski and Zofia Lewinowna,[55] which in fact affirmed in explicitly dissident terms that the Jews fully belong to the Polish nation. Another, more ambiguous book, written by a member of the Jewish Historical Institute and titled *The Forest of the Righteous. A Page in the History of the Rescue of the Jews in Occupied Poland,* was similarly used.[56] The year 1968 therefore marked the first instances of the Israeli term mobilized by the Polish state.

This linguistic appropriation is connected to internal policy, at least in appearance. It was part of the anti-Semitic campaign that led to the expulsion of most of Poland's Jews. More precisely, it was designed to redefine the border between those inside and those outside the Polish national community and was, above all, a foreign policy tool. As a result, it relied on several instruments, including the instrumentalization of history texts. Bartoszewski and Lewinowna's book was translated into English as soon as it was published.[57] In the Poland of the late 1960s, the speed at which the English version spread overseas is a strong indication of how it was distorted, on one hand, and of its place in the diplomatic framework, on the other. In 1970, a translation of the abridged version was widely distributed by Interpress Publishers, which was responsible for disseminating official publications overseas.[58]

In the years that followed, there were no other remarkable references to the Righteous by state representatives. When the term was reactivated, some ten years later, it was once again in the context of foreign policy. In 1978, on the thirty-fifth anniversary of the Warsaw Uprising, the first official medal ceremony to be held on Polish territory was organized by Yad Vashem. The event was conceived as a diplomatic action in the context of the thawing relations between Poland and Israel.[59] A similar ceremony was held in September 1979.[60]

The Polish government and several administrations thus used the term "Righteous" sporadically and then became involved in their commemoration, first in 1968 and then at the end of the 1970s. As was the case with the French appropriation of the Israeli term, the mention of the Righteous by the Polish state provided first a positive counterweight and even a negation of all Polish responsibility in the extermination of the Jews. However, although the presence of this symbolic issue is a point of similarity between the French and the Polish case, the foreign policy perspective of the term in the latter instance is a clear difference.

The regime change in Poland in the 1990s enables us to specify the nature of the political institutions that were behind this difference between the French and the Polish configurations. At the time, the advent of democracy was thought to require the reappropriation of the past and to involve the rejection of all previously imposed official readings of history.[61]

From the 1990s on, the commemoration of the Righteous and the use of the Israeli category by the representatives and administrators of the Polish Republic also became more regular. But this change was purely quantitative. Where references to the Righteous by the state continued to form a counterpoint to any potential accusations of complicity with the Nazis, its connection to foreign policy remained.

From the 1990s on, the official restoration of diplomatic relations with Israel was closely linked to the honors awarded to the Polish Righteous. In his foreign policy speech in the Knesset in May 1991, President Lech Walesa placed his goal to "renew Polish-Jewish dialogue"[62] under the auspices of the Polish Righteous. Similarly, the Polish Righteous were frequently mentioned by the Polish foreign minister, Wladyslaw Bartoszewski, over the course of bilateral meetings between the two countries between March and December 1995 and June 2000 and October 2001.[63] The nomination of Bartoszewski, himself a Righteous and honorary citizen of Israel, to this post is not unrelated to the need to improve diplomatic relations between the two countries. In 2000, on the ten-year anniversary of the restoration of diplomatic ties between Israel and Poland, which involved the same foreign minister visiting Jerusalem, his status as a Righteous was repeatedly held up as a symbol of the event being commemorated.

The permanence of the relation between the commemoration of the Righteous and foreign policy issues finally appears with force in the action undertaken by the Institute of National Memory (IPN). At once academic, political, and legal, this state institution focused on the Righteous among the Nations for the first time in 1992. In 1993, it published a brochure in English titled *Those Who Helped. Polish Saviors of Jews during the Holocaust*,[64] which was destined to be distributed for free in Polish consulates and embassies. One copy was symbolically given to the Israeli prime minister

Itzakh Rabin on 20 April 1993, during his visit to Poland to commemorate the fiftieth anniversary of the Warsaw Uprising.[65]

The brochure began with the transcript of the official speeches given at the reception of the Israeli president at the Polish Parliament on 28 May 1992. In 1995 and 1997 two other editions were published on the same model. Only the declaration of the Israeli ambassador to Poland replaced that of the Israeli prime minister. Since then, references to the Righteous by the IPN have continued to fall within a diplomatic focus.

In 2000, the numerous initiatives by the IPN following the publication of Jan Tomasz Gross's book *Neighbors. 10 July 1941, a Massacre of Jews in Poland* provide the ultimate example. This book tells of how the inhabitants of the village of Jedwabne gathered all their Jewish neighbors together in a barn and burned them alive—even before the German troops arrived.[66] Following this publication, the IPN set to work trying to defend Poland's image overseas. To achieve this, it regularly drew attention to Poland's number one place in Yad Vashem's rankings of the number of Righteous per country.[67] In July 2003, for the celebrations of the sixtieth anniversary of the uprising in Bialystok, the capital of the Jedwabne region, the IPN eventually inaugurated a commemorative exhibition dedicated to the residents of the region who took the initiative to save their Jewish "neighbors." As was the case for the 1993 ceremony, its spokesperson was the Israeli ambassador. In 1990, the establishment of democratic institutions was therefore not associated with genuine change in the use of the term "Righteous."

Memory policy and institutions

However, the institutions with the most influence are not so much the political regimes themselves, but rather the constitutional rules and citizenship regimes that govern attitudes toward minority identities.

Both before and after 1990, the use of the term "Righteous" by the state was indeed framed by the nature of the construction of the Polish nation. The citizenship regime that resulted from this explains the nature of the insertion of the Righteous into the national historic memory since 1945.

Poland was created by the recognition of the countries of the Entente in World War I. On one hand, the birth of this modern Polish nation was enabled by the good will of the other countries, but, on the other hand, it was conditional on Poland's commitment to guarantee equal citizenship for its minorities, of which the Jews had become an international symbol. Signed at the Paris Peace Conference in 1919, the treaty on minorities was seen as a legal means by which to oblige the new state to put an end to the explosion of anti-Semitic violence.[68] These circumstances established "the international dimension" of the "Polish-Jewish question"[69] at the heart of the national rebirth of Poland.

The political conception of Jews as being on the margins of what the Polish nation was to be and the inclusion of Polish-Jewish relations as part of foreign policy were institutionalized here. This original citizenship regime manifested itself in many forms between 1919 and 1939[70] and lasted throughout World War II.[71] The most extreme example of the institutionalization of this structuring of Polish political and national space is possibly that of Zofia Kossak's comments.

Kossak was a founding member of Zegota during the war and has since been awarded the status of Righteous among the Nations. In her public "protest," published in September 1942, Kossak called on the Poles to help the Jews, yet she expressed at the same time her own anti-Semitism. Her commitment to the Jewish cause is first explained by foreign policy concerns—opposing Poland to the rest of the world, on one hand, and Polish people and Jewish people, on the other. Thus, like her action itself, the place that her memory holds in the state narrative of the past from 1968 to after 1990 reflects the ethnic-religious conception of Polish national belonging.

Beyond the strategic logic of the actors, the use of the term "Righteous" therefore results from the actualization of a possibly shared paradigm through the prism of the political institutions managing citizens' individual identities: Belgian pillarization, Polish ethnoreligious nationalism, and French republicanism. Conversely, it is striking to observe that the same interpretation of the commemoration of the Righteous, essentially for diplomatic purposes, is associated with similar citizenship regimes. Although the history of the creation of Israel is clearly different from that of the birth of the Polish state, to the point of almost being its mirror image, the two countries both have a primarily ethnoreligious definition of nation.

Use of a new public action instrument and evolution of institutions

However, although the use of the term "Righteous" by governments and administrations in Poland was consistent between 1945 and after 1990, the development of democracy in the country was not without effect. It led to a modification of the citizenship regime. At the end of the 1990s, the use of the term "Righteous" was thus based on recourse to the law for the first time. The mobilization of a legal instrument that had remained previously unused signaled an important evolution. The choice of legislative support, more directed at the interior and intended to last, marked a break from the former focus on speeches and ceremonies that, although regular, had nonetheless remained sporadic.

In two stages, in 1997 and then in 1999, the Sejm (the Polish Parliament) appropriated the Righteous category for the first time before granting war veteran status to those already awarded the Israeli title. The process of adopting the text reflected the establishment of an increasingly pluralist political space and the modification of the citizenship regime as far as the definition of the nation on ethnoreligious grounds was concerned.

From the mid-1990s on, several organizations weighed in on state policy in the area of awarding honorific status and in the evocation of the past more generally. Established as collective actors shortly after Poland's transition to democracy, the members of these groups had plural identities because of their joint belonging to Poland and to Judaism. This came across strongly in their investment in the official recognition of the Righteous by the Polish state.

From 1990 on, Jewish institutions regained a certain vigor,[72] although the awakening of Jewish culture was much older than this.[73] This renewal of community life, both religious and cultural, was due either to members of the older generation who returned to Judaism (or rather its display in the public space) or to those among the younger generation who henceforth demanded a right to exist—even in the public sphere.[74]

A prime example of this evolution, the Children of the Holocaust organization was created in 1991. It brought together Polish Jews who were hidden as children during the war. Its members demanded both recognition as belonging to Judaism and legitimacy in speaking in the public and political space in Poland.[75] From 1994, this association made several moves to have the Righteous consecrated as national heroes by the state. It was thus responsible for the highest Polish decoration, the Order of the White Eagle, being awarded to Irena Sendlerowa in 2003.[76]

Similarly, Stanislaw Krajewski was one of the leaders of the Union of Jewish Religious Communities, and the Polish Council of Christians and Jews. In 1996, he was invited to speak about the relationship between Polish and Jewish memories. By way of response he put the Righteous among the Nations at the center of the past he wanted to have commemorated:

> Above all we must remember these heroes, these Righteous among the Nations, who helped the Jews. I see two reasons for this. The first is personal: I am a Polish Jew and in my Poland, these heroes are by far more important than the evildoers. The second reason is more general: if I want the communities that I belong to, to be judged according to their best representatives, I have to apply the same rule to Poland and to the Polish. Moreover, in choosing the best and the most worthy representatives of the nation, we can, without fear of lies and injustice, also speak of the evildoers.[77]

Like the Children of the Holocaust, from the mid-1990s onward, Stanislaw Krajewski and the associations he represented began to lobby for the Righteous to be awarded the status of war veterans.

Finally, this interconnection between the mobilization for the appropriation of the Righteous category into Polish law and the affirmation of multiple belongings can be found in the comments of Szymon Szurmiej, the president of the Sociocultural Association of Jews in Poland, another major institution representing Polish Jews, this time descended from communism. In 1996 again, Szurmiej announced:

> I am happy that the ceremony [inaugurating the Kielce Memorial] had a reconciliatory nature. On one hand we talk of the tragedy of the Jewish people and on the other we pay homage to those who risk their lives to save the Jews. We must learn to think of Polish-Jewish relations in other terms . . . anti-Semitism is also anti-Polish.[78]

The transformations of these individuals into social actors, and their demands on the parliamentarians, guided the form that the actualization of the shared paradigm ultimately took in Poland. They introduced a progressive shift of the measures relating to the Righteous, from the foreign policy domain to internal policy explicitly relating to memory. From the establishment of democracy in Poland, the redistribution of national honors was among the possible legal dispositions. On 24 January 1991, the first Polish Parliament voted in a law on war veterans.[79] In the text of this law it outlined their status in strictly military terms but added a status of an "equivalent activity" corresponding to the notion of the civilian resistance, although the term was no longer used.

Although it was considered initially, the proposal to include acts performed in assisting Jews among those granting access to this honorary status was eventually refused. For most of the leaders of the executive as well as the legislative branches, whatever their political allegiances, this remained essentially a foreign policy issue, requiring only symbolic speeches and gestures. During the diplomatic visit by the president of Israel to Poland in 1991, the inclusion of the Righteous among veterans was thus falsely presented as having been already established by the government.[80] In 1994, while visiting Yad Vashem, the president of the Polish Parliament even affirmed that the MPs had recently "ratified a law recognizing the Righteous among the Nations as World War II combatants."[81]

The truth was nothing of the sort, however. Faced with the reluctance of the Committee for Social Affairs (responsible for writing possible amendments to the 1991 text[82]) several organizations publically called for the Righteous to be recognized. In 1994, for example, with support from the Polish Council for Christians and Jews,[83] the Association of Jewish Combatants and Victims submitted an official demand for this recognition to the MPs.[84] This request emanating from social actors encouraged certain MPs to defend their cause.

In November, the persistent refusal of the Committee was weighed against a minority proposal,[85] the initiative of the Freedom Union parliamentary group, a formation stemming from Solidarnosc. Initially this proposition did not break with the established treatment of the commemoration of the Righteous in public policy. It justified its approach with the fact that "each country has honored the Righteous among the Nations in a particular way." Their opponents' arguments were on a diplomatic level, but they arrived at the opposite conclusion; they emphasized the danger of seeing the decision of recognition associated with that granted by a foreign, in this instance Israeli, institute.

On 1 December 1994, the Parliament finally voted in a motion that granted the Righteous the status of war veterans.[86] This time it was vetoed by the Polish president.[87] His spokesperson began by justifying the reticence of the executive branch based on considerations of internal policy and then once again took a position from a foreign policy perspective. He concluded his speech in these terms: "Again, it is not true that other European countries have recognized these heroes as war veterans."[88] The question was only definitively resolved in 1997.

First, the Parliament amended the 1991 law.[89] Henceforth:

> [The Polish state] recognizes [in strictly honorific terms] the merits of all those who, at the risk of their lives, their health, and their freedom, saved people hunted by the German or Soviet Occupation, but also by the Polish authorities in the postwar period up until 1956, because of their actions in favor of Polish sovereignty or independence, as well as for reasons of nationality, religion, or race.[90]

The text mentioned automatic recognition of "Polish citizens distinguished by the medal of Righteous among the Nations, awarded by the Yad Vashem Institute in Jerusalem," as part of this special procedure.

Finally, in 1999, the Poles who had come to the assistance of the Jews became eligible for the status of war veteran. Article 2 of the 1991 laws was eventually modified to include among the "equivalent acts," the act of "sheltering people of Jewish nationality [*sic*][91] or other persons threatened between 1938 and 1945 because of their nationality or their activities in favor of the sovereignty and independence of the Republic of Poland, while these actions were punishable by death."[92]

The use of the term "Righteous among the Nations" in Polish law therefore confirms the role played by political institutions in the development of memory policy. The study of this role allows us to closely identify the nature of the institutions in question and the mechanisms that govern their influences. The citizenship regime in place since the beginning of modern Poland has structured the form and the content of how the commemoration of the Righteous was evoked by the state both before and after 1990. Since 1945, the use of the Israeli category has continuously fallen in the area of foreign policy and has served as a counterpoint to any potential foreign accusations of Poland's complicity in the extermination of the Jews.

However, the establishment in Poland of the rules and structures specific to contemporary European democracies did indeed have an effect.[93] These changes gave rise to a political space where the expression of ethnoreligious pluralism became possible—even if it was not always socially legitimate. This space was invested in by social actors who, through the affirmation of multiple belongings, progressively modified the basis of the citizenship regime:

> In moving away from both the party-state and from the Catholic state of the prewar Polish nation, which were both monolithic and exclusionary, Polish society is today involved in the construction of a democratic political state, a state of law and genuine citizenship that thus creates—in spite of much resistance—the conditions for pluralism to be possible.[94]

In essence, the demand of the social actors to see the Righteous recognized through war veteran status reflected a similar mechanism to that which had led the leaders of the French Committee to call for the Righteous to be eligible for the status of Resistance members. The mechanisms at work here must be once again differentiated from communitarianism. For these individuals, the issue is not simply being recognized as Jewish. For that, the procedure implemented by Israel would be sufficient; it is the expression of a desire to see those who saved Jews honored by the states of which they are citizens, with the help of categories that are part of national memory policy. This reveals the particular role of the state in the contemporary articulation of multiple belongings and identities.

This slow transformation of political institutions has thus led to the commemoration of the Righteous progressively shifting from the domain of state foreign policy to a specific public policy sector related to remembrance of the past. Reciprocally, memorial questions have increasingly come to represent a privileged field for the expression of conflicts and tensions that are possibly due to the ongoing redefinition of the citizenship regime. Thus the polarization of Polish political society that has accompanied access to pluralism can be seen here. The debates and controversies provoked by the discussion of the attitudes of the "neighbors" described in Jan Gross's book provide another example of this.[95]

In 2001, journalist Adam Michnik, a figure of Polish intelligentsia, wrote a tribune in *The New York Times*, expressing his "schizophrenia":

> I am a Pole, and my shame about the Jedwabne murder is a Polish shame. At the same time, I know that if I had been there in Jedwabne, I would have been killed as a Jew. . . . A Polish neighbor might have saved one of my relatives

> from the hands of the executioners who pushed him into the barn. And indeed, there were many such Polish neighbors—the forest of Polish trees in the Avenue of the Righteous in Yad Vashem, the Holocaust memorial in Jerusalem, is dense. For these people who lost their lives saving Jews, I feel responsible, too. I feel guilty when I read so often in Polish and foreign newspapers about the murderers who killed Jews, and note the deep silence about those who rescued Jews. Do the murderers deserve more recognition than the righteous? The Polish primate, the Polish president and the Rabbi of Warsaw said almost in one voice that a tribute to the Jedwabne victims should serve the cause of reconciling Poles and Jews in the truth. I desire nothing more. If it doesn't happen, it will be also my fault.[96]

On the other side of the debate, the commentators of Radio Maryja, an openly anti-Semitic and xenophobic[97] popular radio station in Poland, also began to lobby for the recognition for the Poles who helped the Jews more broadly. But they refused to use the term "Righteous." In reaction to the publication of Gross's book, the directors of the radio station called on their listeners to write "testimonies" about the assistance "really" provided to the Jews. The result was published in a "countermonograph" destined to prove the "greatness" and the "martyrdom" of the "unjustly" accused Poles. The testimonies by those who presented themselves as "saviors" for this project demonstrate strong anti-Semitism. Emphasizing the "ingratitude" of the Jews,[98] the testimonies are clearly in the same vein as the discourses produced by the Polish government in the 1968 campaign, mobilizing stereotypes of avarice and the self-interested search for profit.

Exactly like the conclusions that emerged from the analysis of the vote on the French law on 10 July 2000, we can once again see a clear relation here between the citizenship regime, the democratization of society, and the appropriation of the "Righteous" category by the state.

Our examination of the Belgian and the Polish cases has demonstrated the existence of important differences within the overall paradigm. In this instance, the nationality of memory is not found in its content. Memory policy expresses a national memory inasmuch as it is framed by a citizenship regime and social relations that are crystallized by political institutions, ultimately close to the Durkheimian notion of social morphology. It is therefore through this institutional "subsystem," both physical and symbolic, that the nation constitutes and results in "differences in how social paradigms are spread." It frames the interpretation of a convention and the actualization of a paradigm that manifests itself simultaneously at an international and a transnational level.

At the end of this chapter, we can see that the mode of articulation between the political institutions that govern the possibilities for public debate and the state management of individual belongings and identities has allowed us to understand the institutionalization of the category the Righteous of France. Moreover, it has also provided insight into the institutionalization of French public policy relating to issues of memory more broadly.

Notes

1. Alon Confino, "Collective Memory and Cultural History: Problems of Method," *American Historical Review*, no. 105 (December 1997): 1391.
2. On this point, see the example of the fate of Irena Sendlerowa in different periods. This woman was one of the leaders of the Zegota network, codename of the Council for the Assistance of Jews, a rescue network linked to the exiled Polish government. See Anna Mieszkowska, ed., *Matka dzieci Holokaustu. Historia Ireny Sendlerowej* [Mother of the Children of the Holocaust. A History of Irena Sendlerowa] (Varsovie: Muza Sa, 2004); Irene Tomaszewski and Tecia Werbowski, *Zegota: The Council to Aid Jews in Occupied Poland 1942–1945* (Westmount: Price-Patterson, 1994).
3. Even Denmark, where resistance networks tried to evacuate most Jews to Sweden, did not manage to save all of its Jewish population.
4. As in the previous case, only a few examples are presented here. However, similar evolutions took place in Spain, Sweden, the Vatican, and Turkey, among many others.
5. "A Swiss Woman Steps forward Again to Aid Refugees," *The New York Times*, 14 January 2004.
6. DJYV, File Paul Grüninger and Stefan Keller; Paul Grüninger and Stefan Keller, *Délit d'humanité: l'affaire Grüninger* (Lausanne: Editions d'en bas, 1994). In 1985, another request for posthumous rehabilitation, submitted by the family, was refused.
7. Regula Ludi, "Waging War on Wartime Memory: Recent Swiss Debates on the Legacies of the Holocaust and the Nazi Era," *Jewish Social Studies* 10, no. 2 (2004): 116–52.
8. Speech by Ernst Leuenberger, president of the National Council, Ceremony on 27 April 1998, Federal Assembly, http:/www.parlament.ch. The federal law "on the annulment of the penal sentences against persons who helped the victims of Nazi persecution to flee" was finally voted in on 20 June 2003, https://www.admin.ch/gov/en/start.html.
9. Meir Wagner, *The Righteous of Switzerland. Heroes of the Holocaust*, preface by Joseph Deiss (Hoboken: Ktav, 2001).
10. Cedric Terzi, "'Qu'avez-vous fait de l'argent des Juifs?' Problématisation et Publicisation de la question 'des fonds juifs et de l'or nazi' par la presse suisse, 1995–1998" (Ph.D. dissertation, EHESS, 2004).
11. Wallenberg was a Swedish diplomat appointed to Budapest; he enabled the survival of several thousand Jews, particularly by giving them Swedish passports. In 1945 he was arrested by the Red Army during the arrival of Soviet troops in Hungary on the pretext of spying for the United States. Officially he died in prison in 1947, although his disappearance gave rise to numerous investigations and speculations.
12. http://www.raoulwallenberg.net.
13. In the words of the Canadian heritage minister in the Senate hearing of 5 June 2001, http://www.pch.gc.ca.
14. Document "Hommage/Tribute. Raoul Wallenberg," UNESCO, 10 May to 11 June 1999.
15. Claudine Vidal, "La Commémoration du génocide au Rwanda. Violence symbolique, mémorisation forcée et histoire officielle," *Cahiers d'Etudes Africaines* 44, 3, no. 175 (2004): 588.

16. Aurélia Kalisky, "Mémoires croisées—des références à la Shoah dans le travail de deuil et de mémoire du génocide des Tutsi," *Humanitaire*, no. 10 (Spring–Summer, 2004): 79.
17. "Speech by His Excellency Paul Kagame at the 10th Anniversary of the Genocide in Rwanda," Amahoro Stadium, 7 April 2004. Valérie Rosoux drew my attention to this text.
18. "Gacaca" refers to the traditional justice system in Rwanda, which was reactivated after the genocide to address the sluggishness and powerlessness of the courts. Françoise Digneffe and Jacques Fierens, ed., *Justice et Gacaca. L'Expérience rwandaise et le génocide* (Namur: Presses Universitaires de Namur, 2003).
19. Service National des Juridictions Gacaca, *Système scientifique de collecte, d'acheminement et de classement électronique des informations collectées au cours des séances des juridictions Gacaca, rapport provisoire*, expertise by Joseph Nsengimana, Jean Rubabenga, Gaetan Gatarayiha, and Pierre Claver Zitoni (Kigali, Republic of Rwanda: SNJG, 14 April 2004).
20. Of course, although the existence of this paradigm is considered here as a given, it is in itself the result of social construction. Its emergence could also be deconstructed. Although that is not the project of this book, several researchers have undertaken this task most convincingly. See, e.g., Sandrine Lefranc, Lilian Mathieu, and Johanna Siméant, "Les Victimes écrivent leur histoire," *Raisons politiques*, no. 30 (2008): 5–19.
21. Law no. 97–1019; Law of 28 October 1997.
22. Howard Gilbert, "The Slow Development of the Right to Conscientious Objection to Military Service under the European Convention on Human Rights," *European Human Rights Review* 5 (2001): 554–67.
23. Philippe Mesnard, *La Victime écran: la représentation humanitaire en question* (Paris: Textuel, 2002).
24. Gérard Lopez, Serge Portelli, and Clément Sophie, *Les Droits des victimes: victimologie et psychotraumatologie* (Paris: Dalloz, 2003).
25. Guillaume Erner, *La Société des victimes* (Paris: La Découverte, 2006); Didier Fassin and Richard Rechtman, *L'Empire du traumatisme. Enquête sur la condition de victime* (Paris: Flammarion, 2007).
26. Cf. Douglas E. Beloof, *Victims in Criminal Procedure* (Durham: Carolina Academic Press, 1999).
27. http://www.nobelprize.org/nobel_prizes/peace/laureates/1999/presentation-speech.html.
28. Speech by Jacques Chirac, president of the French Republic, on the occasion of the ceremony awarding honor medals for courage and devotion, Elysée Palace, 28 November 2003.
29. Yves Surel, "Idées, intérêts, institutions dans l'analyse des politiques publiques," *Pouvoirs*, no. 87 (1998): 198. The ellipses replace this text: "neoliberalism in recent times."
30. The Belgian Delegation proceedings, "History and Remembrance of the Shoah in Belgium," *Stockholm International Forum on the Holocaust. A Conference on Education, Remembrance and Research Stockholm*, 26–29 January 2000, p. 110.
31. Royal decree of 6 July 1997 and law of 15 January 1999. *Rapport final de la Commission D'Étude sur le sort des biens des membres de la Communauté Juive de Belgique spoliés ou délaissés pendant la guerre 1940–1945* (July 2001).
32. At the time when the report was submitted and on the occasion of the official commemoration ceremony, this article from the newspaper *Soir* appeared: Christian Laporte, "Assets Returned to Plundered Jews, but Vehofstadt Does Not Mention State Collaboration in the Deportation," 25 September 2000.

33. Particularly Thierry Rozenblum, "Une Cité si ardente. L'Administration communale de Liège et la persécution des Juifs, 1940–1942," *Revue d'histoire de la Shoah. Le Monde Juif,* no. 179 (September–December 2003): 9–49; Lieven Saerens, *Vreemdelingen in een wereldstad. Een geschiedenis van Antwerpen en zijn joodse bevolking (1880–1944)* [Foreigners in a Cosmopolitan City. A Story of Anvers and Its Jewish Population (1880–1944)] (Lannoo: Tielt, 2000).
34. Particularly Maxime Steinberg, "Preface," in *Le Livre des homes. Enfants de la Shoah. AIVG 1945–1959,* by Adolphe Nysenholc I-IX (Brussels: Didier Devillez Editeur, 2004); and an interview with the author 12 February 2004, Noduwez Orp-Jauche, Belgique. Maxime Steinberg played a role comparable to that of Serge Klarsfeld in the reconstitution of the history of the persecution Belgian Jews were subject to. Similarly, the Union of Jewish Students in Belgium organized, e.g., an event titled "The Deportation of Belgian Jews: Was the State Responsible?" Free University of Brussels, 26 November 2002.
35. Law relating to the request for a study on the persecution and deportation of Jews in Belgium during World War II, 8 May 2003; *Moniteur belge,* 2 June 2003.
36. On this point it is remarkable that, in the Belgian case, it was the treatment of the Rwandan case that influenced the treatment of WWII rather than the other way around. This example is worth looking at in more detail in an area of research in which the influences of the memory of the Holocaust on the construction of other memories is considered self-evident.
37. The "presentation of motives" of the first version of the bill establishing new measures for war victims, 18 November 1998, Belgian Chamber of Representatives, no. 1820/1–98/99.
38. Chapter III, Article 6, no. 1820/1–98/99. A second version of the bill was submitted on 17 December 1998 to the Chamber of Representatives; it did not make any amendment to the article concerning the Righteous, no. 1820/4–98/99.
39. Law establishing new measures for war victims, *Moniteur belge,* 26 February 1999.
40. Now Chapter IV, Article 7, Paragraph 1. The second paragraph specifies that "the king determines the conditions and modes of this award of honor."
41. Since 1946, several texts have previously amended this status: law of 9 September 1951, *Moniteur belge,* 9 September 1951; law of 24 July 1952, *Moniteur belge,* 7 September 1951; law of 25 June 1956, *Moniteur belge,* 6 July 1956. None ever used the term "Righteous."
42. Decree law of 24 December 1946; Pieter Lagrou, *Mémoires patriotiques et Occupation nazie* (Brussels: Editions Complexes, 2003), 58, 310n. 53.
43. Report of the ceremony "Public Demonstration to the Belgian People," 5 May 1946, Archives of the Jewish Museum of Belgium (MJB), MM40, Fonds SSP.
44. Extract of the "Record of the 1st Sitting of the Anvers Committee for Homage by Belgium's Jews to Their Heroes and Saviors," MJB, MM36, Fonds SSP.
45. 29 April 2003, at the Palais des Beaux-Arts, Brussels.
46. "Happy as a Jew in Belgium," opinion piece published in *La Libre Belgique,* 13 March 2003.
47. The Belgian Delegation, "History and Remembrance of the Shoah in Belgium," in *Stockholm International Forum on the Holocaust. A Conference on Education, Remembrance and Research Stockholm,* 26–29 January 2000, p. 110.
48. Bernard Poche, "La Belgique entre les piliers et les 'mondes linguistiques.' Quelques réflexions sur la question des formes sociales," *Recherches sociologiques* 23, no. 3 (1992): 43–68. Marco Martiniello, *Culturalisation des différences, différenciation des cultures dans la politique belge,* Les Cahiers du CERI, 20 (Paris: CERI, 1998). On the importance of pillars in the construction of identification with Judaism in Belgium, see Jean-Philippe Schreiber, "L'Israélitisme belge au XIXè siècle: une idéologie *romano-byzantine,*" in *Un*

Modèle d'intégration: Juifs et Israélites en France et en Europe, XIX–XXe siècles, ed. Patrick Cabanel and Chantal Bordes-Benayoun, 77–89 (Berg: Paris, 2004).

49. Liliane Voyé, "Belgique: crise de la civilisation paroissiale et recompositions du croire," in *Identités religieuses en Europe*, ed. Grace Davie and Danièle Hervieu-Léger, 196 (Paris: La Découverte, 1996).
50. Although he does not refer to Belgium, Pierre Birnbaum deals with the differences between the integration and the emancipation of Jews in France and the Netherlands (also characterized by pillarization). He identifies a "French republican culture" and a "Dutch model of citizenship," "ready to make Catholic and Calvinist religious communities pillars of civil society and the state." Birnbaum, *Sur la corde raide. Parcours juif entre exil et citoyenneté* (Paris: Flammarion, 2002), 66.
51. The analysis of the Polish case was conducted with the valuable help and friendship of Agnieszka Niewiedzial. Together we have published our preliminary conclusions in "Figure du Juste et politique publique de la mémoire en Pologne: entre relations diplomatiques et structures sociales," *Critique Internationale*, no. 34 (January–March 2007): 127–48.
52. The Belgian constitution was adopted on 7 February 1831. See "La Naissance de l'etat belge," in *Histoire de la Belgique*, ed. Marie-Thérèse Bitsch, 79–86 (Brussels: Editions Complexes, 2004).
53. Leszek Kuk, *La Pologne du post-communisme à l'anti-communisme* (Paris: L'Harmattan, 2001).
54. Michael C. Steinlauf, *Bondage to the Dead: Poland and the Memory of the Holocaust* (Syracuse: Syracuse University Press, 1997), 75–88; Anna Barbara Jarosz, "Marzec w praise" [March in the Press] in *Marzec 1968. Trzydziesci lat pozniej* [March 1968. Thirty Years Later], vol. 1, ed. Marcin Kula, Piotr Oseka, and Marcin Zaremba, 99–125 (Warsaw: PWN, 1998).
55. Wladyslaw Bartoszewski and Zofia Lewinowna, *Ten jest z ojczyzny mojej. Polacy z pomoca Zydom 1939–1945* [That One Is from My Country. The Poles Who Came to the Aide of the Jews, 1939–1945] (Cracow: Znak, 1969).
56. Szymon Datner, *Las sprawiedliwych. Karta z dziejow ratownictwa Zydow w okupowanej Polsce* (Warsaw: Ksiazka i Wiedza, 1968). Regarding the use of this work, see Anna Bikont, *My z Jedwabnego* [Jedwabne and I] (Warsaw: Proszynski et Ska, 2004), 50–51.
57. Wladyslaw Bartoszewski and Zofia Lewinowna, *Righteous among the Nations. How Poles Helped the Jews, 1939–1945* (London: Earlscourt Publication Limited, 1969).
58. Wladyslaw Bartoszewski, *Le Sang versé nous unit: sur l'histoire de l'aide aux Juifs en Pologne pendant l'Occupation* (Warsaw: Editions Interpress, 1970). This book has also been translated into German.
59. Conscious of the diplomatic stakes, representatives from Yad Vashem went to Warsaw for the event. See Gabriele Nissim, *Il tribunale del bene: la storia di Moshe Bejski, l'uomo che creò il Giardino dei giusti* (Milan: Mandadori, 2003), 276–89.
60. *Zycie Warszawy*, no. 223 (September 1979): 22–23.
61. Alain Brossat, ed., *A l'Est la mémoire retrouvée* (Paris: La Découverte, 1990).
62. Address by the president of the Republic of Poland Lech Wałęsa to the Knesset, Jerusalem, 21 May 1991.
63. Addresses by minister of foreign affairs of the Republic of Poland Władysław Bartoszewski at the Heroes of the Ghetto Kibbutz, Israel, 11 May 1995 and at the Knesset, Tel Aviv, 28 November 2000.
64. Main Commission for the Investigation of Crimes against the Polish Nation, Institute of National Memory, and Polish Society for the Righteous among the Nations, *Those Who Helped. Polish Rescuers of Jews during the Holocaust*, vol. 1 (Warsaw: Agencja Wydawnicza Mako, 1993). Also vol. 2 (1995) and vol. 3 (1997).

65. This copy was given to the National Library of Israel, Jerusalem, where it was consulted by the author.
66. In his book *Neighbors: The Destruction of the Jewish Community in Jedwabne* (Princeton: Princeton University Press, 2001), Jan Tomasz Gross describes the massacre of the Jewish residents of the village of Jedwabne by the Polish population in July 1941. This occurred without any instructions from the German authorities, who had invaded the east of Poland only one month prior to the events. Published in 2001, this book provoked heated controversy in Poland and gave rise to numerous debates.
67. On 1 January 2016, they still held this ranking, with 6,620 individuals recognized by Yad Vashem, ahead of 5,516 awards for the Netherlands, 3,853 for France, 2,544 for Ukraine, and 1,707 for Belgium. Of course, these numbers must be seen in the context of the Jewish populations of these countries and above all in light of the fact that the title Righteous is itself a social construction. On this point, and for a more detailed approach than the one in this book, see Sarah Gensburger, "From the Memory of Rescue to the Institution of the Title of Righteous," in *Resisting Genocides. The Multiple Forms of Rescue*, ed. Jacques Semelin, Claire Andrieu, and Sarah Gensburger (London/New York: Hurst/Columbia University Press, 2011).
68. Marc Levene, "Nationalism and Its Alternatives in the International Arena: The Jewish Question at Paris, 1919," *Journal of Contemporary History* 28, no. 3 (1993): 511–31.
69. Pawel Korzec, *Juifs en Pologne. La Question juive pendant l'entre-deux guerres* (Paris: Presses de la Fondation Nationale des Sciences Politiques, 1980), 62.
70. Gabriele Simoncini, "The Polyethnic State: National Minorities in Interbellum Poland," *Nationalities Papers* 22, no. 1 (1994): 5–28; Jean-Charles Szurek, "Juifs et Polonais (1918–1939)," *Les cahiers de la Shoah*, no. 1 (1994), available at www. http://www.anti-rev.org/textes/Szurek94a/.
71. Pawel Korzec and Jacques Burko, *Le Gouvernement polonais en exil et la persécution des Juifs en France en 1942* (Paris: Cerf, 1997), 27.
72. August Grabski, "Wspolczesne zycie religijne Zydow w Polsce" [Jewish Religious Life in Contemporary Poland], in *Studia z historii Zydow w Polsce po 1945 roku* [Studies on the History of Jews in Poland after 1945], by Grzegorz Berent, August Grabski, and Andrzej Stankowski (Warsaw: Żydowski Instytut Historyczny, 2000), 143–202.
73. Ruth Ellen Gruber, *Virtually Jewish. Reinventing Jewish Culture in Europe* (Columbia/Princeton: University Presses of California, 2002).
74. See Marius Gudonis, "Constructing Jewish Identity in Post-Communist Poland: Part I: 'Deassimilation without Polonization,'" *East European Jewish Affairs* 31, no. 1 (2001): 1–14; Paul Zawadzki, "Transition, Nationalisme et Antisémitisme: l'exemple polonais," in *Théories sociologiques du nationalisme*, ed. Pierre Birnbaum, 103–19 (Paris: PUF, 1997).
75. Paul Zawadzki, "Le Temps de la re-connaissance. Ruptures dans la trame du temps et recomposition des subjectivités juives en Pologne," in *Ecriture de l'histoire et identité juive. L'Europe ashkénaze. XIXe–XXe siècle*, ed. Delphine Bechtel, Evelyne Patlagean, Jean-Charles Szurek, and Paul Zawadzki, 115–16 (Paris: Les Belles Lettres, 2003); and an interview with Anna Drabik, who is responsible for the symbolic recognition of the Righteous among the "Children of the Holocaust," with the help of Agnieszka Niewiedzial, 22 June 2004, Warsaw.
76. "Order of the White Eagle for Irena Sendler," http://www.dzieciholocaustu.org.pl.
77. Stanislw Krajewski, "L'Inventaire des responsabilités," *Le Messager européen*, no. 9 (1996): 219–20.
78. Reported in Dariusz Ryn and Iwona Boratyn, "Rocznica pogromu. Pojednanie i pamiec" [Anniversary of a Pogrom. Reconciliation and Memory], *Gazeta Wyborcza (GW)*, 1 July 1996.

79. Law of 24 January on combatants and certain victims of repression. *Dziennik Ustaw*, no. 17 (1991), heading 75. Following this, all the texts referred to are amendments of this initial law, http://isip.sejm.gov.pl.
80. "Prawa kombatanckie za ratowanie Zydow" [Combatant Status and the Saving of Jews], *GW*, no. 73, 26 March 1992.
81. Archives of Yad Vashem, AM2/1110, press statement, 11 December 1994.
82. Natalia Skipietrow, "Kto bedzie kombatantem" [Who Will Be a Combatant?], *GW*, 17 March 1993; "Spor o kombatantow" [Dispute around Combatants], *GW*, 14 May 1994.
83. Stanislaw Krajewski, "Oddac honor sprawiedliwyn" [Pay Homage to the Righteous], *GW*, 15 November 1994.
84. "Prawa kombatanckie Sprawiedliwym" [Combatant Status for the Righteous], *GW*, 9 November 1994.
85. Sejm, second legislature, form no. 516.
86. Natalia Skipietrow, "Zli i dobrzy ubecy" [Good and Bad "Security Agents"], *GW*, Warsaw, 2 December 1994.
87. Natalia Skipietrow, "Kombatanci czekaja" [The Combatants Are Waiting], *GW*, 26 June 1995; "Projekt noweli ustawy kmbatanckiej UW. Zmiany pilnie wygladane" [Freedom Union Project for the Modification of the Law on Combatants. Impatient for Changes], *GW*, no. 82, 6 April 1995; "Wraca spor o uprawnienia kombatanckie" [Dispute around War Veterans], *GW*, 3 July 1995.
88. Intervention by Adam Dobronski, Sejm, second legislature, session of 11 January 1996.
89. "Uprawnienia kombatantckie nie przysluguja" [Veteran Status Does Not Apply], *GW*, 26 April 1997.
90. Law of 24 January 1991, Article 20^2. Amendment of 25 April 1997, *Dziennik Ustaw*, no. 68 (1997): heading 436.
91. The conception of Judaism as an ethnonational identity is clearly visible here and may go some way to explaining why it was considered exclusive and incompatible with Polish ethnonational identity.
92. Amendment of 4 March 1999, Article 2, paragraph 3, title 1, *Dziennik Ustaw*, no. 77 (1999): position 862.
93. On this point, see, e.g., the 1990 creation of the Commission of National Minority Affairs (*Monitor Polski*, no. 34 [1990]), several of the results of its work, and the ratification in 2000 of the 1995 Strasbourg Convention on the protection of national minorities (*Dziennik Ustaw*, no. 22 [2002]: heading 209. See also the adoption on 6 January 2005 of the law on national and ethnic minorities and regional languages (*Dziennik Ustaw*, no. 17 [2005]: position 141).
94. Paul Zawadzki, "Juifs de Pologne: malaise dans la filiation," *Les Cahiers du judaïsme*, no. 1 (Spring 1998): 41; Geneviève Zubrzycki, *The Crosses of Auschwitz: Nationalism and Religion in Post-Communist Poland* (Chicago: University of Chicago Press, 2006); Geneviève Zubrzycki, "Religion, Religious Tradition and Nationalism: Jewish Revival in Poland and 'Cultural Heritage' in Quebec." *Journal for the Scientific Study of Religion* 51, no. 3 (2012): 442–55; Geneviève Zubrzycki, "What Is Pluralism in a 'Monocultural' Society? Considerations from Post-Communist Poland," in *After Pluralism: Re-imagining Models of Interreligious Engagement*, ed. Courtney Bender and Pamela Klassen, 277–95 (New York: Columbia University Press, 2010).
95. Surveys conducted after the controversy revealed the polarization of these positions. "Trend Reports, Poles' Opinions about the Crime in Jedwabne—Changes in Social Consciousness," *Polish Sociological Review* 1, no. 137 (2002): 117–28.
96. Adam Michnik, "Poles and the Jews: How Deep the Guilt?" *New York Times*, 17 March 2001, republished in Antony Polonsky and Joanna B. Michlic, eds., *The Neighbors*

Respond. The Controversy over the Jedwabne Massacre in Poland (Princeton: Princeton University Press, 2004), 438–39.

97. Ireneusz Krzeminski, ed., *Czy Polacy sa antysemitami?* [Are Poles anti-Semitic?] (Warsaw: Oficyna Naukowa, 1996); and its updated version, "Przybylo nam antysemitow" [Increasing anti-Semites], *Rzeczpospolita,* 19 July 2003.
98. *Godni synowie naszej Ojczyzny* [Worthy Son of Our Homeland] (Warsaw: Wydawnictwo Siostr Loretanek, 2003).

Chapter 6

Memory Policy and Institutions

The commemoration of the Righteous of France

The study of the emergence of the Righteous of France category may seem to end with the vote on the law of 10 July 2000. However, there is one final step to take. As one member for Parliament (MP) remarked during the debates in the National Assembly, "this national day will take on its full meaning when initiatives for remembrance and homage abound in every French town." This is also true for the specific terms established by the adoption of the text.

If the emergence of the term "Righteous of France" results from a combination of strategic, cognitive, and institutional factors, it remains clear that once established, this new term may give rise to more traditional usage. We have seen the limits of the explanations emphasizing the existence of pressure groups and the rise of communitarianism as well as those assimilating the state's action to a top-down narrative of the past in the developments leading to the vote of 10 July 2000. But what happened after the vote?

A commemorative coproduction

The sole article moving the national day to 16 July was published in the *Journal Officiel* on 11 July 2000.[1] Although a few days later homage was immediately paid to the Righteous of France at the site of the former Vel d'Hiv[2] cycling stadium in Paris, this tribute was largely absent from regional ceremonies. The application decrees were published only two years later.[3] The relevant minister was in no hurry to provide them.[4] The first national commemorative day incorporating this new title was not held until July 2002.

However, several state services took advantage of the February 2000 text and its vote in the National Assembly. For this, they relied on the social actors who participated in the specific configuration, first among them the French Committee for Yad Vashem. Together they coproduced the public action for the commemoration of the Righteous of France.

Implementing a tribute to the Righteous of France

Following the first vote on the text, and even though the Senate had not yet made an announcement on the subject, the National Assembly once again joined with the French Committee for Yad Vashem in order to host a ceremony to present the medals. Unlike in 1994, the date of their first partnership, the initiative came from the MPs this time. The event was held on 2 May 2000. The organization of this event was conceived by its promoters as a means of implementing a new tribute.

Thus, the *Activity Report for the National Assembly* for the year 2000 did not directly evoke the adoption of the 10 July law, but referred to it only in passing in the description of the demonstrations on 2 May. It applauded at length the "sacred memory," the "work of memory, symbol of republican humanitarianism" of the French Committee for Yad Vashem.[5] What was claimed to be the first implementation of the "homage to the Righteous of France" was thus based on a partnership with actors outside the administrative-political sphere. Here the action of the state is accomplished via the work of social actors, who are subject to modifications in status and structure by the state. One could hypothesize that the choice of this co-production resulted from the partial adoption of the law that had not yet received Senate approval.

This was not the case, however. The methods for implementing the final text were identical. Starting in July 2000, the National Office for Veterans and Victims of War (Office National des Anciens Combattants et Victimes de Guerre [ONAC]) expressed its interest in organizing this new national day.[6] This Office is one of the links in the administrative chain responsible for what is referred to as "state memory policy." It has seven principal missions: "commemoration, pedagogy, historic information, publishing and production of films, museums, tombs and memorials, and finally the valorization of heritage and tourism linked to memory."[7] In fact, its departmental delegations assist the prefectures in carrying out commemorative tasks, among which figure the organization of national days of commemoration. In the terms of the law, the Office takes its instructions from the High Council of Veteran Remembrance (Haut Conseil de la Mémoire Combattante), which has been responsible for determining the direction of memory policy since its creation in 1997.[8]

However, ONAC's investment in the homage to the Righteous of France was not an instruction from above. Mainly made up of representatives from veteran circles, the High Council showed scarcely any interest in promoting these civilian heroes.[9] ONAC's central office became involved in this new national day of its own accord. This "spontaneous" mobilization can be largely explained by the Office's need to demonstrate its usefulness and its competence in a period when its status and its budgetary allocations were the subject of negotiations with its supervisory minister.

Moreover, Serge Barcellini, the cabinet director of the Secretary of State for Veterans' Affairs, at the time of the preparation of the bill left his position in March 2000 during a ministerial reshuffle. He then took up a position at the head of ONAC, so he was particularly aware of the existence, the potential, and the implications of this new commemorative day. He was aware, for example, of the amount of room for maneuvering left open by the text, and he intended to pursue his previous action from his new administrative position. He feared that the state would be dispossessed in this respect, to the benefit of social actors.

He thus took the initiative and set up several partnerships, which seemed to him to be the best way to influence and control the action of the social organizations that he feared would ultimately be in competition with the public authorities. As he explained to us during the interview:

> Once we had said, "recognition for the Righteous," we then had to have something to say. Well it was in this context that I set up my assistance to the French Committee for Yad Vashem. I helped them find the traces of the families to give a human reality to the ceremonies. I did that for the Righteous and so that they were present. To make sure that the Righteous become a part of France's collective memory.[10]

Following the vote on the law, the departmental direction of the Office contacted the French Committee to obtain information on the civil status and contact details of the Righteous. It therefore anticipated the requests for information that would be addressed to them by the services of the prefectures wanting to incarnate the commemoration. The Prefecture of Mayenne, for example, wrote to the association as early as 18 July 2000 with a request for contact details.[11]

In return, the French Committee for Yad Vashem turned toward ONAC. For its members, this cooperation was seen as an opportunity to improve public knowledge of the Righteous, to see its own action in France recognized, and to maintain a form of control over the use of the Israeli honorific title. It was the result of more than one practical necessity. The vote of 10 July led to a considerable increase in demands for information relating to the Righteous of France. Staffed by only a handful of volunteers, the French Committee was unable to meet this demand. At the time it did not have an up-to-date register of all the Righteous still living, their addresses, and the identity of their beneficiaries. ONAC, and its network of delegations, took on this task in their place.

Already longstanding, the interaction between the French Committee and the public authorities thus became more intense. It also changed in nature. Like ONAC, the administrations were no longer content with reacting (positively for the most part) to possible solicitations by the French Committee; instead they took the initiative. From 15 May 2000 on, for example, the departmental director of ONAC in Mayenne fell into step with the MPs who had just held the second major ceremony in the National Assembly building. He set up an important file for the recognition of the town of Fougerolles du Plessis as Righteous among the Nations.[12] He included individual testimony, extracts from books, archival documents, and many indirect accounts of protagonists. In so doing, he carried out the work that was ordinarily done by the French Committee.

An official partnership convention between ONAC and the French Committee for Yad Vashem was finally signed on 30 June 2003.[13] It aimed to "catalog and honor the Righteous of France in associating them in particular with the ceremonies organized on the occasion of this national day." Although the use of the status of resistant had been excluded by the law, the Righteous of France eventually fell under the responsibility of the Secretary of State for Veterans' Affairs. This requalification occurred indirectly through the establishment of a partnership.

The coproduction of the commemoration can be explained first by cognitive factors. As we saw at the moment of the vote on the law of 10 July 2000, the reading of the title of Righteous by the members of the French Committee for Yad Vashem brings it closer to the status of resistant, with which ONAC was familiar. The existence of a kind of shared minimalist interpretation between the different partners facilitated this collaboration.

There was also a number of simultaneous strategic factors that came into play. In this process, each party relied on the legitimacy and resources of the others to affirm its own role and position. The French Committee gained visibility and became more representative. In 2000, its president joined the executive office of the Representative Council of Jewish Institutions in France (CRIF) and the administrative council of the Foundation for the Memory of the Shoah. The following year, he spoke for the first time in the name of the "Jewish community," during the newly named national commemoration on 16 July. Finally, on 25 January 2005, the day of the inauguration of the Memorial of the Shoah, he was personally thanked by the president of the French Republic[14] for his activities in the area of memory. He went on to become the new president of the CRIF in 2008.

Conversely, these specific administrations relied on this partnership to found their legitimacy for action in an area that they had long been absent from. The use of a coproduction was accompanied by a genuine appropriation of the action of the French Committee for Yad Vashem, presented and defended as public action. When questioned on all their initiatives relating to the Righteous, both the prefectures and the ONAC delegations regularly mentioned, alongside the organization of the national day on 16 July, the medal ceremonies for the Israeli award organized by the French Committee in different municipalities in the area. To this annual recognition can also be added what they call "periodic recognition."[15] The prefecture in Vendee added, for example, these "medal ceremonies for the Righteous" to the "traditional ceremonies of 16 July" to describe all their "actions undertaken."[16] Out of the sixty-six services who responded to the questionnaire, twenty-three included these specific events among the activities relating to the Righteous that they counted as being within the scope of the administration.

However, this formal appropriation does not imply the production and imposition of new content for this narrative of the past. The administrations in fact mobilize almost none of the instruments that they have traditionally used to conduct state memory policy.[17] The vectors[18] that are ordinarily used to transmit a state-controlled reading of the past are not used here. The *Report by the High Council of Veterans' Remembrance 2001*[19] envisaged the creation of only two physical supports for this homage to the Righteous of France. It advised the writing of an initial brochure on the 16 July commemoration that would include a presentation of the Righteous of France and that would be distributed to those attending annual ceremonies. Another brochure, with the prospective title "A Village against: Le Chambon-sur-Lignon," was planned but never written by the Department of Memory, Heritage and Archives (DMPA).

The school curricula, like the various circulars put out by the minister for national education, did not launch any further discussion of the Righteous. Written in 1995, and updated in 2001 and 2004, the general history curriculum was not modified.[20]

The publication of the Dictionary of the Righteous of France

The only genuine support for the commemoration to be created was, once again, a coproduction. From as early as 1999, the French government participated in the preparation of the *Dictionary of the Righteous of France,* which was finally jointly published in 2003 by the Institute Yad Vashem and the publisher Fayard.

The creation of a "glossary of Righteous among the Nations" was envisaged back in 1953 by Israeli MPs. In the spirit of its promoters, it aimed to provide brief summaries with the names and deeds of each of the Righteous recognized to date in each country. The writing of the *Encyclopedia of the Righteous among the Nations* was not really begun until 1995, however. The director of the Department of the Righteous at the Institute was the initiator of this project; he sought both to promote his work and to ensure the survival of his department.[21] Unlike in the previous period, by this time he was indeed able to draw support from the growing interest that an increasing number of states and transnational actors began to show in this commemoration.

Thus, starting in 1998, the European Union provided financial support for the publication project.[22] Several of its member states even did so individually. In 2000, for example, the Netherlands sent a researcher from the Dutch Institut voor Oorlogsdocumentatie (Institute for War, Genocide, and Holocaust Studies) to Yad Vashem for three years. In September 2004, *The Encyclopedia of the Righteous among the Nations: The Netherlands* was finally published.[23] It was the same as the other volumes in the collection.

Things went differently in the French case. Unlike other countries, France's participation in the project was not limited to financial support. It took the form of a genuine coproduction of a new vector of memory. This process occurred in parallel with the discussions that led to the vote of 10 July 2000.

On 2 August 1998, the French ambassador gave the president of Yad Vashem a check representing "the contribution of the Prime Minister, Mr. Lionel Jospin to the publication of the book of the Righteous among the Nations in France." [24] Four years later the words used had changed and the book had become the *Dictionary of the Righteous of France.*

The first volume of the *Encyclopedia* to be actually published, the French edition was the only one to adopt a different title. It therefore broke away from the standardized form of the title that simply added the name of the country in question to the generic "Encyclopedia of the Righteous among the Nations." The title that was ultimately chosen provided the opportunity to draw attention to the Righteous of France. Related to this, and in keeping with the financing agreement in 1999, the head of state wrote its preface.[25] This was a review of all the elements present in the presidential speeches given previously and in the statement of motives for the law of 10 July 2000. It was therefore under the auspices of the French state that the Righteous—now officially "of France"—were placed.

The legislative creation of the category "Righteous of France" thus led to the state's implementation of commemorative action. However, this did not consist in a direct and unilateral diffusion of historic memory imposed from above on to passive recipients. On one hand, like the presidential discourses before it, the adoption of the text by the parliament led to legitimacy and opportunity effects even within the public sphere. On the other hand, in correlation with this, the mobilization of consecutive state services were deployed in a partnership with the social actors involved.

Cognitive and strategic factors came together to shape the implementation of the commemoration of the Righteous. This coproduction was first made possible by the existence of an interpretative space that was as minimalist and polysemic as possible, to be shared by its different protagonists. Next, it involved an appropriation by the public authorities of actions produced by members of "civil" society, who also found an interest for themselves in the social recognition they gained from cooperation with the state.

National commemoration and community discourses

The hypothesis might therefore be made that the implementation of memory policy shifted the object of the state's instrumentalization. This would no longer concern memory but instead the social actors working in the area. However, the study of the actual evolution of the national day shows that this "instrumentalization" appears instead to be an instrument of state policy. If the participation of social actors in the implementation of state commemoration did indeed reinforce state commemoration, the state did not control either the shape or the extensions of this remembrance.

On 1 July 2001, the State Secretary for Veterans' Affairs finally sent the prefectures a circular relating to the organization of a new national day of commemoration.[26] These instructions were supposed to provide the framework for the application of the law of 10 July 2000; yet the framework was empty. These instructions only had one thing in common: the order of the establishment of partnerships. From this perspective it was expected that the communities spoke in the name of the state to a certain extent.

Memory, nation, and communities

In this specific circular, the meaning given to the ceremony was still not made explicit. Only the 16 July 1995 and November 1997 speeches of the president of the Republic were included in the regulatory text. It was suggested that the decentralized services could find meaning in them. The circular focused above all on the wide margins left to the prefects in order that "the representatives of the persecuted communities, Jewish and Romani, may be involved in the organization as much as possible."

Although, as we saw in Chapter 4, French law recognizes neither race nor religion, the state services responsible for its application are able to give a central place to ethnoreligious groups as such. Just as in the period leading up to the vote on the bill, political institutions were an additional factor, working alongside strategies and cognitive frameworks to explain the shape of the implementation of the text. The tension between a citizenship regime that affirms universality and laicity, on one hand, and pluralization of society and the public expression that accompanies it, on the other, structure the concrete implementation of memory policy here

This governmental directive goes along with that which ONAC sent to its departmental services. The Office in turn sought to encourage the latter to make contact with local Jewish organizations, on one hand, and with local Righteous, on the other.[27] In 2002, the date of the sixtieth anniversary of the deportation of the French Jews, the place that the state intended to accord civil society, in this instance before all the representatives of Jewish communities, was again affirmed. Making reference to the CRIF's request to be able to participate in the regional ceremonies, in this particular year, a special circular of the Minister of the Interior thus called once again on the prefects to pay the utmost attention to this request and to respond according to the local history and situation. The prefects had to allow the state services to "define the content of [their] message."[28]

A study of the 2002 ceremony allows us to see how this empty framework is filled up through the event itself. First, the speeches by the prefects who represented the state during the ceremony allow us to see the meaning that was finally given to it. In this respect it is striking to note that in spite of the lack of explicit instructions, these speeches were quite similar from one area to another. The content of these speeches focused on two main interconnected themes.

First, in keeping with the presidential speeches, the place accorded to the Righteous was presented as a counterpoint to the state's complicity in the deportations. Second, these speeches spurned all military and patriotic themes and instead proclaimed the values of human rights, made references to the Republic, and presented the example of "active solidarity" in all of the sixty-nine speeches collected. The humanitarian rhetoric systematically filled the void left by the secretary of state's failure to make the values to be promoted explicit. The cabinet director for the prefect of the Oise region's response to my open question on the meaning of this commemoration perfectly sums up this dominant interpretation: "The action of the Righteous of France remains current today and is part of the republican conception of the nation, in fraternity and solidarity. It also shows the courage of those who helped the Jews at the risk of their lives, by resisting a totalitarian regime based on exclusion."

This time in keeping with the instructions of the supervisory minister, this affirmation of a reference to human rights and republican principles goes along with the practice of putting the Jewish community at the center of the event. Indeed, the relevant services seized on the opportunity to involve the representatives of Jewish institutions and, to a much lesser extent, the Righteous. In fact, the Righteous or their beneficiaries attended less than 20 percent of the ceremonies. Only two of them, the president and vice president of the Association of the French Righteous spoke publically at these events.[29] The Righteous and their families in fact did not have much of a role in this event that was supposed to pay tribute to them.

Inversely, it emerged that out of the ninety-eight ceremonies, only sixteen did not include speeches by local leaders of the Jewish community. In other words, where there was an identifiably Jewish organization, it was systematically invited to the ceremony and in most cases its representatives made a speech. Out of the sixty-nine departments we have information about, forty-five ceremonies included this kind of speech. The speeches generally included few specifically Jewish religious or cultural references, instead promoting the "French values" and human rights that the collaboration of the Vichy regime betrayed.

As a part of the implementation of the state's homage to the Righteous of France, the management of the meaning of this commemoration by civil society actors was not purely discursive. The implication of representatives of Jewish institutions was actively sought by the administration prior to the event and was a part of its conception. In the Yvelines, the site was chosen after a commission was established regrouping the main qualified members of the community.[30] In Indre, "The choice of 16 July rather than the following Sunday, corresponded to the desire of the Israelite cultural association."[31]

Elsewhere, the representative of the local Jewish community was referred to me as the person to contact for further information about the organization of these events by the public authorities.[32] Conversely, the small scale of the ceremonies is seen here as linked to the weak presence, investment, or interest of these associations.[33] The response ONAC received from the Aube region sums up, implicitly, the position of these administrations: "Know that the CRIF is not established in our department and that the local community associations are not by any means substantial. I am beginning to put together the documents, however."[34]

In turn, the concrete implementation of the law of 10 July 2000 in the organization of national days did not take the form of a unilateral understanding of an official truth that the state sought to impose. Like the legislative text itself, these events were produced in collaboration with other social actors. This foundation of the implementation of state memory policy on the development of partnerships with social actors is not specific to the establishment of the Righteous of France category. This is a genuine desire to coproduce public commemoration on the part of the administrations responsible for what they themselves call "memory policy."

This goes back a long way. After World War I, the development of war memorials and commemorations for veterans in French towns had already resulted from shared action by the state and the veterans' associations.[35] In 1954, the vote on the bill creating a "national day of memory for the victims and heroes of the deportation" and its implementation were also the result of interaction between the "Network of Memory" organization and the MPs.[36] Moreover, research conducted since 2007 within DMPA suggests that this is still the dominant approach to conducting public action in the area of memory today.

This position can be seen, for example, in the case of the selection of several dates for the national day. In 2006, the choice fell on 10 May as the annual commemoration of slavery and its abolition. This day was chosen by an ad hoc committee and was not a reference to the past to be remembered but rather evoked the action of the state itself. It corresponds to the day in 2001 the elected representatives of the French Republic unanimously adopted the text, which after a final reading in the Senate became the law of 21 May 2001, by which France recognized slavery and the slave trade as a crime against humanity.

A similar mechanism had been used for the choice of the date for the national day of homage to those who "died for France" during the Algerian War and the battles in Morocco and Tunisia. In 2003, the ad hoc administrative commission had not managed to bring the various associations to an agreement. Faced with a stalemate, the state finally decided to not decide. The date of 5 December that was finally chosen does not refer to the past but once again to the action of the state. It is nothing more than a reference to the inauguration of the memorial in honor of the military dead of the Algerian War, which the French president presided over on 5 December 2002.[37]

The coproduction of commemoration, and more broadly of memory policy, can therefore not be reduced to a recent increase in "communitarianism" and pressure by the said communities to impose their objectives by lobbying the state. The interaction between "civil society," governing bodies, and administrations responsible for memory predates the contemporary affirmation of ethnic-religious pluralism and is not limited to this area alone. It also concerns the commemoration of war and veterans in much the same way.

It seems that this method of implementation of public action stems from the nature of French political institutions. On one hand, they do not leave any legal space for the recognition of the particular, whatever its nature. On the other hand, their functioning is based on the affirmation of democratic principles that are not very compatible with the prescription of a unilateral narrative of the past that would verge on propaganda. The development of partnerships appears to be a specific mode of social regulation through memory. In this institutional configuration and from a strategic point of view this time, the coproduction of commemoration also appears to be the best way to ensure the latter's success.[38]

As the entity responsible for making the major directions in this area, the High Council of Veterans' Remembrance also talks about the need for partnerships, as a "condition of success":

> Because the memory of contemporary conflicts concerns the whole nation, because the defense of republican values concerns all citizens and is expressed through various supports, the minister of defense envisages his missions in these areas as part of partnerships that are as broad and diverse as possible.[39]

Beyond the promotion of social actors as an instrument for policy, the general comments of the High Council also summarize the two main traits of the implementation of the 10 July 2000 law. On one hand, the memory of the nation first targets the defense and diffusion of republican values. The national is conveyed through a reference to human rights. On the other hand, this universalist goal can only be realized through the participation of a large range of social actors in the state's policy in this area. The resolution of this tension between the nation and the community, or more broadly between the universal and the particular, which is at the heart of French political institutions, occurs through the delimitation of a space for legitimate commemoration in which the state services expect to be supported by civil society actors. In this respect, the potentially communitarian nature of some of these actors—here the leaders of the Jewish community—are not specific. They result from the French public authorities' ordinary approach to managing issues of memory.

Propaganda and communitarianism are thus connected here by a mechanism different from that described by most analysts of the contemporary relations between memory and politics. The specificity of the construction of the French nation, through a constant reference to the universal, has a driving role in this. Here, it is the services of the state that have undertaken a potentially communitarian reading of the event, while most of the community speeches in fact refer to universal values and other human rights that evoke the honor of the French Republic.

If the birth of the Righteous of France category and the implementation of the tributes due to these people indeed reveal a close interconnectedness between politics and memory and the management of individual group memberships, this is distinguished from the linear evolution of individual and community memory to the detriment of shared national memory. It stems first from the logic of coproduction and the state appropriation of the initiatives of social actors that is characteristic of the way memorial questions are dealt with by public authorities.

Institutions and implementation of memory policy

This particular articulation between memory policy and the state management of individual belongings and their expression emerges strongly in one final presidential speech. On 8 July 2004, the head of state chose Le Chambon-sur-Lignon, the "town of the Righteous,"[40] to launch a wake-up call against intolerance. As the title of the event shows, the public intervention in the area of memory constituted an indirect and ultimately derivative way for the state to act in an area that had no legal existence in terms of political institutions.

Given that French political institutions recognize neither race nor religion, they cannot be concerned with the coexistence of these factors. Questioned on the reasons for this new remembrance of the past, the services of the presidency told us that the head of state "wanted to remind people that the Republic is the common good of every citizen, with equal rights and responsibilities whatever the origins and beliefs of each of us."[41] Whereas the establishment of the 16 July national day consisted in giving voice to the ethnic-religious communities to evoke the past, talking of the past constitutes an instrument of intervention in social relations between citizens with various ethnoreligious belongings.

In this speech, the term "Righteous" and the historic remembrance of the past are intended to illustrate the "Declaration of the Rights of Man" and "shared humanity":

> The history of the towns of the "plateau" follows that of the fight for freedom of conscience and for tolerance. . . . To confront this [religious intolerance], Protestantism had to fight a painful fight, a fight for a nation, a fight that led to freedom of religion being inscribed in our Declaration of the Rights of Man. . . . then, [under the Occupation], in anonymity, discretion, in the simple enthusiasm of the outstretched hand, shared fraternity and humanity, refusing the law of hate. "The Plateau," Righteous among the Nations, made France grow. . . .

After a long reiteration of the "values of the Republic," the president finished his speech with comments linked to a figurative past bearing universal values and destined to enable the state's management of particular belongings:

> Faced with the risk of indifference and passivity on a daily basis, I solemnly call on each French man and woman to be vigilant. In the face of danger, this is a wake-up call. In the face of rising intolerance, racism, anti-Semitism, refusal of differences, I ask that they remember a history that is still near to us. I tell them to remain faithful to the lessons of history, a history still so recent. I invite them to always remind their children of the mortal danger of fanaticism, exclusion, cowardice, and giving in to extremes. I ask them to strongly demonstrate our resolve, our ability to live in harmony and respect. I ask them to always bear our heritage with pride. As the birthplace of human rights, France has written in the stone of its great building the universal values of humanity. It has made liberty, equality, and fraternity the motto of the Republic. Let us remind our children that the whole history of the French nation is marked by these battles—sometimes terrible battles, the battles that made tolerance and the protection of the weak central to our principles. These were the battles of those great minds and these great principles that forged our culture. There were also more humble battles, which often remained anonymous, whose engagement—sometimes with the ultimate sacrifice—made the honor and greatness of France and the French. A few days away from 14 July, the symbol of our fraternity, I call on each of you to unite so that together, faithful to our values, we may know how to keep a certain idea of humanity alive, a certain idea of France.[42]

This speech reused certain formulations and parts of phrases that were already present in the speeches of 16 July 1995 and 2 November 1997 and in those that presented the motivations for the law of 10 July 2000. However, in this case, these elements of language no longer served an explicit memory policy but rather a policy of managing ethnoreligious belonging by another name.

Although the exceptional and presidential nature of the event left less room for the shared management of the event than previous examples, there were nevertheless voices other than the president's. Joseph Atlas, a French citizen hidden as a Jewish child in the village, was invited to speak by the municipality who had coorganized the ceremony. He took the podium to share his story. This discourse in particular focused on the values of the Republic; it paid deeply felt tribute to the "school system, laic, co-ed, tolerant and fraternal."[43] Once again the interaction between the representative of the nation and the spokesperson of the community was accompanied by a reference to universal republican principles.

But this partnership is selective. Only social actors sharing a minimalist interpretative space with the state are likely to be involved in coproducing the commemoration. Thus, certain members of the specific configuration were not associated with the preparation of the event. This was also the case for the Foundation of the Friends of Le Chambon, which played an important role in the attribution of the title "Righteous among the Nations" to the village, as we saw in Chapter 2. On 6 July 2004, President Pierre Sauvage wrote to all those who were involved with the evocation of the French Righteous from the United States, where he lives.

He wanted to share his opinion on the imminent visit of the French president to the village. He began by celebrating the announcement of the presidential visit before explaining that it "filled him with pride and gratitude toward all those, inhabitants or former refugees, who carried in their hearts this little corner of France that never stopped being free under the Occupation." But immediately, through an imaginary description of the future presidential ceremony, he shared his own frames of interpretation both of the past and of the event:

> The president will surely know to take into consideration the fact that it was hardly the values of the Republic that motivated the Righteous of the Le Chambon-sur-Lignon region: everyone agreed that what was done in Le Chambon and its surroundings was done out of much more personal priorities. My friend Joseph Atlas, invited by the mayor of Le Chambon-sur-Lignon to speak before the president in the name of the former Jewish refugees of the Plateau, will perhaps not hesitate to evoke the religious, or even "communitarian" dimension of the rescue action he benefited from.[44]

The divergence between Pierre Sauvage's comments and the interpretation of the past prescribed by Jacques Chirac, like that expressed by his "friend" and former hidden child Joseph Atlas, reveals the limits of both coproduction and historic memory. If the investment of the state and the appropriation it undertook in the context of these partnerships is able to direct or influence the action of social actors, it relies on the preexistence of an interpretative framework of the past that is partly shared by them. Indeed, the narrative prescribed through the implementation of memory policy is not necessarily imposed on actors, whether they remain isolated individuals or unite for collective action. "Fundamentally, in terms of memory, like in other areas, society conserves an important degree of autonomy in relation to the authorities or groups established."[45]

In July 2001, the first national day in memory of the victims of the racist and anti-Semitic crimes of the French state and homage to the Righteous of France in fact provoked some negative reactions. Scarcely a week after the ceremony, the Canadian president of the Offshore Coordination of Jewish Children Survivors of the Holocaust having lived in France violently criticized the French Committee for Yad Vashem as well as the president of the CRIF for their participation in the event. Through them he condemned the public policy transfer of which the creation of the Righteous of France category was the final stage. "It is not your role to obey the French injunctions that seek to amalgamate the crimes committed by the French police against French Jews and the devotion of more than 2000 French citizens who helped save a few of them. The well-deserved recognition of the Jewish people regarding those 2000 French Righteous must be expressed on another occasion."[46]

These two examples of divergent reactions encourage us to consider the overarching role played by political institutions in establishing the coproduction we have observed and, more broadly, in the different forms of appropriation of this category, including its rejection. We saw in the previous chapter that the institutional organization of relations between the state and particular belongings structures the way memory public policies are elaborated and implemented. In this respect the form of the partnerships established by the state, and the divergences in perspectives observed, demonstrate the distance between French and U.S. political institutions in this area.

The president of the Foundation of the Friends of Le Chambon and the Off Shore Coordination both lived in France during the Occupation, and they share the same migratory trajectory. Pierre Sauvage's story is revealing in this respect. He was born in Le Chambon-sur-Lignon during the war and was hidden there as a baby. After the liberation, his path diverged from that of Joseph Atlas; he left France with his parents to go and live in the United States. Brought up as an atheist by parents who had chosen to set aside their Judaism, he lived in New York and then in Los Angeles. At the beginning of the 1970s, he returned to the Cevennes region of France. At the time, Sauvage was following the traces of his birth to make a documentary. On several occasions he described the way in which this encounter with the people of Le Chambon converted him, not to Christianity but to religion. In his eyes, which are those of an individual whose socialization primarily occurred in the United States, the assistance of the villagers during the Occupation was a Huguenot commitment in favor of Jews.[47]

The differences between the institutions overseeing the relationship between the state and individual belongings seem to play a driving role in the divergences observed here as well as in the possibility of a coproduction of this public commemoration.

A new approach to the relations between memory and public policy

It nonetheless remains true that the expression of critical perspectives on the development of a policy of commemoration of the Righteous of France is rare. There was no controversy here over what constitutes an instrument of memory public policy and its entrepreneurs, ordinarily described as an instrumentalization by the analysts of memory as well as by participants in the public debate. Because we have seen that subscribing to historical memory is not automatic, it is important to close the present study with a look at the construction of the apparent convergence between public action and individual perspectives.

How does the influence of this translation play out on these actors from varying social positions? Which social mechanisms govern the interaction between recall and memory policy? We do not seek to establish a list of the possible effects of the public policy transfer in the genesis of the category the Righteous of France. The use of this term would suppose the existence of a frontier between the public sphere and civil society, a frontier that we have seen would be ineffective. Chapter 3 has, for example, shown the circular nature of relations between public and social actors that governed such effects. In this respect, this final stage is nothing more than a shift in the focal point of our analysis, to look at the birth of the Righteous of France category from a new angle.

The object of this book was constructed precisely in such a way as to offer several angles from which to observe these mechanisms. In carrying out the fieldwork that has been analyzed here, particular attention was paid to the sources likely to allow us to understand public policies of commemoration on the Righteous of France based on the viewpoints of some of the social actors. The question of the articulation between the universal and particular, on one hand, and between nation and community, on the other, thus emerges in a new light.

Public action and the expression of memories

The applications for Righteous status put together at Yad Vashem for the nomination of French citizens are among the sources constructed in which public policy and social actors interact. Once again, in order to be registered, each application needs at least one Jewish person to make a specific request to Yad Vashem and to testify about their experiences. The study of these documents reveals a strong correlation between the situation in 1995, the beginning of the appropriation of the term "Righteous among the Nations" by the French state and the increase in individual use of this honorific title in talking about the past. The year 1996 saw a historic high in the number of annual nominations of French Righteous, with 194 awards compared to just 115 the previous year. Several individual applications, each opened following a new stage in the French translation of the term "Righteous among the Nations," seem to suggest that the coincidence observed reflects a causal relationship.

In 1999, a number of press articles reported on the submission of the bill behind the text of 10 July 2000, and this led several French citizens to write to the MPs who had proposed it.[48] Most of these letters are from Jews who see themselves as having been helped by non-Jews. In their letters, they systematically express an expectation that they see as being fulfilled by the creation of a French title. For example, in October 1999, one woman wrote to the MPs explaining:

> I have wished for nearly fifty years that homage be paid to the family in Tours, thanks to whom I was saved from the deportation, and it was with great interest that I read in the *Express* of 26 August 1999 that you have filed a proposition for a law to award the title of Righteous of France to the French citizens who saved victims of Nazi persecution during World War II. I ardently hope that this bill comes to fruition because I have always regretted not being able, until now, to have this act of courage and heroism publically recognized.[49]

Sometimes the authors of these letters also initiated a procedure for nomination with Yad Vashem. For this woman, the chronology of these two actions reveals the way in which the intervention of the state in the configuration was a reference point from which to use the Righteous category as a way of publically expressing her memory. She later finally applied to Yad Vashem to honor her rescuers.

Another of these letters was written by a man who was rescued as a child by a French family. He wrote to the MP Jean Le Garrec in October 1999 seeking to express his desire to see—in the context of the future nomination procedure for the title Righteous of France—recognition for those "who, aware of the risks they took and without ulterior motives, housed [him] for two years while [his] family was deported" and who "also for a time hid a fellow Jew who had escaped a roundup." As though this man sought to take a stand without explaining the nature of the title to which he himself referred, he "point[ed] out that this family was not counted among the 1720 Righteous and there were other examples in the village too."[50]

It was thus knowingly and by choice that this man seemed to prefer the solution proposed by the French state over the existing one offered by Israel. However, it was as though for this man this first step and the enthusiastic response of the French MP signified the national legitimation of the Israeli title. He ultimately began an official application for Yad Vashem Righteous status with the French Committee the following November.[51] Here, the reminder of the past and the affirmation of ethnoreligious belonging that accompanied it—it was as a Jew that this man testified before Yad Vashem—occurred through the intermediary of the French state. A similar mechanism can be seen in each one of these stages that, between 1995 and 1999, preceded the vote on the law of 10 July 2000.

In the documents of the archives of the French Committee was another notable example: a letter from a man rescued as a child with his brother by a family in the town of Vieille-Tursan. From as early as 1994, even before the presidential declaration of July 1995, this man had decided to express his recognition of those he considered his saviors. On 8 May he organized a ceremony in the town where he had found refuge during the Holocaust. For this event he brought together the local elected officials and most of the population. He spoke before the war memorial and played the Marseillaise through his own personal loudspeaker. At the time when he was publically making his own personal thanks in his own way,[52] he had recently become the leader of the Jewish community of Laon. It is thus reasonable to think that he was aware of the existence of the Righteous among the Nations title. Yet during his ceremony he never used the Israeli term.

The term "Righteous" did not take on its meaning for this man until three years later, following the 1997 inauguration of the memorial to the Righteous of France jointly organized by the Central Consistory and the French state. He thus responded to the call for testimonies launched by the Consistory for this event, hoping to bring together stories in the perspective of creating a new honorific status.[53] Here the simultaneous intervention of the cultural representative of French Judaism and the French public authorities in the configuration seems to have allowed this individual the specific social position to recognize himself in an appropriation of the Israeli category that thus corresponds to his frames of interpretation of the past, such as they appeared from 1994 during the local ceremony that he organized. The symbolic meaning of the expression "Righteous among the Nations" was sufficiently altered to allow this man to finally be able to use it.[54]

Finally, an identical process was also at work the day after the president's declaration on 16 July 1995. The archives enable us to retrace another example, one that was a direct consequence of the presidential speech. On 17 July, a man who had been sheltered with his cousin during the war in the town of Varetz decided to honor those who had protected him from deportation. In order to do this, he did not initially approach the French Committee for Yad Vashem but instead wrote directly to the mayor of the town. Speaking of the remaining survivors among those who he considers his benefactors, this man concluded his letter in these terms:

> They have a right to our deeply affectionate admiration and recognition. Allow me, Mr. Mayor, to remind you of the heroic behavior of this family, which was able to express its patriotism at risk of their lives. Fifty years later, while the whole of France celebrates the Nazi defeat, I have the honor of asking you to intervene with Mr. Prefect, to ask that a national recognition be awarded to them. This solemn gesture would be the symbol of a vibrant homage to all those, who through their courage and their abnegation, saved the honor of France.[55]

The president's evocation of the Righteous among the Nations served to liberate this man's public position, and he recognized this.

From this starting point, both local and national, he contacted various state representatives and territorial agencies in order to obtain "national honors" for those he saw as his saviors. He ultimately turned to the title of Righteous among the Nations. In doing so he took the path that his various contacts in the public sphere incarnating traditional state memory policy had proposed to him. Nearly two years after having solicited the state to obtain a form of recognition for those who had sheltered him, he wrote to the French Committee for Yad Vashem. Through them, he obtained the nomination of "his" Righteous in October 1998. It seems that his previous contacts were in fact steps that enabled him to embed his memories.

One final example allows us to specify the mechanism at work here. In fact it benefits from a specific, and at first sight paradoxical, status. It reveals the relation between a political policy nonaction and the appropriation of this policy by the actors. We conducted a number of interviews with Jews who were saved in France during the Occupation and who, even though they were aware of the procedure proposed by Yad Vashem, chose to not use it. Each time, their comments reveal their expectations that it should be the responsibility of the French state, and not only the state of Israel, to establish an honorific status for the Righteous.

During one of the interviews, our contact immediately explained that for him it is very important to talk about the Righteous:

> We have to emphasize these actions, particularly for the young. Really, we must! That is why I'm talking now if you like. Because Papon, well Papon was one thing, Papon followed Pétain, he was a sort of. . . . He didn't know anything, he didn't think. He was just there. And that is why we must talk about the Righteous, that's why! Because they were the *silent majority,* those people! The policemen who came to warn people: "I'm coming to arrest you, go quickly, I'll come back!" You see, *that's* France.

However, when we asked him, bearing in mind his previous statements, if he had already considered filing an application to have these people recognized as Righteous among the Nations, he responded:

> No, I haven't done it. But I could do. I've never done it, never. But you know, it is only recently that I decided to talk about it. And I think that people like me who were not too young can talk about it best because they have the stable memories of an adolescent. But would one person or another be Righteous? I'm not a fan of decorations you know.

When we replied, "And what of a medal from the French state . . . ?"[56] he immediately interrupted, with a completely different attitude:

> Oh yes! Yes! That, yes! That I can understand, understand very well! I would do that, yes. The Republic must do that, it must recognize—yes I would feel much better about that! Yes, that kind of medal would be great. The Republic must recognize those who acted, in the moment, with courage, against the control of the authorities. A decoration like that, yes, that I would do.[57]

His reservations about "decorations" were now completely gone.

The comments of this interviewee show the connection between the social position of this man, his refusal to resort to the Israeli title, and his support for the creation of a French equivalent. Indeed, the interviewees who were waiting for the creation of a republican medal shared the same situation. Although they identify with Judaism in cultural terms, they do not really practice it, and sometimes they claim militant secularism. They have no close or family ties with Israel, and for the most part they have never been there. Some even declare themselves "anti-Zionist." Indeed, they all have close connections with the world of non-Jews, sometimes even matrimonial links. The man in the previous example was born in France into a Jewish family from Alsace, which had lived there since the sixteenth century. As a nonpracticing Jew, he married a non-Jewish woman, and he therefore had a specific place within the social morphology that makes up the fabric of French society.

The failure to create a Righteous of France title implicitly reveals the mechanism by which memory policy plays out on actors. This last example shows just how the appropriation of memory policy by social actors involves the way in which individuals articulate their different belongings, here to Judaism, to France, and to a form of symbolic space connected to the state of Israel. The expression of memories and the form that they take, like the formation of representations of the past, do not stem from the rejection or acceptance of a narrative prescribed by the state so much as from the social positions of the respective actors regarding their simultaneous belongings to different political spaces and groups. Thus, it is above all because individuals recognize themselves in the reference points provided by memory policy that the latter has an effect on them.[58]

Translation, polysemy, and diversity

It is therefore possible to understand by which mechanisms the different stages of the public policy transfer, initiated by the state in 1995, were able to lead to the construction of an agreement. While, over the course of the 1990s, "the slow rise of cultural pluralism considerably changed the place of Jews in French society,"[59] the renewal of the term "Righteous" by the French state allowed an increasing number of individuals to reconcile their different belongings through memory and, reciprocally, to remember while being able to situate themselves at the intersection of the different spaces of identification that are relevant for them.

Indeed, the birth of the Righteous of France category occurred in parallel to the birth of a kind of naturalization of the relationship to Israel for many French Jews. The work of Doris Bensimon shows that although before the end of the 1980s, Israel progressively became a pole of identification for French Jews, this relationship was not yet unequivocal. Over this first period "there was a non-negligible proportion (some 15–20%) of French Jews that were quite critical and sometimes even hostile toward Israel."[60]

This polarization has since evolved and eventually disappeared. One important mode of Jewish identification occurs through "solidarity with Israel that was strongly and publically manifested for the first time in 1967 in the face of fears for the survival of Israel, but of which the importance seems to have declined since the end of the 1980s." Since the beginning of the 1990s, "the relation with Israel has become banal, it has been 'de-ideologized.'"[61] The same is true for the public affirmation of Jewishness in French society.

The previous examples, as well as the range of interactions between social actors and public authorities that played a driving role in the institutionalization of the category of the "Righteous of France," suggest that the rise of this pluralism did not occur necessarily alongside or against the state, but, on the contrary, was founded on it. The process was identical to what Pierre Birnbaum showed in his study of the decisions made by Jewish social actors during the French Revolution:

> Instead of appearing as a zero-sum game where the centralization of one occurred, as we long thought, to the detriment of the other, revolutionary centralization of society, paradoxically evolved along with that of certain particularisms controlled by the state in the global process but nonetheless able to preserve their own ends. . . . As though, strangely, the control of the state made it possible for certain particularistic practices to survive in the private space.[62]

In a word, this revolutionary example "appears to be quite crucial for understanding the contemporary quarrels regarding a hypothetical 'plural France,' of which the possible birth would mean the end of the emancipatory model just described."[63]

Similarly, it is because the French state has been continually operating a translation of the Israeli title Righteous among the Nations since 1995, that this has become meaningful for an increasing number of French Jews who are identifying more and more with a form of collective Jewish identity and with Israel. Public institutions and their representatives play a mediating role in this process. This constant also allows us to understand why, in the different national cases concerned and even though this linguistic category was simultaneously adopted by all European countries in the second half of the 1990s, it was only in France that there was a significant increase in nominations of the Righteous.

This evolution was indeed different from that observed, for example, in the Polish, Belgian, and Dutch cases, in which this simultaneous trend was absent. There is a specificity in the French national construction in the relation between the nation and the reference to the universal and to human rights and thus in the structure of the political institutions in this area. This allows the actors involved to jointly proclaim their belonging to the humanitarian paradigm, Judaism, and a form of identification both with France and Israel.[64]

Each of these dimensions has a different place for different individuals, however. The translation, in the emergence of the Righteous of France category, was thus only the object of a relative consensus because it allowed polysemic interpretations able to give each person a reference point in relation to his or her own particular social position. The translation process was, as we have seen, in the specificity of the instruments that it mobilized leading to the creation of a composite memorial term. Depending on the points of view, this term could be seen as being close to its Israeli cousin or to the status of Resistance member, on one hand, and as being Israeli or French, on the other. This hybrid term was thus susceptible to being appropriated by individuals from very different social positions.

The description of the medal award ceremonies by the interviewees concretely reveals this mechanism. Depending on their social positions, these individuals grant different places to the political participants and symbols in their narratives. One of these examples is particularly extreme, from a woman who had attended the medal ceremony for those whom she had nominated as Righteous. The ceremony took place in the Senate in March 1995. During the interview, she described it in these terms:

> Well, at the ceremony there were several Righteous to be honored; the Israeli ambassador presented them with the medal. I thus got to make a speech for two minutes and thirty seconds. So with my husband that's what we did. It was very important for me. Well you'll see what I said. Among other things I said something that, two and a half years ago, it was two years or three years. I don't remember. Something very bold: I said among other things, at the time there were Nazis, sixty years ago they killed my father but their descendants killed my son [She had described to me earlier how her "son was stabbed to death by

> Arabs." She went to get her speech to read it to us.]: "Sixty years ago Nazism tried to exterminate the people of Israel, six million men, women, and children went up in smoke and among them my dear father whom I hardly knew. Today, thank God, we have our state, we live free in the land of our fathers, and the yellow star has become the blue star of the flag of Israel. But now, by a phenomenon of evolution, the demons of the forces of Evil reappear in new forms: terrorism, Hezbollah, Hamas . . . but their goal is the same as the Nazis: throw us into the sea, take away our land, massacre us, men, women, and children. Among the thousands of innocent victims they have managed to assassinate was our beloved son, E., only twenty-six years old. But today, as then, the barbarians will not succeed in extinguishing our will to live, nor our boundless recognition for the Righteous to whom we owe our lives. Thank you!" You know, sometimes you feel the electricity in the air, and I say to myself that I was very brave to say that, in the Senate. But we had the proof with 11 September so there you go [*silence*]. In fact, this medal is the opposite of ingratitude. I don't know what else I could have done. No, what I would have liked to do, and that still holds, is to have them come here, to Israel, to my place and all that. But he was very moved. It was for his parents. But he remains my big brother. I'm still his little sister. We hugged. I would like him to come to Israel. And for me particularly because I think that, alas, alas, they are a minority of humanity, the Righteous. That is why it is all the more important to say that they existed. And I remember after the war, when I went home to Mother, she spoke Yiddish and always talked about the "goyim." And I felt that in that, I had the impression that there was something pejorative in that. I couldn't stand it when she called them "goyim." But well, it's true that they were "goyim!"[65]

The symbolic space of the ceremony as it was interpreted by this woman is completely different from the physical space of the Senate. It became a diplomatic enclave of the state of Israel. Simultaneously, the importance of the distinction between Jews and non-Jews, these "goyim," was again reiterated. This woman's perspective on the past, her focus point on the commemorative event, and her specific social position form a whole. This woman immigrated to Israel in the 1960s, practices Orthodox Judaism, and lives in the Old City in Jerusalem. Of course, her comments were made before the veritable initiation of a French translation of the Israeli title. Since 1995 precisely, the proportion of French Jews resorting to the Israeli title has increased considerably, to the detriment of those who have become Israeli citizens and who for a long time made up an important portion of the people providing their testimony to Yad Vashem to honor the French who saved them.

The study of the implementation of the different stages of the public policy translation and transfer in the birth of the Righteous of France category thus reveals the way in which memory policy has an impact on individuals. In its evolution over time, it has offered a range of reference points with which actors are able to identify, in a given social configuration, and that they are able to mobilize in conceiving the past. Simultaneously, and given the diversity and pluralism that characterize contemporary society, they are only the object of a relative agreement when they are able to allow for polysemic interpretations. To do this, they must run through specific public action instruments that are able to leave both the commemorative event, and the past to be commemorated, at least partly open for interpretation.

Of course, it is possible to object that this conclusion is based on very specific examples. We could have focused only on those testimonies bearing personal experience and not paid attention to representations of those with no connection to the past evoked by the term "Righteous of France." It would have been possible, for example, to conduct an additional survey, by questionnaire or qualitative fieldwork, in order to gauge the impact and the effects of the 2000 law on French citizens who were not institutionally legitimate witnesses nor potential Righteous.[66] The decision to not construct this kind of source was deliberate however. It seemed to us that by its construction at the intersection of individual spheres and public action, our approach reveals the broader mechanisms at work and, on the contrary, obliges us to reverse the way social sciences approach memory.

As Roger Bastide has said, "If the other is necessary for our remembering, it is because our memories are interconnected with the memories of others in a well-adjusted game of reciprocal images."[67] The linguistic categories mobilized by memory policy are only appropriated when they are recognized, in other words, only if they echo preexisting categories of meaning, categories that will themselves induce a rereading, a retranscription of the memory apparently transmitted or prescribed. These categories are thus the cognitive product of institutional structures, present interactions, social frames,[68] and past socializations that have accompanied the trajectories and governed the social positions of the actors over the course of their lives. It is also possible to hypothesize that it is ultimately the narrative and continuously interpreted nature of the past, and thus its possible hybridization and intrinsic polysemy, that is behind the current success of the notion of memory.

Notes

1. Law no. 2000–644 of 10 July 2000, *Journal Officiel. Lois et décrets*, no. 159.
2. The velodrome where the victims of the raids on the Jewish community in Paris, on 16 and 17 July 1942, were confined.

3. Decree no. 2002–994 of 11 July 2002 implementing law no. 2000–644 of 19 July 2000, which established a national day in the memory of the victims of racist and anti-Semitic crimes of the French state and homage to the Righteous of France. *Journal Officiel. Lois et décrets*, no. 164, 16 July 2002.
4. The calendar of the year 2000, published in the *Rapport du haut conseil de la Mémoire Combattante* in 2001, indeed shows the intermediary status of this project. For the date of 16 July it mentions the "commemoration of the racist and anti-Semitic persecutions committed under the de facto authority of the so-called 'Vichy Government' and homage paid to the Righteous of France," a mixed formulation that borrows both from the 1993 decree and from the law of July 2000.
5. Activity report of the National Assembly 2000, *Rapport d'activité de l'Assemblée nationale 2000*, "L'Assemblée gardienne de la mémoire républicaine. L'Hommage aux Justes de France," p. 44.
6. Converging interviews with Serge Barcellini, 3 October 2002, and Stéphane le Borgne, 7 May 2003, Paris, also with Mr. Mouly, head of the office for associations and ceremonies at the Department of Memory, Heritage and Archives (DMPA), and Emmanuelle Lenoir, head of the associations section, and Mr. Fleury, head of the section responsible for monuments and plaques, DMPA, 8 November 2002, Paris. Finally, in the sometimes fortunate collection of various documents at the prefectures, no document suggested that any measures were considered by the High Council and its administration, which is the DMPA.
7. Report by the Commission of Finances, general economy and the plan on the finance bill for 2003, no. 256, distributed 8 November 2002, "Annexe no. 10: Anciens Combattants."
8. Decree no. 97–11 of 9 January 1997 establishing the High Council for Veteran Remembrance, *Journal Officiel de la République française. Lois et Décrets.*
9. *Rapports du Haut Conseil de la Mémoire Combattante*, 7 February 2003 and 19 February 2002.
10. Interview with Serge Barcellini, 3 October 2002, Paris.
11. There were also demands addressed to the French Committee for Yad Vashem from the departmental services of Poitou-Charentes (August 2000), Haute-Savoie (September 2000), Loire (September 2000), and Cantal (February 2001), CFYV.
12. Application "Fougerolles du Plessis," sent 15 May 2000, CFYV. There were a few similar initiatives, although we cannot be exhaustive here: letter from the subprefect in Poitou-Charentes, the prefecture of Vienne, in August 2000; demand to ONAC by Haute Savoie, 26 October 2000; demand to ONAC by Mayenne, July 2000 and 14 May 2001; demand to ONAC by Haute-Marne, June 2000; demand to ONAC by Loire; demand to ONAC by Cantal, 15 February 2001, CFYV.
13. *ONAC Info* (newsletter of ONAC), no. 20, September 2003 and *Lettre d'information du CFYV*, September 2003.
14. Speeches by Jacques Chirac, president of the Republic on the occasion of the inauguration of the Memorial of the Shoah, Paris, 25 January 2005.
15. Letter of 16 May 2003, response to questionnaires.
16. Letter of 17 May 2003, response to questionnaires.
17. Jean-François Chanet, "La Fabrique des héros. Pédagogie républicaine et culte des grands hommes de Sedan à Vichy," *Vingtième Siècle. Revue d'Histoire*, no. 65 (January–March 2000): 13–34; Claude Amalvi, *De l'Art et la manière d'accomoder les héros de l'histoire de France. De Vercingétorix à la Révolution. Essai de mythologie nationale* (Paris: Albin Michel, 1998).
18. The term is borrowed from Henry Rousso, who looked more specifically at "vectors of memory" in the form of cinematographic works. Henry Rousso, "Pour une histoire

de la mémoire collective: l'après-Vichy," in *Histoire politique et sciences sociales,* 243–64. Cahiers de l'IHPT, no. 18 (Paris: Centre national de recherché scientifique, 1991), 171. Elsewhere, he uses the expression "vector of recollection," which seems equivalent. Henry Rousso, *Le Syndrome de Vichy* (Paris: Seuil, 1990), 251. To me, however, it seems that the formulation does not imply the reality and effectiveness of the memory that is supposedly transmitted. It is useful, therefore, only as a generic term to refer to the ensemble of tools established.

19. *Rapport du haut commissariat de la mémoire combattante,* 2001, p. 63 and 2002, p. 22.
20. *Bulletin officiel du ministère de l'education nationale et du ministère de la recherche,* special issue no. 3, 30 August 2001 and special issue no. 7, 3 October 2002.
21. "Discussion Paper. Anthology of the Righteous among the Nations," YV, AM2/1016.
22. Donation made in 1998, *Yad Vashem Quarterly Magazine,* Spring 1998, 17.
23. Jozeph Michman and Bert Jan Flim, eds., *The Encyclopedia of the Righteous among the Nations: Rescuers of Jews during the Holocaust. The Netherlands* (Jerusalem: Yad Vashem, 2004).
24. *France-Israel Information,* Juillet-août 1998, 8.
25. Israël Gutman, ed., "Préface de Jacques Chirac," in *Dictionnaire des Justes de France* (Paris: Fayard, 2003), 9.
26. This document was sent to me simultaneously by the prefectures of Corrèze, Isère, and Eure in response to the questionnaires.
27. Circular of 2 July 2001, sent by ONAC, Saône-et-Loire, in response to the questionnaire.
28. Circular of 27 June 2002, simultaneously sent by the prefectures in Cantal and Corrèze in response to the questionnaire.
29. The former spoke during the ceremony in the Bouches du Rhône, the latter during that in Haute-Savoie.
30. "Note to Mr. Prefect of the Yvelines regarding the memorial sites of the anti-Semitic persecutions in the department of the Yvelines," addressed by the departmental services of the Yvelines, 30 March 2003.
31. Note sent by ONAC, Indre, in response to the questionnaire.
32. Letters from the Cabinet of the Prefect of Puy-de-Dôme, 8 April 2003, and the Cabinet of the Prefect of Maine-et-Loire, 6 May 2003.
33. In response to the questionnaire, the director of the departmental services of the Vosges explained, e.g., that "the Jewish community is more than 80 percent dispersed and is also very discrete, and the commemoration ceremony for the Vel d'Hiv roundup, although organized as intended by the prefecture and associated with a homage to the Righteous, was poorly attended by the descendants of the victims."
34. Email response, 11 April 2003, from the historic information officer of ONAC in Aube.
35. Antoine Prost, "Monuments to the Dead," in *Realms of Memory,* ed. Pierre Nora, 307–23, vol. 2 (Columbia: Columbia University Press, 1996).
36. Claire Andrieu, "La Commemoration des dernières guerres françaises: l'élaboration de politiques symboliques, 1945–2003," in *Politiques du passé. Usages politiques du passé dans la France contemporaine,* ed. Claire Andrieu, Marie-Claire Lavabre, and Danielle Tartakowsky, 39–46 (Aix-en-Provence: Publications de l'Université de Provence, 2006).
37. For a more systematic study of this issue, see Sarah Gensburger, "Comprendre la multiplication des 'journées de commémoration nationale': étude d'un instrument d'action publique de nature symbolique," in *L'Instrumentation de l'action publique. Controverses, résistances, effets,* ed. Charlotte Halpern, Pierre Lascoumes, and Patrick Le Gales, 345–65 (Paris: Presses de Sciences Po, 2014). For insights regarding the Italian case, see Andrea Cossu, "Memory, Symbolic Conflict and Changes in the National Calendar in the Italian Second Republic," *Modern Italy* 15, no. 1 (2010): 3–19.

38. Even though, as we will see, once the memory policy was elaborated, in part with actors considered as being the most involved, we have to ask, by which criteria should we judge its influence and its effects?
39. *Rapport du haut conseil de la mémoire combattante,* 19 February 2002, p. 6. The same approach is reiterated every year in the document.
40. "Le Chambon-sur-Lignon. Village de 'Justes,'" *La Croix,* 8 July 2004, cover and pp. 3–5.
41. Email sent by the French presidency, 9 August 2004.
42. Speech by Jacques Chirac, president of the Republic, Le Chambon-sur-Lignon, Haute-Loire, 8 July 2004.
43. *Le Monde,* 10 July 2004.
44. Email circular of 6 July 2004, sent by Pierre Sauvage, titled "Visit to Chambon-sur-Lignon on Thursday 8 July by the President of the Republic."
45. Robert Frank, "La France des années noires: la mémoire empoisonnée," *Les Cahiers français,* no 303, juillet-août 2001 p. 65.
46. Letter of 23 July 2001, CFYV.
47. Interview by Pierre Sauvage in the opening of the DVD *Armes de l'Esprit* and interview with Pierre Sauvage, 4 March 2004, Paris.
48. *Le Figaro,* 13 August 1999; *L'Express,* 26 August 1999; *Le Nouvel Observateur, Information Juive,* no. 190, July 1999; *Le Monde,* 1 March 2000; *Le Point,* 24 March 2000. No systematic inventory was made of these articles, and they should not be considered representative of collective memory. We simply mention their publication as an element of context in considering some of the reactions they provoked.
49. Letter from Ms. X, Neuilly, 15 October 1999, Archives Le Garrec.
50. Letter from Yvon C., 6 October 1999, Archives Le Garrec.
51. CFYV, File Ernest and Marie Androuin, no. 9083, title awarded in 2000.
52. Nicolas Rebière, "Commémorations à Vielle-Tursan," *Sud-Ouest,* 10 May 1994.
53. "Consistory," letter from G.G., 4 November 1997, CFYV.
54. CFYV, Application Jean-Baptiste and Marie Lalanne, no. 7982, title awarded 26 March 1998.
55. Photocopy of letter from C.G. to the mayor of Varetz, 17 July 1995, CFYV, Application Henri and Marie-Louise Rouland, no. 8203, title awarded 15 October 1998.
56. A prompt that, an hour and a half into the interview, appeared to be coherent with the comments of this interviewee up to that point. On this methodological approach, see Gérard Grunberg, Nonna Mayer, and Paul M. Sniderman, eds., *La Démocratie à l'épreuve. Une Nouvelle Approche de l'opinion des français* (Paris: Presses de Sciences Po, 2002).
57. Interview conducted in Paris, 8 June 1998.
58. The term is borrowed from Roger Bastide, who talks about "reference points to hang memories on." Roger Bastide, "Les Problèmes de la mémoire collective," in *Les Religions africaines au Brésil,* by Bastide (Paris: PUF, 1995), 337.
59. Pierre Birnbaum, *La France imaginée: déclin des rêves unitaires?* (Paris: Gallimard, 2003), 32.
60. Doris Bensimon, *Les Juifs de France et leurs relations avec Israël. 1945–1988* (Paris: L'Harmattan, 1989), 169.
61. Martine Cohen, "Les Juifs de France. Modernité et Identité," *Vingtième Siècle. Revue d'Histoire,* no. 66 (April–June, 2000): 91, 105.
62. Pierre Birnbaum, "Les Juifs entre l'appartenance identitaire et l'entrée dans l'espace public: la Révolution française et le choix des acteurs," *Revue française de sociologie* 30 (1989): 500, 509.
63. Ibid., 499.

64. Maurice Kriegel, "Trois Mémoires de la Shoah: États-Unis, Israël, France. À propos de Peter Novick, L'Holocauste dans la vie américaine," *Le Débat*, 117 (November–December 2001): 71.
65. Interview conducted 11 June 2003 in Jerusalem.
66. For an example of this approach, see Amy Corning and Howard Schuman, "Matters. The Anniversaries of 9/11 and Woodstock," *Public Opinion Quarterly* 77, no. 2 (2013): 433–54.
67. Bastide, "Les Problèmes," 343.
68. Here Maurice Halbwachs's concept of frames of memory truly echoes Erving Goffman's frame analysis.

EPILOGUE

The "Righteous of France" in the Pantheon

Public policy and sites of memory

One of the results of the creation of the "Righteous of France" category reveals some of these interactions between memory policy and representations of the past—beyond the reactivation of memories of lived experience—particularly well. On 18 January 2007, a "National Homage to the Righteous of France" was organized within the walls of the Pantheon, and an honorific inscription was placed in the crypt of this temple of the Republic. The ceremony was broadcast live on French television, and access to the monument was free for seven days following the event. During that time, more than forty-two thousand people came to see the new commemorative plaque.[1]

In light of what had preceded it, this event was only one of the many addendums to the public policy transfer that was behind the creation of the Righteous of France category. In this respect it remained an epiphenomenon to the long-term evolution we have analyzed over the course of this book. Indeed, the research that was the basis for this book was completed more than six months before the ceremony was held at the Pantheon.

However, this event also has particular significance. First, the organization of formal ceremonies at the Pantheon is one of the oldest instruments for state action in terms of memory.[2] Secondly, this instrument has been intensely reactivated over the past thirty years—along with the creation of national days of commemoration.[3] Between 1958 and 1987 only the ashes of Jean Moulin were enshrined in the Pantheon, but since then six more transfers have been made.

The double status of this National Homage to the Righteous of France means that its analysis serves as a kind of epilogue to this now-completed study of the French translation of the Israeli "Righteous Among the Nations" category. Moreover, it provides the opportunity to reformulate some of the questions that structure the dominant approach to the relationship between memory and politics in the social sciences today.

This final chapter therefore makes it possible to explore a dimension of memory policy that has not yet been studied here. Since Pierre Nora's publication of the first volume of his book titled *Realms of Memory*,[4] this notion has become an important concept in the social sciences; it has also become a frequent and legitimate term in public policy.[5] What can we learn from the state's use of this now ordinary instrument in conducting the commemoration of the Righteous of France?

A French ceremony

Following the vote on the law of 10 July 2000, the president of the French Republic continued to pay homage to those who, in the terms of the law, are now figures of the historical memory of the Occupation. He did this, for example, during his call for tolerance in July 2004 in Le Chambon-sur-Lignon. Later, the public speeches by the head of state systematically occurred at the inauguration of what the administrations responsible for them call "sites of memory." Initially, these sites were not exclusively, or even primarily, consecrated to the commemoration of the Righteous.

On 25 January 2005, the Memorial of the Shoah was inaugurated in Paris. During the ceremony, the president of the Republic explained that he was thinking of all those who had perished in the death camps but also "of the Righteous, the conscience and honor of our country, thanks to whom three quarters of the Jews were saved." Two days later in Poland, during the sixtieth anniversary of the liberation of Auschwitz, he oversaw the inauguration of the new museology of the French pavilion and once again referred to "these thousands of Righteous, these French men and women, of all social conditions."

But the law of 10 July 2000 also led to new sites exclusively dedicated to the Righteous of France. Once again, the parliamentary vote created a space for legitimacy and led to opportunity effects for a certain number of actors, both individual and social. Between 2000 and 2003, three separate "Avenues of the Righteous" were inaugurated in France.

In partnership with the future Memorial of the Shoah (which was then still known as the Memorial of the Unknown Jewish Martyr—Center for Contemporary Jewish Documentation) the Municipality of Paris changed the name of the pedestrian street running alongside the building.[6] It was inaugurated as the "Avenue of the Righteous" (Allée des Justes) on 8 October 2000 in the fourth district in Paris. The Central Consistory of France, through its specific association,[7] joined together with the town of Nancy to create an Avenue of the Righteous there. In 2001, due to the geographical situation of the space made available, it was in fact a "Square of the Righteous" that was jointly inaugurated by the mayor of the town and Gérard Blum, then president of the Consistorial Association and responsible for the Jewish community of the town. Finally in 2003 it was Toulouse's turn, in association with the regional branch of the Conseil Représentatif des Institutions juives de France, to inaugurate an Avenue of the Righteous.

The expression "Avenue of the Righteous" is an explicit reference to the avenue inaugurated in 1962 at Yad Vashem in Jerusalem. As we have seen, originally the planting of an honorific tree was the only commemorative instrument envisaged by the Israeli state. The fact that this term was adopted here shows a desire to embed this public policy transfer, constituted by the creation of the Righteous of France category within the French social and geographical space. However, since 1990 the Israeli Institute no longer uses this avenue. It has been replaced by the inscription of the laureates' names on a wall situated in a commemorative garden dedicated to the Righteous. This is part of the same territorial logic of the public policy transfer that led to the inauguration of a "Wall of the Righteous" in France in the summer of 2006. Indeed, on 14 June 2006, in Paris, in the side street now known as the "Avenue of the Righteous," an official ceremony was organized to reveal the names of the Righteous of France engraved on the outside wall of the Memorial to the Shoah. The creation of this new site of memory, as it is referred to by its creators, did not overlook the national origin of the term "Righteous." The new wall was jointly inaugurated by the French prime minister and his Israeli counterpart.

The ceremony in the Pantheon just a few months later was part of this dynamic of territorializing the commemoration of the Righteous. It marked a new step in emancipation from the Israeli model. The addition of the inscription "National Homage to the Righteous of France" in the crypt thus represents the genuine completion of the progressive embedding of this term on French soil.

The choice of the Pantheon first and foremost marks a break from the previous sites of commemoration. It is no longer a matter of finding French equivalents of places in Israel. The Pantheon is a monument that is specific to France. It is dedicated entirely to the memory policy of the French state.[8] This final stage in the national appropriation of the Israeli category can also be seen on a typographic level. The inverted commas that frame the word "Righteous" in the expression "'Righteous' of France" in the law of 10 July 2000 have been removed. It is no longer necessary, or at least no longer desirable, to signal the borrowing of the term.

We can also see this shift in the commemorative stamp that was produced in January 2007 for the occasion. At the request of the French president, the postal service designed an image intended to honor the Righteous of France inspired by the origin of the term. The image featured a white tree on a green background; the graphic influence of the Israeli title was explicit (Figure 7.1). The reaction of the services of the presidency to this initial project reveals the territorial and symbolic emancipation that is played out in the entry of the Righteous of France into the Pantheon. This initial design never went on sale; another hastily replaced it. The aesthetic and semantic reference to the origin of the term "Righteous" was removed and replaced by a view of the Pantheon, over which the name of the event was simply inscribed.

Following a mechanism already encountered between 1989 and 1998, and fueled by the legitimacy resulting from the participation of the various social actors involved (along with representatives of Israel at previous manifestations and inaugurations), the presidency shed all remnants of the Israeli connection during the ceremony of 18 January 2007. The ambassador of Israel was not involved in the preparation of the event, nor was he particularly encouraged to attend. Finally, following heated exchanges that verged on becoming a diplomatic incident, a representative of the embassy was authorized to come to the Pantheon, but he was not granted any official status during the ceremony.

On the other hand, the French state involved several of its administrations in the project, working simultaneously for the first time. The Ministry of Culture is responsible for the Pantheon,[9] and it supported the services of the presidency. Similarly, the office of the Secretary of State for Veterans' Affairs used its publications and networks to attract attention to the event. The Ministry of Education was also involved; it centered its annual circular on pedagogic activities relating to the memory of genocide and the prevention of crimes against humanity on this homage to the Righteous of France.[10] It also constructed a website dedicated to the ceremony at the Pantheon to help teachers in their mission.

Finally, as though this distancing from Israel and the nationalization of the Righteous of France category that accompanied it profoundly changed the nature of the commemoration, the Ministry of Foreign Affairs used their commemoration for the first time in foreign policy. The internet site of the French embassy in Israel gave an account of the ceremony in both French and English. The minister for foreign affairs wanted the artistic work commissioned for the

Figure 7.1. Stamps successfully created by the French postal service to honor the Righteous of France. Stamp on the left created by Yann Gafsou, La Poste, 2007. Stamp on the right created by Tanguy Besset, La Poste, 2007.

occasion by the minister for culture, a video installation by Agnes Varda, to be exhibited overseas. From March 2007, barely two months after the ceremony, the French diplomatic authorities exported Varda's installation piece to the United States, through a project by the French consulate in New York and in cooperation with the American Jewish Committee.[11]

The form of the ceremony was in fact a tool to finalize the nationalization of the term "Righteous" and the embedding of the commemoration of these actors in French national territory. Fundamentally, the narrative of the past inscribed on the plaque in the Pantheon is also part of a relationship of emancipation regarding the meaning Israel awards to the title of Righteous among the Nations.

The text in the crypt reads:

> National Homage to the Righteous of France.
>
> Under the cloak of hatred and darkness that fell over France during the Occupation, thousands of lights refused to be extinguished. Named Righteous among the Nations, or remaining anonymous, women and men of all social conditions, saved Jews from anti-Semitic persecutions and the extermination camps. Braving the risks involved, they incarnated the honor of France, its values of justice, tolerance, and humanity.

This reading of the actions of the Righteous of France is directly opposed to Israel's interpretation of them. The personal recognition of individuals, who are presented as being an exceptional minority, was replaced with the recognition of numerous anonymous figures seen as representing a more collective attitude. Moreover, the Israeli category reflected the principle of hostility by non-Jews toward Jews and toward Israel. Yet this homage to the Righteous of France instead affirms the dominance of values such as tolerance and humanity in French society both under the Occupation and today.

The discourse of the past conveyed through Agnes Varda's installation shares this semantic evolution. The work in itself consists of a video installation incorporating several different elements. At the heart of the Pantheon, under the dome, Agnes Varda set up photographs on a circular platform. These presented portraits and images of Righteous figures, dating from the time of their rescue actions and from after the war. Images of anonymous people photographed by the artist on the street in 2006 are also included without any details or explanation. Diametrically opposed to the symbolic discourse of Yad Vashem, this installation conveys the message that "we are all (potentially) Righteous."

As though through a magnifying glass, the National Homage to the Righteous of France provides an image of the appropriation at work here. In this respect, it was the first genuinely national ceremony dedicated to the commemoration of the French Righteous. Finally, this epilogue to the transfer of public policy in the form of the institutionalization of the Righteous of France illustrates the conclusions that most studies of these contemporary transfers have reached: "Transfers are never identical to the model that is imported and external loans are always subject to an internal logic of appropriation,"[12] which are themselves governed by existing institutions.

A cosponsored ceremony

In this instance, the internal logic of appropriation emerged in the context of a coproduction of public action. The completion of the French adoption of the Righteous was not the work of a government and administration that imposed, top-down, a memory policy conceived unilaterally and in isolation. On the contrary, like the other moments of the institutionalization of this category before it, the National Homage of January 2007 was based on close collaboration between the state and social actors. The traditional functioning of the Pantheon accentuated this mechanism here. Indeed, it is often the case that ceremonies are suggested by associations and other collective actors who are then involved in coproducing the event.[13]

In 2009, on its blog, the French Committee for Yad Vashem congratulated itself on having helped "re-establish historical truth" regarding the period of the Occupation through its participation in the ceremony.

However, the contours of the event are precisely the result of the modifications to the configuration of the recognition and evocation of French Righteous figures and the place of the French Committee for Yad Vashem had become marginal in this.

"This homage was proposed to the president of the Republic by the Foundation for the Memory of the Shoah."[14] The Foundation for the Memory of the Shoah was created in 2000 following the recommendations of the Mattéoli Commission, which was charged with providing an assessment of the looting of French Jews and the compensations and restitutions they were to benefit from.[15] The funds wrongfully held by state services were then transferred to this new Foundation in the form of an endowment of 393 million euros. As a private body, the Foundation is managed by an administrative council made up in equal portions of representatives of public authorities, representatives of France's Jewish institutions, and other qualified persons. It was recognized immediately as being of public interest.[16]

Its statutory tasks make reference to the Righteous:

> The Foundation aims to shed light on this terrible period and to warn, particularly younger generations, about what can happen when we give up and give free range to anti-Semitism, racism, and xenophobia, and when, on the other hand, following the example of the "Righteous" and the Resistance, we have the heart and courage to rise up and fight back.[17]

From its very creation, the Foundation thus invested the terrain that was previously occupied exclusively by the French Committee for Yad Vashem. First, it began financing projects related to the commemoration of the Righteous on a case by case and continuous basis. As an example of this, in 2002, it supported the organization of a day of Homage to the Righteous as part of the International Festival of Films on the Resistance at the Museum of the Resistance in the Côte d'Azur. In 2003, it assisted in the publication of a book dedicated to *Bishop Théas, the Jews, and the Righteous*.[18]

Because of its financial weight and its proximity to the French political authorities, the Foundation rapidly acquired legitimacy and power that progressively brought it to equal status with the French Committee for Yad Vashem in several of the latter's missions. In 2003, it subsidized the promotion and launch of the *Dictionary of the Righteous of France* as part of the radio show "Shared Destinies: The Rescue Actions by Righteous and Jews," which was jointly produced by one of the Jewish community radio stations and the French Committee for Yad Vashem.[19] Each time, either Simone Veil, the president of the Foundation, or one of her representatives spoke publically. The Foundation thus appropriated several projects initiated by the Committee. It also finally asserted itself as a new and important actor in the configuration of the commemoration of the Righteous of France.

Although the Foundation is a direct actor, this positioning has occurred through the action of the Memorial for the Shoah. Indeed, since its creation, the Foundation has subsidized up to 80 percent of this institution's budget. The initiatives of the Memorial therefore reflect the engagement of its directors and the Foundation in the commemoration of the Righteous. The major stages in this were October 2000, with the creation of an Avenue of the Righteous; April 2005, with the opening of a section on the Righteous within the permanent exhibition; and finally June 2006, with the inauguration of a Wall of the Righteous, along with a temporary thematic exhibition.

On each one of these occasions, tension emerged between the Memorial, the Foundation and the French Committee for Yad Vashem. If by nature the Foundation had links with the Israeli Institute, it was primarily anchored in French institutional and administrative space. This new slippage of the center of gravity in the configuration of the actors in the commemoration of the French Righteous explains the decisive nationalization of the Righteous category that occurred through the ceremony at the Pantheon.

This ultimate shift from Israel to France also appears in the series of initiatives behind the event, but it is no use searching for the very first decision. Although this national homage was indeed decided, it is primarily explained by the evolution that preceded it and in which it is situated over the long term. Retracing the process that led to the organization of this ceremony in the short term is nothing more than a way of understanding what is at work here.

It seems that the first move toward the enshrinement of the Righteous in the Pantheon was made by Lucien Lazare, former member of the French Volunteers and francophone rapporteur for the Committee for the Designation of the Righteous among the Nations at Yad Vashem.[20] From 2003, Lazare sought a hearing with the president; his project was to choose someone who was deceased and who had been recognized as Righteous among the Nations by the Israeli Institute, whose ashes could be enshrined in the Pantheon. Over the course of interactions, the project evolved, and this evolution saw the removal of Lazare and with him the French Committee from the project, to the benefit of the Foundation for the Memory of the Shoah and its president.

On 24 January 2006, Simone Veil sent the head of state a "note concerning the Foundation's proposition to have the Righteous of France enter the Pantheon." Through this presentation of her intentions, she took a position that was in total convergence with the narrative and interpretation of the past proposed by Jacques Chirac since 1995. She thus radically transformed the contours of the project initially formulated by Lucien Lazare. The transfer of ashes, the main ceremonial medium of the Pantheon, was replaced by an honorary inscription. Inscriptions on the walls of this temple of the Republic were not unprecedented, but up until then they had consisted of plaques upon which lists of specific names were engraved.[21] This commemoration was thus set apart by the anonymous nature of the homage. Like the process that governed the vote for the law of 10 July 2000, the individual nominative recognition that was intended initially ended up transformed into a collective and anonymous tribute.

In this note, the date of 16 July was once again envisaged. However, the French president refused this suggestion on the grounds that it fell during the summer holidays. This date would have meant the national education system could not be involved and would have prevented widespread media coverage. The choice thus fell on 27 January, which although not an official national day of commemoration has an intermediary status. Since 2002, at the initiative of the European Council, this date has been celebrated in the schools of member states as International Holocaust Remembrance Day to prevent future genocides. For practical reasons relating to the availability of key figures, 18 January was finally chosen for the ceremony.

The very principle of a National Homage to the Righteous of France was therefore a coproduction. The same was true of its implementation. Both the presidency and the minister of culture put in place teams responsible for press relations, but communication about the event was first and foremost the domain of the Foundation. Thus it is important that the press conference destined to announce the ceremony brought together Simone Veil, Renaud Donnedieu de Vabres, the French minister of culture, and Agnès Varda. Veil spoke first, and it was once again she who answered most of the journalists' questions, along with the general director of the Foundation. Moreover, the Foundation directly subsidizes two print titles—*Le Monde des Ados* and *Je lis des histoires vraies*—two publications directed at young people, which brought out special issues related to the event. The latter was distributed for free to all students in CM2 (the final year of primary school) as well as to all high school libraries.

As part of this implementation, the French Committee for Yad Vashem was reduced to managing the contacts for the Righteous for whom it continued to be the point of contact. However, on the day, it was neither the French Committee nor one of the state services that was responsible for welcoming the Righteous who came to Paris to receive their homage. The Foundation paid their travel expenses, and a visit to the Memorial of the Shoah and film screenings were organized for them. Finally, all the people present on 18 January in the Pantheon received an updated copy of the catalog of the exhibition *Righteous of France,* which had been held at the Memorial of the Shoah the previous year. While the Foundation brought legitimacy to the state and allowed it to definitively appropriate the term "Righteous," it in return relied on the latter to cement its status and establish itself as one of the principal actors in the "memory of the Shoah" in France and overseas.

If, as we have seen in the first part of this epilogue, the ceremony of the Pantheon was a French ceremony, in that it broke away from the Israeli loan, this was primarily because it was coproduced with social actors who nevertheless represent a specific social group. According to a mechanism that we have seen several times in this book, this community perspective once again carried a national message. This articulation was based on a shared reference to general and universal values that were simultaneously evoked by the representatives of the state, in this instance the president of the Republic, and by those of the Foundation in the figure of its president.

Indeed, only two speeches marked this National Homage to the Righteous of France, first one by Simone Veil and then one by Jacques Chirac. The analysis of these two discourses reveals a total convergence on the narrative of the past that they present.

First, although the texts of these speeches are distinctly longer than those at previous presidential speeches, neither mentions Israel. The original expression itself, "Righteous Among the Nations" is only used once by Jacques Chirac and without any mention of its origin. The mention of the official title is indeed accompanied by a reduction in its breadth: "Some have been recognized as Righteous among the Nations while others remain anonymous, either because they gave their lives to help others, or because in their modesty they haven't sought recognition for their acts."[22]

Finally, and in correlation with this new configuration, the president went to the logical extreme of the narrative that had governed the syllogism that structured his discourse since 1995. On this occasion he claimed national pride:

> To all, in this place where it honors its great men, the nation today testifies to its respect and its esteem. You are the incarnation of France in its most universal aspect, in the faithfulness to its founding principles. Thanks to you, thanks to other heroes throughout the centuries, we can look France in the eye and look at our history face on: for sometimes we see very dark moments there. But we also and above all see the best and the most glorious. We must take our history as a single block. It is our heritage; it is our identity. It is based on this, and by forging new paths, that we can walk with our heads high toward the future. Yes, we can be proud of our history! Yes, we can be proud to be French![23]

On this point, the discourse of Simon Veil perfectly echoed that of the president. They both connected, and in the same way, the evocation of a particular past, pride in being French, and the promotion of values that are presented as being universal:

> Certain French people take pleasure in smearing the past of our country. I have never been one of them. I have always said, and I repeat it solemnly here tonight, that there was Vichy France, responsible for the deportation of seventy-six thousand Jews, including eleven thousand children, but there were also all those men, all those women, thanks to whom three quarters of the Jewish population of France escaped capture. Elsewhere, in the Netherlands, in Greece, 80 percent of Jews were arrested and exterminated in the camps. In no other country occupied by the Nazis, with the exception of Denmark, was there a wave of solidarity comparable with what happened here. You all, the Righteous of France to whom we pay homage today, you illustrate the honor of our country, which, thanks to you, once again found the meaning of fraternity, justice, and courage.[24]

The use of "we/our" in this last phrase indicates the double role of the Foundation in this national ceremony. The first "us" refers to a form of Jewish collective or, more specifically, to those who Veil lists at the beginning of her speech. She explains her position "in the name of the Foundation for the Memory of the Shoah, and in the name of all those who owe their lives to you, I come to you tonight, to express our respect, our affection, our gratitude." But in the extract cited above, as in several places in her speech, the "us" and the "ours" also refer to the national collective, "our country." As was the case for the mechanism that operated during the implementation of the law of 10 July 2000, the community affirmation passed through national affirmation here.

Moreover, the comparison of the discourse finally read by Veil, with the version that had been previously written for her by a famous writer, reveals the way in which the expression of a form of particular belonging is simultaneously based on identification with the nation. The first text was indeed set aside because it contained too many biblical references. Thus, paradoxically, the only religious reference during the ceremony was to the Talmud. It was made by the president.

This epilogue to the institutionalization of the Righteous category thus confirms the need to consider that, as long as they exist, demands for memory that are addressed to the state may be part of a more complex mechanism than the work of *homo actans* and pressure groups, whether they are community groups or others. This encourages us to reverse this perspective to ask: To what extent do the increasing demands for commemoration that are addressed to the French government reflect an unequivocal atomization or fragmentation of identities? Or, on the contrary, do they reflect a form of integration into shared space, where this space is political and possibly conflictual and made up of vectors of previously unvoiced past experiences?[25]

The analysis of the coproduction of this National Homage to the Righteous of France thus confirms the combination between cognitive, strategic, and institutional factors, which as we have seen govern the implementation of the current memory public policy. Pierre Muller and Yves Surel conclude:

> Governance appears both as a mode of government (the latter being understood in the broadest sense), in which the coherence of public action . . . does not occur through the action of a relatively homogenous politico-administrative elite (which tends to lose its relative monopoly in the construction of cognitive and normative matrixes of public policy because of this) but through the establishment of multilevel and multi-actor forms of coordination, of which the perpetually uncertain result depends on the capacity of public and private actors to define a space of shared meaning.[26]

An appropriated ceremony

This space of meaning jointly produced by the Foundation for the Memory of the Shoah and the state is also shared by others to varying degrees. Once again, this ceremony does influence the representations of actors to the extent that they recognize themselves in the contours of the event. In this instance, the appropriation of the National Homage to the Righteous of France is an exact reflection of the transformations of the configuration that made the event possible.

For the first time, negative reactions were expressed in public through the media. They came from Israeli citizens. One woman attended the ceremony as a member of the Israeli association of children hidden in France, Aloumim. She said that commemorating the Righteous of France in the Pantheon provoked a strange uneasiness in her:

> Quite simply because there was no mention of the fact that the Israeli state was the one to have awarded the Righteous medal and simply because it was Yad Vashem in Jerusalem, in Israel, that created a committee more than twenty years ago to recognize the Righteous who saved Jews from an atrocious death during this black period and risked their lives. Simply because the plaque in the Pantheon, placed by the French president, makes no mention at all of the Israeli origin of this recognition.[27]

This woman's perception can be directly explained by the lessened presence of Israel and its commemorative symbols in the implementation of memory policy. Up until then, however, this woman had warmly accompanied and commended the different speeches and state initiatives designed to honor the Righteous. In 1997, at the heart of the state appropriation of the Israeli term, she personally awarded the Righteous medal to those she considered to have saved her life. Ten years later the political transfer was complete and the hybridization was insufficient for this woman to identify with the public action for the commemoration of the Righteous.

Those recognized as the Righteous of France see it differently, however. All the Righteous who were still alive (or their family members who were invited to represent them if necessary) accepted the presidential invitation. After the ceremony, they were awarded the medal of the Legion of Honor at the Easter promotion.[28] These different forms of homage correspond to an expectation formulated by the members of the Association for the Righteous.[29] As early as 2003, and even though neither the Pantheon event nor the nomination for the title of the Legion of Honor were yet envisaged, the president of the Association of the Righteous of France for Yad Vashem very clearly inserted the recognition of the Righteous into the question of the attribution of national insignia. During the interview he gave us, and even before he was questioned on this point, he said directly:

> You see that we turned to Veterans' Affairs. Because there is something I must tell you that in all the investigations I've made, people think that all the Righteous, they just saved Jews and that's all. But according to the information I have, they also had an overwhelming involvement in the Resistance, and in your dissertation you have to say that, if you can record that it would give us a lot of pleasure. Because, for example, we'll talk in a little bit about Paul Grimaldi, he was an officer of the Legion of Honor as a soldier, he had the Cross of War and so forth. . . . I want to emphasize this, above all for your work, in your research. Well, as you have seen, before I even saved any Jews, I was in the Resistance, and I was, as I said, the liaison agent for General Schmidt, who was the chief of the Secret Army, and actually the forward to my book was written by his son, General Schmidt, Chief of the General Defense Staff.

When prompted about what he meant by "turn to the Veterans' Affairs," he continued:

> Well I turned to, you'll see it in there [indicating the 2003 annual report of the Association], I mean I attended all the Veterans' Meetings, because I'm also a Knight of the Legion of Honor myself, and I have the Cross of War and, you see, I also say here. . . . [he gets out a document] Here it is, 27 April, General Assembly of our Association for those awarded the Legion of Honor, in the section for risking one's life . . . the Professor Ivan Beltrami is appointed administrator and

> represents the Righteous. I just hope that one day the Righteous as a whole will be awarded the Legion of Honor.[30]

In fact, even those who were not members of the Association appropriated the event because they were offered the attribution of the Legion of Honor. Following the ceremony, several of them accepted the organization of official award ceremonies for this new medal; one such was held on 4 July 2007 at the town hall of the nineteenth district in Paris.

Between these two poles, between rejection of and identification with the event, the actors each appropriated it in different ways but according to a single mechanism. Indeed the fact that the event was coproduced allowed different reference points to be attached to it according to the trajectories and social positions of the actors. As we saw at the end of Chapter 6, the very fact of expressing one's memories and the form that they take (such as the formation of representations of the past) do not stem so much from the rejection or acceptance of a narrative prescribed by the state as from the simultaneous belonging of actors to both political spaces and particular groups.

Reading the visitors' book of the event reveals the mechanism at work here.[31] Signed during the week when the Pantheon was open to the public, it takes the form of two thick notebooks, and they reveal the diversity of reactions. Some are critical, as we can see in this laconic message: "3,000 Righteous. 70,0000 deported, including 11,000 children"; another reads, "As the son and daughter of deported Jews, we are alive thanks to French citizens. But our whole families were deported by the French and did not return."[32] These critical messages are a minority, however.

The visitors' book above all contains many thanks for the homage paid to the Righteous. These thanks are sometimes addressed to the president, to Simone Veil, or to the Republic and sometimes to a combination of two, or even three, of them.

Also, a large number of visitors transformed these pages into a record of the names of the Righteous of France. This method was a compensation for the impossibility of identifying them all with the official recognition procedure provided by the Yad Vashem Institute, or as a complement to it. Indeed, many French Jews used the book to record the names of those who they considered to have rescued them. One man "66 years old today" wrote: "Many thanks to the inhabitants of 25 rue St Vincent de Paul, Paris 10th district, for having saved our lives."

Another visitor stipulated, "I have looked closely. Among the anonymous Righteous there were Mr. and Mrs. Abiln in Lassy, and we slept in a cave until the liberation. As children we had only good memories of these marvelous and courageous people." Elsewhere, the son of a Righteous of

France wrote, "I think of the anonymous ones! Of Alain Mossé, of Mrs. Chomette, of my mother! Of the village in Savoie that did not hesitate to allow Jewish children to live happily there for months. I think of the priest who provided baptism certificates. They are all Righteous too!"

These notebooks, set out at the entry of the Pantheon, were not used solely by those who had directly experienced the events being commemorated. Reading them also allows us to complete the analysis in Chapter 6 by taking into account the interaction between memory policy and representations, instead of the memories of experiences of the past to be commemorated. It enables us to explore the process of secondary witnessing.[33] A nun thus saw the National Homage to the Righteous of France on a religious level. In her eyes, the people honored were all "saints": "Each man is a sacred story. I am very moved and congratulate the French nation for this historic and humane work. Saints of God, pray for us."

Unfortunately, the very nature of the visitors' book means that we only rarely know the background of those expressing themselves in it. This source was thus complemented by fieldwork observation and short interviews with the visitors at the Pantheon during the week the building was freely open to the public.[34] These interviews reveal the exact same process. Social, local, national, religious, or gender identities clearly influence the visitors' perceptions of the Righteous of France and the homage paid to them. Often these different perspectives are combined in a single individual and are presented separately here for clarity. For example, visitors from outside of Paris only retained from the ceremony the portraits of the Righteous who were from their own town or region. For example, one farmer told of how he had visited the agricultural show the previous year and, in searching for elements that could symbolize the Limousin region where he was from, he had discovered that Righteous individuals had worked in that area. He came to the Pantheon especially to pay homage to them.

Similarly, the women interviewed tended to draw attention to the fact that there were more women than men among the Righteous of France. Correspondingly, they also emphasized the figure of Simone Veil, whose role in the vote on the legalization of abortion was mentioned several times.

Those who declared themselves practicing Catholics accentuated the Christian and moral engagement of these Righteous figures, who were often described as "saints." A couple of Comorian tourists, whose clothing indicated strict Islamic practice, also said they recognized themselves in this homage and described the Righteous as "martyrs."

Finally, we spoke to a student at the prestigious preparatory class at the Lycée Henri IV, which is just next to the Panthéon. He spoke of the

Righteous as being the descendants of Voltaire and Hugo, whose ashes are also in the Pantheon. For him their actions illustrated "the essence of the Lumières." Another student, a Moroccan national in France for his studies, spoke at length of the king of Morocco who "showed solidarity" with the Jews. He added that for him the attitude of the Righteous shows the possibility of understanding between religions, including between "Islam and Judaism."

In light of these few examples, again it seems that the narrative of the past presented by the state and the linguistic categories that it mobilizes make sense to the actors only if they are appropriated through the prism of their own social representations, which are closely linked to their present social positions and past trajectories. The mechanism at work here is identical to that documented for the particular case of the expression of past experiences. Commemorative public action that is at the crossroads of the prescription of a narrative of the past and global representations of actors is vastly different from a situation of the transmission of memory to a passive recipient.[35] A French coproduction, the ceremony of 18 January was also appropriated by its audience.

At this point, it is important to return to the notion of "sites of memory." In 1984, while Pierre Nora was building this concept, he established the principle that "there are *lieux de mémoire,* sites of memory, because there are no longer *milieux de mémoire,* real environments of memory."[36] This epilogue and the developments that led to it result in a tangibly different observation, however. In 1963 in Israel, as in 2007 in France, these sites of memory created by the states did not convey any kind of national memory (of which we have seen the limits). The study of the various appropriations of these sites suggests that the environments of memory remain operative in that they refer above all to the social environments in which the actors are embedded. Susan Crane summarizes it in these terms, "Every narrative, every text remains an object, as long as it is not 'read' or taken as a reference point by individuals."[37] It is therefore as an anchorage point from which to interpret the possible appropriation of memory policy by individuals—ranging from absolute rejection to total acceptance—that these "sites of memory" are able to become operational for contemporary research on memorial questions.[38] This approach is diametrically opposed to the conception of those people who use these sites as public policy instruments.

Like the analysis of the origin of the Righteous of France category before it, the study of the appropriation of the National Homage to the Righteous of France ceremony ultimately demonstrates what public policies are used for and by what mechanisms they produce their effects. "They constitute spaces (forums) within which the different actors concerned construct and express a 'relationship with the world' that reflects the way in which they perceive the real, their place in that world and what that world should be."[39]

A consensual ceremony

The space created by the ceremony at the Pantheon appears in this instance to be essentially consensual. Although it provoked some critical reactions, they were nonetheless rarely expressed in public. The two Israeli tribunes mentioned above are exceptions to this. The coverage and treatment of the event by French journalists showed genuine media support for this National Homage to the Righteous of France. Press articles were systematically limited to a positive description of the commemoration, which was in itself seen as self-evident.

This apparent consensus was all the more remarkable because it was totally out of step with the terms of the public and scientific debates as they had formed in France over the course of 2005. In that year, the controversy sparked by the vote on article 4 of the law of 23 February indeed gave rise to the formation of a new configuration of actors. From different positions and multiple modalities, several individuals—mostly historians—mobilized to fight against the "use" and "instrumentalization" of the past by public authorities.[40] These new social actors have since sounded the alarm several times in this respect, as we can see in the controversy surrounding the 2007 decision of the new president to have Guy Moquet's letter ceremoniously read to all senior school students at the beginning of the school year.[41]

A few months earlier, however, none of these actors had judged it pertinent to alert public opinion to the organization of a ceremony that was indeed based on the same public action instruments—sites of memory, public education circulars, and law—as those it ordinarily considered to be political uses of the past.

When the public authorities emphasized the "positive role" of colonization, the political use was constituted by the fact that this prescribed narrative of the past was in contradiction to the reality of the past documented by historians or, more precisely, to the representations that most of the social actors involved have, historians first and foremost. When, according to an identical process and with the same instruments, the state celebrated the positive role of the French civilian population faced with the extermination of the Jews, the mechanism at work was entirely different. The Righteous category, although constructed by similar public policies, was adopted by historians.

In 2004, for example, in his book *La France et les Juifs* (France and the Jews), Michel Winock uses the term as a given as well as the interpretation provided by the French state. He writes, "More than two thirds" of French Jews were "saved." This "grand rescue of the Jews was due . . . to the courage, the will, and the humanity of many French people—those who Israel recognized as 'Righteous' in different European countries where non-Jews saved Jews."[42] One year later, however, this same historian was among the signatories and instigators of the petition "Freedom for History," which criticized the way in which the state tried to influence memory, history, and the teaching of the past.[43]

This discrepancy between public positions and the scientific study that should precede them reveals a specific understanding of memory. The question of the instrumentalization of memory has a paradoxical place here: it is both central and partial (in both senses of the word). In this case, the use of the term "Righteous" and the syllogism the French state used in popularizing it were not seen as problematic because they were in keeping with representations shared by a large number of actors, apparently including French historians. Thus the law of 10 July 2000 was not considered one of the "memorial laws" that the signatories of the petition "Freedom for History" were demanding the abolition of. Similarly, Tzvetan Todorov, as the inventor of the concept "abuse of memory,"[44] is today regularly solicited to analyze and discuss contemporary issues of memory.[45] Yet he in turn engages in the near glorification of the memory of these "acts of concern" that accompanied those who helped the Jews, who he himself refers to as "Righteous."[46]

The study of the consensus[47] that surrounded the National Homage to the Righteous of France, and the transfer of the Israeli category to France more generally, thus reveals the limits of what can be called the "paradigm of strategic memory."[48] In light of the latter, it is not the actors involved or the instruments concerned that constitute the political nature of this utilization of the past. It is first and foremost the nonconformity of the historic memory thus prescribed with what is considered history as it happened or with the representations of those—historians or witnesses—who have social legitimacy to talk about the past.

If explanations in terms of political utilization of the past and instrumentalization constitute clear and distinct ideas today, the thick description[49] of institutionalization of the Righteous of France category underlines the importance of breaking away from them. "In an extremely problematic period, where numerous mutations are occurring, where individuals seem to have difficulty accepting change, the theories that move beyond historical uncertainty acquire *reassuring virtue.* And the lack of a grasp on the real is compensated on the level of logical certitudes or behavior that is transferred to the register of social imaginary."[50]

Public action relating to memory cannot be reduced to phenomena of competition between pressure groups or other communities, nor to manipulation or other strategies that are limited in linear or vertical terms by "established powers" and other "power holders."[51] The conclusions of this epilogue concur with those of Jeffrey Olick regarding his own research. They "demonstrate the continual process of social construction without ignoring strategic and historical factors." They encourage us to take a path that is neither instrumentalist nor essentialist in order to seize contemporary relations between memory and politics.[52] This path would benefit from passing through political science and public policy analysis.

Yet the development of the Righteous of France category over more than half a century encourages us to be prudent regarding the effectiveness of change on this issue. Between 1942 and 2007, from Israel to France, the concrete modalities of public action were modified of course, but several of the mechanisms—cognitive, strategic, and institutional—that made this possible were identical in different times and different places. In light of what we have seen, it is also possible to hypothesize that the analyses that promote a radical change of both the memorial regime and public policies are based on the transformation not of the objects of study but rather of the way they are perceived. As Jean-Claude Passeron and Jacques Revel have remarked, "When the descriptive concepts of an empirical observation produce knowledge, it means that they allowed us to observe phenomena that were not *observable* before the theoretical reconfiguration of the concepts that made them *describable*, made them *understandable*."[53]

Notes

1. This was the official number given by the Pantheon administrator at the end of January 2007.
2. Mona Ozouf, "Le Panthéon. L'Ecole normale des morts," in *Les Lieux de Mémoire*, vol. I *La République*, ed. Pierre Nora (Paris: Gallimard, 1984), 139–66; Avner Ben-Amos, "The Sacred Center of Power Paris and Republican State Funerals," *Journal of Interdisciplinary History* 22, no. 1 (1991): 27–48; Avner Ben-Amos, *Funeral, Politics and Memory in Modern France, 1789–1996* (Oxford: Oxford University Press, 2000).
3. Sarah Gensburger, "Comprendre la multiplication des 'journées de commémoration nationale: étude d'un instrument d'action publique de nature symbolique," in *L'Instrumentation de l'action publique. Controverses, résistances, effets*, ed. Charlotte Halpern, Pierre Lascoumes, and Patrick Le Gales (Paris: Presses de Sciences Po, 2014), 345–65.
4. Pierre Nora, ed., *Realms of Memory: Rethinking the Past*, 3 vols. (New York: Columbia University Press, 1996), first published in French as *Les Lieux de Mémoire* (Paris: Gallimard, 1984).

5. The Department of Memory, Heritage, and Archives maintains and creates these "sites of memory," which are promoted through a magazine titled *Paths of Memory*.
6. Memorial for the Unknown Jewish Martyr, Center for Contemporary Jewish Documentation, *Rapport moral 1999*, p. 14.
7. French Association for Homage to the Righteous among the Nations, see Chapter 3 for more details.
8. Patrick Garcia, "Panthéonisation," in *Dictionnaire des politiques culturelles de la France depuis 1959*, ed. Emmanuel De Waresquiel (Paris: CNRS Editions, 2001), 473–74.
9. Patrick Garcia, "Les Panthéonisations sous la Vème République: redécouverte et métamorphoses d'un ritual," in *Façonner le passé. Représentations et cultures de l'histoire (XVIe–XXIe siècle)*, ed. Jean-Luc Bonniol and Maryline Crivello (Aix-en-Provence: Publications Universitaires de Provence, 2004), 87–106.
10. Circular, no. 2006–216 of 27 December 2006, *Official Journal of the Education Department*, no. 1, 4 January 2007. In 2002 the European education ministers, in response to the suggestion by the European Council, chose 27 January as the date of Holocaust Remembrance Day.
11. "Les Justes de France arrivent aux Etats-Unis," *French Morning US*, 4 March 2007.
12. Thierry Delpeuch, "L'Analyse des transferts internationaux de politiques publique: un état de l'art," *Questions de Recherche/Research Question*, no. 27 (December 2008): 61.
13. Garcia, "Les Panthéonisations."
14. The expression used by Renaud Donnedieu de Vabres, minister for culture and communication, during the conference.
15. Founding statutes, *Annual Report 2002*. Also, interviews with several of those responsible for this creation: with François Bernard, 30 December 2003; with Jean Mattéoli, 15 January 2004; and with David Kessler, 8 January 2003, in Paris. The successive versions of the statutes were given to me by François Bernard. For historical information of the robbing of the Jews, see Martin Dean, *Robbing the Jews. The Confiscation of Jewish Property in the Holocaust, 1933–1945* (New York: Cambridge University Press, 2008); Sarah Gensburger, *Witnessing the Robbing of the Jews. A Photographic Album, Paris, 1940–1944* (Bloomington: Indiana University Press, 2015).
16. Decree of 26 December 2000 acknowledging the Foundation as an establishment in the public interest.
17. Decree of 26 December 2000 acknowledging the Foundation as an establishment in the public interest.
18. The Foundation's activity reports published from 2003 are available on the website. They contain the lists of projects that are supported every year.
19. This information is taken from the public activity reports of the Foundation as well as from the fieldwork and participant observation of this period in the French Committee for Yad Vashem.
20. The following information results from participant observation fieldwork conducted within the French Committee for Yad Vashem and from the reflexive approach during the Homage itself in the different interactions with the directors of the Foundation for the Memory of the Shoah. On one hand, this Foundation contacted me to write "a book on the Righteous" for the Pantheon and, on the other hand, they financially contributed to a conference I co-organized in 2004, initially titled "The Righteous." See, respectively, Sarah Gensburger, "La Sociologue et l'actualité. Retour sur 'l'Hommage de la Nation aux Justes de France,'" *Genèses*, section "knowledge," no. 68 (September 2007): 116–31; Andrieu Claire, Sarah Gensburger, and Jacques Sémelin, *Resisting Genocides. The Multiple Forms of Rescue* (New York: Columbia University Press, 2011),

21. E.g., the two homages to writers who died during the two world wars. See Nicolas Beaupré, "Du Bulletin des Ecrivains de 1914 à l'Association des Ecrivains combattants (AEC): des combats à la mémoire, 1914–1927," in *La Politique et la guerre. Pour comprendre le XXème siècle. Hommage à Jean-Jacques Becker*, ed. Stéphane Audouin-Rouzeau, Annette Becker, Sophie Coeuré et al. (Paris: Agnès Viénot, 2002), 301–15.
22. Jacques Chirac's speech 18 January 2007.
23. Jacques Chirac's speech 18 January 2007.
24. Once again, the objective here is neither to validate nor to criticize this reading. For a critical approach, see Robert O. Paxton, "Jews: How Vichy Made It Worse," *The New York Review of Books*, 6 March 2014.
25. On this point, see the similar conclusions of William M. Johnston, *Celebrations: The Cult of Anniversaries in Europe and the United States Today* (New York: Transaction Publisher, 1991).
26. Pierre Muller and Yves Surel, *L'Analyse des politiques publiques* (Paris: Montchrestien, 1998) 3296–97.
27. Jacqueline Schochat-Rebibo, "Etrange Malaise," *Site Primo*, Jerusalem, 29 January 2007. Also see Tsilla Herscho, "Questions sur le prochain hommage aux Justes au Panthéon," *Guysen Israël News*, 15 January 2007.
28. The Legion of Honor is a national order of merit and the highest national distinction in France. It is divided into several different ranks and recognizes service to the nation, either military or civilian. The award ceremony is held at Easter for civilians.
29. Association of French Righteous for Yad Vashem; see Chapter 3.
30. Interview with Ivan Beltrami, 18 March 2003, Marseille. Cf. Ivan Beltrami, *Mémoire d'un Juste* (Marseille: self-published, 2000).
31. This was initially consulted in situ during the daily visits to the Pantheon to conduct interviews and observational fieldwork. A complete copy was finally given to me by the Pantheon administrator on my request.
32. Of course we cannot consider the messages in this visitors' book as representative of the opinion of French people regarding the ceremony. We can hypothesize that visiting the site in itself presupposes a positive attitude, which is partially reflected in the book. It is simply a matter of using the book to reveal the mechanisms that govern the perception of the event, whether they lead to rejection or acceptance. See Sharon McDonald, "Accessing Audiences: Visiting Visitor Books," *Museum and Society* 3, no. 3 (2005): 119–36.
33. Dora Apel, *Memory Effects: The Holocaust and the Art of Secondary Witnessing* (New Brunswick: Rutgers University Press, 2002).
34. This brief wave of interviews was conducted with the help of Michèle Baussant, a CNRS colleague and anthropologist. Michèle Baussant, *Pieds-Noirs: mémoires d'exils* (Paris: Stock, 2002).
35. This conclusion answers some of the issues at the core of the birth of memory studies as an integrated research field. See Kervin Lee Klein, "On the Emergence of 'Memory' in Historical Discourse," *Representations*, no. 69 (2000): 127–50; Wulf Kansteiner, "Finding Meaning in Memory: A Methodological Critique of Collective Memory Studies," *History and Theory* 41, no. 2 (2002): 179–97.
36. Pierre Nora, *Representations, No. 26, Special Issue: Memory and Counter-Memory* (Spring, 1989): 7–24
37. Susan Crane, "Writing the Individual Back into Collective Memory," *American Historical Review*, no. 105 (December 1997): 1381.
38. Indeed, this approach was used for the first time by Maurice Halbwachs, *La Topographie légendaire des Evangiles en Terre sainte. Etude de mémoire collective*, Marie Jaisson, ed. (Paris: PUF, 2008).

39. Muller, "L'Analyse cognitive," 195.
40. As an example, a Committee for Vigilance Regarding the Public Use of History was created in June, and in December an association called "Freedom for History" was created.
41. "Encart. 22 octobre: commémoration du souvenir de Guy Môquet et de ses 26 compagnons fusillés," *Bulletin officiel de l'Education Nationale,* no. 30, 30 August 2007.
42. Michel Winock, "La Part des Justes," in *La France et les Juifs. De 1789 à nos jours* (Paris: Seuil, 2004), 258.
43. *Libération,* 13 December 2005.
44. Tzvetan Todorov, *Les Abus de la mémoire* (Paris: Arléa, 1995).
45. Emmanuel Terray, *Face aux abus de la mémoire* (Arles: Actes Sud, 2006).
46. Tzvetan Todorov, *Facing the Extreme: Moral Life in the Concentration Camps* (New York: Holt Paperbacks, 1997).
47. A consensus is always relative of course. Yet apart from the interview published prior to the event by a U.S. historian specializing in the Holocaust, and not of its "memory," the media consensus appears substantial. Saul Friedländer, "La Shoah ou la solitude des Justes," interview by Nicolas Weill, *Le Monde,* 6 January 2007.
48. The expression was first used in Sarah Gensburger, "Les Figures du Juste et du Résistant et l'évolution de la mémoire historique française de l'Occupation," *Revue Française de Science Politique,* no. 2 (September 2002), 291–322.
49. Clifford Geertz, "Thick Description: An Interpretative Theory of Culture," in Geertz, ed., *The Interpretation of Cultures* (New York: Basic Books, 1973), 3–30.
50. George Balandier, *Sens et puissance* (Paris: PUF, 2004), 8–9.
51. These recurrent terms are used in particular by Jocelyn Létourneau and Bogumil Jewsiewicki, "Politique de la mémoire," *Politique et Sociétés* 22, no. 2 (2003): 5; Paul Ricoeur, *La Mémoire, l'histoire, l'oubli* (Paris: Seuil, 2000), 97.
52. Jeffrey Olick, "Memory and the Nation—Continuities, Conflicts, and Transformations," *Social Science History* 22, no. 4 (1998): 385.
53. Jean-Claude Passeron and Jacques Revel, eds. *Penser par cas* (Paris: Éditions de l◉EHESS, 2005), 43–44.

CONCLUSION

Memory Politics as Public Policy

This epilogue has provided an overview of the principal mechanisms that presided over the institutionalization of the Righteous of France category. Institutional, strategic, and cognitive factors came together to enable this term to be transferred from Israel to France. Together they established a dynamic of hybridization that unfolded over more than a decade. Over the course of this book we have seen the significance of the coproduction of policy as well as the references it mobilizes but also the importance of time in the institutionalization of public policy. As conclusive as it is, this epilogue in turn provokes two further remarks.

Strengths and weaknesses of the genealogical approach

The first of these questions relates to the issue of the time frame for any public policy analysis. This approach set out to trace the genesis of the Righteous of France category. Over the course of the analysis it emerged, however, that from a methodological perspective, the genealogical approach, although useful, risks preventing us from grasping the continued mechanisms of reinterpretation and hybridization because it leads us to focus on an "initial" time. The notion of institutionalization, on the other hand, has the advantage of taking the time frame of public policy into account without necessarily presupposing the existence of an original period that would have a founding role in the phenomena to be studied.

In this respect, the term "epilogue" itself has to be relativized. It is in fact impossible to date the beginning or the end of the dynamic of institutionalization of the Righteous of France category. Emerging in 1942 in Israel and then in 1986 in France, this dynamic did not end with either the vote of 10 July or the plaque in the Pantheon. The ceremony in January

2007, therefore, in turn produced incentive and opportunity effects that, combining institutional, strategic, and cognitive factors, led to changes in the configuration of actors as well as in the translation of the Israeli term. In 2007, following the tribute to the Righteous of France at the Pantheon, several municipalities inaugurated Avenues of the Righteous: in Nice on 26 April, in Epinay on 29 April, and in Evry on 7 October.

Similarly, many social actors saw this National Homage to the Righteous of France as an encouragement for collective mobilization in a different form from that proposed by the Yad Vashem Institute—this time embedded in the French social and geographic space. Certain French Jews thus adopted several of the key terms used by the president on 18 January 2007. In so doing they fed the conception of the Righteous of France category as being collective and anonymous. Some set up the association "Homage to the Villages of France," which was intended to "identify villages that took in and saved Jews hunted by the Nazis and to honor them." Others, along with non-Jews, founded the association the "Anonymous, Righteous, and Persecuted of the Nazi Era" in order to "provide an open platform for contributions, exchanges and encounters between all people wanting to contribute their testimonies in order to enrich, complete and publicize a story or an incident of rescue during World War II."

Although these initiatives explicitly claim to have been inspired by the Pantheon ceremony, it is possible that, in turn, they will contribute to the evolution of the Righteous of France category. The institutionalization of this category is thus an ongoing and complex process; it is never completely finished and is sometimes reversible. A composite entity, depending on time periods, sites, and levels of analysis, it is likely to take on one of the four forms codified by Ronald L. Jepperson: the formation of institutions, the development of institutions, deinstitutionalization, and reinstitutionalization. In light of this, the conclusion to this book can only be partial and temporary.

The analysis of memory public policy

The second of these two final remarks relates to the nature of the generalization of the conclusions drawn from this case study. Because of the questions we have explored through this study, the analysis has revealed the knowledge that is to be gained from the banalization of memory as a normal research topic, on the one hand, from the use of political science to approach it, on the other. It encourages a certain scientific normalization of the social sciences study of memory, the analysis of which too often remains a prisoner to normative and moral preconceptions.

Although this book applies public policy analysis to an object that is most often reserved for the new field of memory studies, it concludes that it would be highly relevant to include the theme of memory among the legitimate objects of public policy. In other words, it encourages us to overturn the currently dominant perspective of the relations between memory and politics. We should avoid estimating the relevance of particular uses of the past—or judging their efficiency—and instead investigate the way in which memory policy has indeed become a category of state and public intervention since the beginning of the 1980s. It is with the help of this term that, over the past twenty years, the French state and other public actors have promoted most of the politicoadministrative initiatives that have to do with remembering the past.

Thus it is not without basis that in July 1999 the newspaper *Le Monde* questioned the possible "creation of a Ministry for Memory," following the presence of the president of the French Republic and the prime minister at the commemorative ceremonies in Oradour-sur-Glan and in Auschwitz. The Department of Memory, Heritage, and Archives was established later that same year to "[conduct] actions in areas of policy concerning the remembrance of war and contemporary conflicts and the promotion of sites of memory and historic monuments."

But the action of successive governments extended beyond the activities of this specific service alone. Like the commemorations of the abolition of slavery and the slave trade, which have at different times been the responsibility of the Ministry of Culture, or the Ministry of Overseas Territories, or the Ministry for Education, this memory policy is relevant to several branches and administrations of the executive.

The remembrance of the past is also an area of frequent parliamentary intervention. Romain Bertrand has shown how, in the case of the vote on the law of 23 February 2005, several members of Parliament presented their action as part of memory policy; yet this policy was not "invented" for the occasion. For several years prior to this, "memory policy," as it is called, had already been a regular subject of debates, reports, and parliamentary evaluations. In this respect, and although the emergence of the term "memory laws" over the course of the year 2005 should be the subject of a specific critical study, it is an indication of the progressive institutionalization of the investment of the legislative branch in this area.

Proposing that political science take on these questions does not, however, mean unilaterally defining a new public policy sector. Memory public policies as a research topic cannot be restricted to borders drawn by governing bodies alone. The work of categorization, particularly linguistic, that actors are involved in, depending on the sites and periods, must also be an integral part of the analysis. The conclusions of this study on the institutionalization of the Righteous of France category encourages us, for example, to focus on the likely slippages between this area that claims to be public policy and other sectors.

It also means asking what might be at stake, other than memory, in these public policies supposed to be dedicated to this. By the same token, does the evocation of the past by public authorities actually aim to act on memory, or is it instead a simple instrument that is mobilized to serve public actions in other areas of state intervention? Does the politics of memory ultimately have something to do with the purpose of governing memory?

Finally, beyond the conclusions this case study has enabled us to reach, it has also allowed us to see how establishing memory as a social issue is fully part of the contemporary sociology of public policy. Far beyond France, the establishment of memory as a sector of public policy and as a political issue has occurred simultaneously in a number of countries as well as at an international and transnational level. That is why this book calls for more political science and public policy analysis of this evolution. It is worth wagering that memory studies have much to learn from the concepts and methods of political science. Similarly, the latter may find in issues of memory a means of tackling some of its current challenges, such as the symbolic nature of public policy, policy feedback, or the borders of the state.

APPENDIX A

METHODOLOGY AND CORPUS

This book revisits and extends part of the conclusions of research that I undertook and defended at the Ecole des Hautes Etudes en Sciences Sociales ([EHESS] Advanced School in Social Sciences) in 2006—a sociological study of a topic of interest to historians—which ultimately led to a book in political science, notably due to the diversity of disciplinary perspectives on the object. This study is based on a corpus that is very diverse, covering more than five countries. Alongside the use of interviews and the analysis of official texts, which are standard analytic tools in public policy, this book also mobilized participant observation and archival methods. These methods are fundamental to treating an object that is deliberately constructed as the articulation of the private and the public, on one hand, and in a midterm perspective, on the other.

With the hypothesis that the community sector may be particularly relevant for the observation of interactions between individuals, social actors, and public actors, I took advantage of the opportunity to join the team of volunteers working for the French Committee for Yad Vashem. From July 1999, when I had been working there for several months, this association became the French state's main contact on the issue, both in the context of the vote on the law of July 2000 and during the preparation of the ceremony at the Pantheon seven years later. Moreover, the choice of participation as a method to observe public action, outside state services, allowed me to include data in the corpus that are often excluded from both public policy analysis and memory studies.

Different kinds of archives were consulted for this research, with different objectives. Points of articulation between the expression of individuals' memories, the institutional action of Yad Vashem and the respective state policies of Israel and France, and the administrative files and applications for the attribution of the title of Righteous among the Nations immediately attracted my attention. They were subjected to both qualitative and quantitative analysis. I also consulted fourteen archive centers in five different countries. This was in part made necessary by the very nature of the object; the internationalization of the fieldwork also stemmed from the desire to provide a comparative basis for the study of contemporary memory public policy.

Although the French situation is central throughout the case study of the evolution of the Righteous of France category, the fact that the term "Righteous" spread much more widely meant that it was also necessary to look closely at the Belgian and Polish examples. This encouraged me to identify sources that enabled me to question the respective roles of the processes of globalization, Europeanization, and localism in the contemporary institutionalization of the "memory" public policy category. The fortunate discovery of and access to several private archives, particularly from associative leaders and members for Parliament, increased this corpus of archival material.

Finally, conducting interviews and collecting official publications complemented retrieving materials from the first two types of sources. The identification of and access to public speeches, legislative or regulatory texts, and statutory documents or journal articles, all stemming from the French, Israeli, Belgian, Polish, or U.S. contexts between 1942 and 2008, were also an important part of this corpus. Roughly fifty interviews were then conducted with actors who participated, to one degree or another in the evocation and recognition of the Righteous either by the French or, to a lesser extent, overseas' authorities. The identification of these actors stemmed essentially from the participant observation conducted over three years in the French Committee for Yad Vashem.

It also resulted from attending numerous Righteous among the Nations medal ceremonies between 1997 and 2007. These interviews were essentially informative and thus directive. However, whenever possible, and although several people who were met on these occasions turned out to have testified for Yad Vashem, particular attention was paid to the representations and social trajectories of these actors, who were initially met in the context of their political associative or institutional roles. Beyond this, the interviews allowed me indirect access to official documents, which although part of the state archives are not yet accessible as such.

Finally, in 2005, a questionnaire was sent to all the prefectures and departmental services of the National Office for Veterans and Victims of War, which is responsible for the annual commemorative day established by the law of 10 July 2000. They were asked to describe the procedure and organization of the event, to specify the instructions and circulars they had received on this subject, and to summarize all the other possible initiatives relating to the evocation of the Righteous in these regions. The return rate was close to 66 percent. Once again, these responses provided access to several internal administrative documents that would otherwise have been inaccessible. Although uneven in their degree of precision and relevance, these responses were subject to both qualitative and quantitative analysis.

Finally, but most importantly, the research that provided the material for this book also led to more than sixty nondirective interviews—in France, Belgium, Israel, the United States, and Poland. These were interviews with Jewish people who had testified in the process of attributing Righteous status and with those who had deliberately chosen not to use this procedure. Although these interviews are taken into account in this book, because of the desire to study the intersection of the private and the public within public policy, they are not central here as they were in most of the original dissertation. Nevertheless, the complexity and diversity of this testimony provide a fundamental interpretative background for this analysis.

Corpus used for the analysis of the vote on the 10 July 2000 law (Chapter 4)

In addition to public documents, this analysis is based on private sources. At the end of my visit to his home, Daniel Marcovitch, who has not been a member for Parliament since 2002, allowed me to accompany him to his office in the Paris town hall, where he kept a box of all the documents relating to this bill, which he entrusted to me. In addition, following my interview with Jean Le Garrec, I met with him a second time so that I could consult the documents he had kept in his office. These two types of sources are referred to as the "Marcovitch Archives" and the "Le Garrec Archives." The oldest document among them is a letter dated 4 December 1997 from the director of the Research and Information Service of the National Assembly to Daniel Marcovitch in response to Marcovitch's request concerning the writing of his bill.

Corpus used in the analysis of the implementation of the 10 July 2000 law (Chapter 6)

This analysis is based on three main sources. The first is made up of the responses to the "prefecture questionnaire" mentioned above. The second source is the "Overview of the national day in memory of the victims of the racist and anti-Semitic crimes by the French state and in homage to the Righteous of France," which was made annual by the central services of the National Office for Veterans and Victims of War based on files sent by their departmental services. This overview was given to me by Stéphane Le Borgne, assistant to the head of the Department of Veteran Remembrance, in this office in an interview of 7 May 2003 in Paris. Finally, the brochures put out by the Conseil Représentatif des Institutions juives de France, the Foundation for the Memory of the Shoah, and the Association des Fils et Filles de Déportés Juifs de France (Association of the Sons and Daughters of Jews Deported from France) in July 2002 on the sixtieth anniversary of the deportation of French Jews, presented a "collection of the speeches given at the commemorations of the roundups of summer 1942."

Appendix B

Detailed References of Official Texts

Texts referred to as "memorial laws" by the various protagonists in the controversy over article 4 of the law of 23 February 2005 on the "positive role of colonization":

- Law number 90–615 of 13 July 1990, the so-called Gayssot Law: "repressing any racist, xenophobic, or anti-Semitic act."
- Law number 2001–70 of January 2001, of which the sole article states, "France publically recognizes the Armenian genocide of 1915."
- Law number 2001–434 of 21 May 2001, the so-called Law Taubira: "leading to France's recognition of slavery and the slave trade as a crime against humanity."
- Law number 2005–158 of 23 February 2005, the so-called Mekachera Law: "providing recognition by the nation and national contributions regarding repatriated French citizens."

Texts establishing national days of commemoration adopted since 2001[1]:

- Law number 2001–434 of May 2001 recognizing the slave trade and slavery as crimes against humanity.
- Decree number 2006–388 of 21 March 2006 specifying the date of the annual commemoration of the abolition of slavery in metropolitan France.
- Decree of 31 March 2003 establishing a national day of homage to the *harkis* and other auxiliary units.

- Decree number 2003–925 of 26 September 2003 establishing a national day of homage on 5 December each year to those who died for France during the Algerian War and fought in Morocco and Tunisia.
- Decree number 2005–547 of 26 May 2005 establishing a national day of homage on 8 June each year to those who died for France in Indochina.
- Decree number 2006–313 of 10 May 2006 establishing 18 June each year as the national day for the commemoration of the historic speech by General de Gaulle to refuse defeat and continue the fight against the enemy.

Commissions and other working groups on *questions mémorielles* (memorial issues) in 2008:

- Working group number 5 for the *Livre Blanc sur la défense et la sécurité intérieure* (White Paper on Defense and Interior Security) includes memory as one of its themes for reflection.
- Act of 31 October 2007 on the creation of the commission responsible for organizing the celebration of the ninetieth anniversary of the end of World War I.
- Act of 12 December 2007 on the creation, by the secretary of state for Veterans' Affairs, of the study commission on the modernization of public commemorations.
- Information mission on *questions mémorielles* (memory issues), created by the Conference of Presidents of the National Assembly, 25 March 2008.
- Education mission on the teaching of the Shoah in primary schools, established 27 February 2008.

Notes

1. For a systematic study, see Sarah Gensburger, "Comprendre la multiplication des 'journées de commémoration nationale': étude d'un instrument d'action publique de nature symbolique," in *L'Instrumentation de l'action publique. Controverses, résistances, effets*, ed. Charlotte Halpern, Pierre Lascoumes, and Patrick Le Galès (Paris: Presses de Sciences Po, 2014), 345–65.

Bibliography

Amalvi, Claude. *De l'art et la manière d'accommoder les héros de l'histoire de France. De Vercingétorix à la Révolution. Essai de mythologie nationale.* Paris: Albin Michel, 1998.

Andrieu, Claire. "La Commémoration des dernières guerres françaises: l'élaboration de politiques symboliques, 1945–2003." In *Politiques du passé. Usages politiques du passé dans la France contemporaine,* edited by Claire Andrieu, Marie-Claire Lavabre, and Danielle Tartakowsky, 39–46. Aix-en-Provence: Publications de l'Université de Provence, 2006.

Andrieu, Claire, Sarah Gensburger, and Jacques Sémelin. *Resisting Genocides. The Multiple Forms of Rescue.* New York: Columbia University Press, 2011.

Apel, Dora. *Memory Effects: The Holocaust and the Art of Secondary Witnessing.* New Brunswick: Rutgers University Press, 2002.

Balandier, George. *Sens et puissance.* Paris: PUF, 2004 [First edition 1971].

Bartoszewski, Wladyslaw. *Le Sang versé nous unit: Sur l'histoire de l'aide aux juifs en Pologne pendant l'occupation.* Warsaw: Editions Interpress, 1970.

Bartoszewski, Wladyslaw and Zofia Lewinowna. *Righteous among the Nations. How Poles Helped the Jews, 1939–1945.* London: Earlscourt, 1969.

Bartoszewski, Wladyslaw and Zofia Lewinowna. *Ten jest z ojczyzny mojej. Polacy z pomoca Zydom 1939–1945* [That One Is from My Country. The Poles Who Came to the Aide of the Jews, 1939–1945]. Cracow: Znak, 1969.

Baruch, Marc Olivier. *Des Lois indignes? Les Historiens, la politique et le droit.* Paris: Tallandier, 2013.

Bastide, Roger. "Les Problèmes de la mémoire collective." In *Les Religions africaines au Brésil.* By Bastide. Paris: PUF, 1995 [first ed. 1960].

Bauer, Yehuda. *American Jewry and the Holocaust: The American Jewish Joint Distribution Committee, 1939–1945.* Detroit: Wayne State University Press, 1981.

Baussant, Michèle. *Pieds-Noirs: Mémoires d'exils.* Paris: Stock, 2002.

Beaupre, Nicolas. "Du Bulletin des Ecrivains de 1914 à l'Association des Ecrivains combattants (AEC): Des combats à la mémoire, 1914–1927." In *La Politique et la guerre. Pour comprendre le XXème siècle. Hommage à Jean-Jacques Becker,* edited by Stéphane Audouin-Rouzeau, Annette Becker, Sophie Coeure et al., 301–15. Paris: Agnès Viénot, 2002.

Becker, Howard. "Moral Entrepreneurs." In *Outsiders. Studies in the Sociology of Deviance.* New York: Free Press of Glencoe, 1963, 147–65.

Beloof, Douglas E. *Victims in Criminal Procedure.* Durham: Carolina Academic Press, 1999.

Beltrami, Ivan. *Mémoire d'un Juste.* Marseille: self-published, 2000.

Ben-Amos, Avner. "The Sacred Center of Power Paris and Republican State Funerals." *Journal of Interdisciplinary History* 22, no. 1 (1991): 27–48.

Ben-Amos, Avner. *Funeral, Politics and Memory in Modern France, 1789–1996.* Oxford: Oxford University Press, 2000.

Bensimon, Doris. *Les Juifs de France et leurs relations avec Israël. 1945–1988.* Paris: L'Harmattan, 1989.

Bertilotti, Paola. "Italian Jews and the Memory of Rescue (1944–1961)." In *Resisting Genocide. The Multiple Forms of Rescue,* edited by Jacques Sémelin, Claire Andrieu, and Sarah Gensburger, 127–44. New York: Columbia University Press, 2010.

Bertrand, Romain. *Mémoires d'empire. La controverse autour du "fait colonial."* Bellecombes-en-Bauge: Éditions du Croquant, 2006.

Bikont, Anna. *My z Jedwabnego* [Jedwabne and I]. Warsaw: Proszynski and Ska, 2004.

Bilsky, Leora. *Transformative Justice. Israeli Identity on Trial.* Ann Arbor: University of Michigan Press, 2004.

Birnbaum, Pierre. "Les Juifs entre l'appartenance identitaire et l'entrée dans l'espace public: La Révolution française et le choix des acteurs." *Revue française de sociologie* 30, nos. 3/4 (1989): 497–510.

Birnbaum, Pierre. "Etre Juste et fonctionnaire? Oui, c'était possible." *L'Arche* 482, March 1998.

Birnbaum, Pierre. *Sur la corde raide. Parcours juif entre exil et citoyenneté.* Paris: Flammarion, 2002.

Birnbaum, Pierre. *La France imaginée: Déclin des rêves unitaires?* Paris: Gallimard, 2003.

Bitsch, Marie-Thérèse. *Histoire de la Belgique.* Brussels: Editions Complexes, 2004.

Blanchard, Pascal and Isabelle Veyrat-Masson. *Les Guerres de mémoires: La France et son histoire, enjeux politiques, controverses historiques, stratégies médiatiques.* Paris: La Découverte, 2008.

Borraz, Olivier and Patricia Loncle-Moriceau. "Permanences et recompositions du secteur sanitaire, les politiques locales de lutte contre le sida." *Revue française de sociologie* 41, no. 1 (2000): 37–60.

Brog, Mooli. "In Blessed Memory of a Dream: Mordechai Shenhavi and Initial Holocaust Commemoration Ideas in Palestine, 1942–1945." *Yad Vashem Studies* 30 (2002): 297–336.

Brog, Mooli. "Victims and Victors: Holocaust and Military Commemoration in Israel Collective Memory." *Israel Studies* 8, no. 3 (2003): 65–99.

Brossat, Alain, ed. *A l'est la mémoire retrouvée.* Paris: La Découverte, 1990.

Callon, Michel. "Some Elements of a Sociology of Translation: Domestication of the Scallops and the Fishermen of St Brieuc Bay." In *Power, Action and Belief: A New Sociology of Knowledge?* edited by J. Law, 196–223. London: Routledge, 1986.

Chalandon, Sorj and Pascale Nivelle. *Crimes contre l'humanité. Barbie, Touvier, Bousquet et Papon.* Paris: Plon, 1998.

Chandernagor, Françoise and Pierre Nora. *Liberté pour l'histoire.* Paris: CNRS Editions, 2008.

Chanet, Jean-François. "La Fabrique des héros. Pédagogie républicaine et culte des grands hommes de Sedan à Vichy." *Vingtième Siècle. Revue d'Histoire,* no. 65 (January–March 2000): 13–34.

Charvolin, Florian. *L'Invention de l'environnement en France.* Paris: La Découverte, 2003.

Chaumont, Jean-Michel. *La Concurrence des victimes. Génocide, identité, reconnaissance.* Paris: La Découverte, 1997.

Clifford, Rebecca. *Commemorating the Holocaust: The Dilemmas of Remembrance in France and Italy.* Oxford: Oxford University Press, 2013.

Cohen, Erik. "Les Résultats de la grande enquête sur les Juifs français." *L'Arche* 538, December 2002, 52–79.

Cohen, Erik. "Une Communauté inscrite dans la socialité. Valeurs et identité des Juifs de France." *L'Observatoire du monde juif*, nos. 10/11 (May 2004): 7–14.

Cohen, Martine. "Les Juifs de France. Modernité et identité." *Vingtième Siècle. Revue d'Histoire*, no. 66 (April–June 2000): 91–106.

Commaille, Jacques. "Sociologie de l'action publique." In *Dictionnaire des politiques publiques*, edited by Laurie Boussaguet, Sophie Jacquot, and Pauline Ravinet. Paris: Presses de Sciences Po, 2004.

Conan, Eric and Daniel Lindenberg. "Pourquoi y-a-t-il une affaire Jean-Moulin?" *Esprit*, 198 (January 1994): 5–18.

Conan, Eric and Henry Rousso. *Vichy, un passé qui ne passe pas.* Paris: Gallimard, 1996 [1st edition 1994].

Confino, Alon. "Collective Memory and Cultural History: Problems of Method." *American Historical Review* 105 (December 1997): 1386–403.

Corning, Amy and Howard Schuman. "Matters. The Anniversaries of 9/11 and Woodstock." *Public Opinion Quarterly* 77, no. 2 (2013): 433–54.

Cossu, Andrea. "Memory, Symbolic Conflict and Changes in the National Calendar in the Italian Second Republic." *Modern Italy* 15, no. 1 (2010): 3–19.

Crane, Susan. "Writing the Individual Back into Collective Memory." *American Historical Review*, no. 105 (December 1997): 1372–85.

Datner, Szymon. *Las sprawiedliwych. Karta z dziejow ratownictwa Zydow w okupowanej Polsce.* Warsaw: Ksiazka i Wiedza, 1968.

Dean, Martin. *Robbing the Jews. The Confiscation of Jewish Property in the Holocaust, 1933–1945.* New York: Cambridge University Press, 2008.

Delpeuch, Thierry. "L'Analyse des transferts internationaux de politiques publique: un état de l'art." *Questions de Recherche/Research Question*, no. 27 (December 2008).

Digneffe, Françoise and Jacques Fierens, eds. *Justice et Gacaca. L'Expérience rwandaise et le genocide.* Namur: Presses Universitaires de Namur, 2003.

Don-Yehiya, Eliezer. "Memory and Political Culture: Israeli Society and the Holocaust." *Studies in Contemporary Jewry* 9 (1993): 139–62.

Douglas, Lawrence. *The Memory of Judgment. Making Law and History in the Trials of the Holocaust.* New Haven: Yale University Press, 2001.

Erner, Guillaume. *La Société des victims.* Paris: La Découverte, 2006.

Fassin, Didier and Richard Rechtman. *L'Empire du traumatisme. Enquête sur la condition de victime.* Paris: Flammarion, 2007.

Favre, Pierre. "Qui gouverne quand personne ne gouverne?" In *Être gouverné. Études en l'honneur de Jean Leca*, edited by Pierre Favre, Jack Hayward, and Yves Schemeil, 257–71. Paris: Presses de Sciences Po, 2003.

Feldman, Jackie. *Above the Death Pits, beneath the Flag: Youth Voyages to Poland and the Performance of Israeli National Identity.* New York: Berghahn Books, 2010.

Felman, Shoshana. *The Juridical Unconscious: Trials and Traumas in the Twentieth Century.* Cambridge, MA: Harvard University Press, 2002.

Fine, Gary Alan. "Reputational Entrepreneurs and the Memory of Incompetence: Melting Supporters, Partisan Warriors, and Images of President Harding." *American Journal of Sociology* 101, no. 5 (1996): 1159–93.

Fogelman, Eva. *Conscience and Courage. Rescuers of Jews during the Holocaust.* New York: Anchor Books, 1995 [1994].

Fralon, José-Alain. *Aristide de Sousa Mendès. Le Juste de Bordeaux.* Bordeaux: Mollat, 1998.

Frangi, Marc. "Les 'Lois mémorielles' de l'expression de la volonté générale au législateur historien." *Revue du droit public, de la science politique en France et à l'Etranger* 1 (2005): 241–66.

Gamzon, Robert, alias Worried Beaver [Castor soucieux]. *Les Eaux claires. Journal 1940–1944,* Paris: EIF, 1981.

Garcia, Patrick. "Panthéonisation." In *Dictionnaire des politiques culturelles de la France depuis 1959,* edited by Emmanuel De Waresquiel, 473–74. Paris: CNRS Editions, 2001.

Garcia, Patrick. "Les Panthéonisations sous la Vème République: redécouverte et métamorphoses d'un rituel." In *Façonner le passé. Représentations et cultures de l'histoire (XVIe–XXIe siècle),* ed. Jean-Luc Bonniol and Maryline Crivello, 87–106. Aix-en-Provence: Publications Universitaires de Provence, 2004.

Geertz, Clifford. "Thick Description: An Interpretative Theory of Culture." In *The Interpretation of Cultures,* ed. Clifford Geertz, 3–30. New York: Basic Books, 1973.

Gensburger, Sarah. "Les Figures du Juste et du Résistant et l'évolution de la mémoire historique française de l'Occupation." *Revue Française de Science Politique,* no. 2 (September 2002): 291–322.

Gensburger, Sarah. "Essai de sociologie de la mémoire. L'Expression des souvenirs à travers le titre de "Juste parmi les nations" dans le cas français: entre cadre institutionnel, politique publique et mémoire collective." Ph.D. dissertation, Ecole des hautes études en sciences sociales, Paris, 2006.

Gensburger, Sarah. "La Sociologue et l'Actualité. Retour sur 'L'Hommage de la Nation aux Justes de France.'" *Genèses,* no. 68 (September 2007): 116–31.

Gensburger, Sarah. "Fragments de mémoire collective: les Justes parmi les nations." In *La Topographie légendaire des Evangiles en Terre sainte (1941),* edited by Maurice Halbwachs, 99–112. Coll. "Quadrige/Grands textes," reedition edited by Marie Jaisson. Paris: PUF, 2008.

Gensburger, Sarah. Review of *Mémoires d'empire. La controverse autour du "fait colonial",* by Romain Bertrand. *National Identities* 10, no. 4 (2008): 453–55.

Gensburger, Sarah. "L'Émergence progressive d'une politique internationale de la mémoire: l'exemple des actions publiques de 'partage' de la mémoire." In *Traumatisme collectif pour patrimoine. Regards sur un mouvement transnational,* ed. Bogumil Jewsiewicki, 25–42. Laval: Presses de l'Université Laval, 2008.

Gensburger, Sarah. "From the Memory of Rescue to the Institution of the Title of Righteous." In *Resisting Genocides. The Multiple Forms of Rescue,* edited by Claire Andrieu, Sarah Gensburger, and Jacques Sémelin. New York: Columbia University Press, 2011: 17–26.

Gensburger, Sarah. "The Righteous among the Nations as Elements of Collective Memory." *International Social Science Journal*, nos. 203/204 (March–June 2012): 135–46.

Gensburger, Sarah. "Comprendre la multiplication des 'journées de commémoration nationale': étude d'un instrument d'action publique de nature symbolique." In *L'Instrumentation de l'action publique. Controverses, résistances, effets*, edited by Charlotte Halpern, Pierre Lascoumes, and Patrick Le Gales, 345–65. Paris: Presses de Sciences Po, 2014.

Gensburger, Sarah. *Witnessing the Robbing of the Jews. A Photographic Album, Paris, 1940–1944.* Bloomington: Indiana University Press, 2015.

Gilbert, Howard. "The Slow Development of the Right to Conscientious Objection to Military Service under the European Convention on Human Rights." *European Human Rights Review* 5 (2001): 554–67.

Goldman, Ariel. "Lettre ouverte aux Justes qui ont sauvé mes frères." *Tribune Juive* 1423, 24 November 1997.

Grabski, August. "Wspolczesne zycie religijne Zydow w Polsce" [Jewish Religious Life in Contemporary Poland]. In *Studia z historii Zydow w Polsce po 1945 roku* [Studies on the History of Jews in Poland after 1945], edited by Grzegorz Berent, August Grabski, and Andrzej Stankowski, 143–202. Warsaw: ZIH, 2000.

Gross, Jan Tomasz. *Neighbors: The Destruction of the Jewish Community in Jedwabne.* Princeton: Princeton University Press, 2001.

Gruber, Ruth Ellen. *Virtually Jewish. Reinventing Jewish Culture in Europe.* Berkeley: University Presses of California, 2002.

Grunberg, Gérard, Nonna Mayer, and Paul M. Sniderman, eds. *La Démocratie à l'épreuve. Une Nouvelle Approche de l'opinion des Français.* Paris: Presses de Sciences Po, 2002.

Grüninger, Paul and Stefan Keller. *Délit d'humanité: l'affaire Grüninger.* Lausanne: Editions d'en bas, 1994.

Gudonis, Marius. "Constructing Jewish Identity in Post-Communist Poland: Part I: 'Deassimilation without Polonization.'" *East European Jewish Affairs* 31, no. 1 (2001): 1–14.

Gutman, Israël, ed. *Dictionnaire des Justes de France.* Paris: Fayard, 2003.

Hacking, Ian. *The Social Construction of What?* Cambridge: Harvard University Press, 2000.

Halbwachs, Maurice. *La Topographie légendaire des Evangiles en Terre sainte. Etude de mémoire collective.* Edited by Marie Jaisson. Paris: PUF, 2008 [1941].

Hall, Peter A. and Rosmary C.R. Taylor. "Political Science and the Three New Institutionalisms." *Political Studies* 44 (December 1996): 936–57.

Hallie, Philip. *Lest Innocent Blood Be Shed: The Story of the Village of Le Chambon and How Goodness Happened There.* New York: Harper and Row, 1979.

Hammel, Frédéric, alias Camel [Chameau]. *"Souviens-toi d'Amalek": témoignage sur la lutte des Juifs en France 1938–1944.* Paris: CLKH, 1982.

Hartog, François. *Des Régimes d'historicité. Présentisme et Expériences du temps.* Paris: Seuil, 2002.

Hassenteufel, Patrick. "De La Comparaison internationale à la comparaison transnationale. Les Déplacements de la construction d'objets comparatifs en matière de politiques publiques." *Revue française de science politique* 55, no. 1 (2005): 113–32.

Heran, François. "Rite et Méconnaissance. Notes sur la théorie religieuse de l'action chez Pareto et Weber." *Archives de sciences sociales des religions* 39, no. 85 (1994): 144.

Herscho, Tsilla. "Questions sur le prochain hommage aux Justes au Panthéon." *Guysen Israël News*, 15 January 2007.

Jablonka, Hanna. "After Eichmann. Collective Memory and the Holocaust since 1961." *The Journal of Israeli History*. Special issue 23, no. 1 (2004): 1–17.

Jablonka, Hanna. *The State of Israel vs. Adolf Eichmann*. New York: Schocken Books, 2004.

Jansen, Robert S. "Resurrection and Appropriation: Reputational Trajectories, Memory Work, and the Political Use of Historical Figures." *American Journal of Sociology* 112, no. 4 (2007): 853–1007.

Jarosz, Anna Barbara. "Marzec w praise" [March in the Press]. In *Marzec 1968. Trzydziesci lat pozniej* [March 1968. Thirty Years Later], edited by Marcin Kula, Piotr Oseka, and Marcin Zaremba. 2 vols. Warsaw: PWN, 1998.

Jobert, Bruno. "Représentations sociales, controverses et débats dans la conduite des politiques publiques." *Revue française de science politique* 42, no. 2 (1992): 227.

Johnston, William M. *Celebrations: The Cult of Anniversaries in Europe and the United States Today*. New York: Transaction Publishers, 1991.

Kabalek, Kobi. "The Commemoration before the Commemoration: Yad Vashem and the Righteous among the Nations (1945–1963)." *Yad Vashem Studies* 39, no. 1 (2011): 169–211.

Kahn, Jean. *L'Obstination du témoignage*. Paris: Plon, 2003.

Kalisky, Aurélia. "Mémoires croisées—des références à la Shoah dans le travail de deuil et de mémoire du génocide des Tutsi." *Humanitaire* 10 (Spring–Summer 2004): 79.

Kansteiner, Wulf. "Finding Meaning in Memory: A Methodological Critique of Collective Memory Studies." *History and Theory* 41, no. 2 (2002): 179–97.

Kapel, René. *Un Rabbin dans la tourmente*. Paris: Editions du CDJC, 1986.

Kedar, Nir. "Ben-Gurion's Mamlakhtiyut: Etymological and Theoretical Roots." *Israel Studies* 7, no. 3 (2002): 117–33.

Kenan, Orna. *Between Memory and History. The Evolution of Israeli Historiography of the Holocaust, 1945–1961*. New York: Peter Lang Publishing, 2003.

Klarsfeld, Serge. *Vichy-Auschwitz. La 'Solution finale' de la question juive*. Paris: Fayard, 2001 (1st ed. 1983).

Klarsfeld, Serge. *Le Calendrier de la persécution des Juifs de France*. Paris: Fayard, 2003.

Klein, Kervin Lee. "On The Emergence of 'Memory' in Historical Discourse." *Representations*, no. 69 (2000): 127–50.

Korn, Eugene. "Gentiles, the World to Come and Judaism: The Odyssey of a Rabbinic Text." *Modern Judaism* 14 (1994): 265–87.

Korzec, Pawel. *Juifs en Pologne. La Question juive pendant l'entre-deux guerres*. Paris: Presses de la Fondation Nationale des Sciences Politiques, 1980.

Korzec, Pawel and Jacques Burko. *Le Gouv pas d'espace ernement polonais en exil et la persécution des Juifs en France en 1942*. Paris: Cerf, 1997.

Krajewski, Stanislaw. "L'Inventaire des responsabilités." *Le Messager européen*, no. 9 (1996): 219–20.

Kriegel, Maurice. "Trois Mémoires de la Shoah: États-Unis, Israël, France. À propos de Peter Novick, *L'Holocauste dans la vie américaine*." *Le Débat* 117 (November–December 2001): 59–72.

Krzeminski, Ireneusz, ed. *Czy Polacy sa antysemitami?* [Are Poles Anti-Semitic?]. Warsaw: Oficyna Naukowa, 1996.

Kuk, Leszek. *La Pologne du post-communisme à l'anti-communisme*. Paris: L'Harmattan, 2001.

Lagrou, Pieter. *Mémoires patriotiques et occupation nazie*. Brussels: Editions Complexes, 2003.

Lascoumes, Pierre and Patrick Le Galès, eds. *Gouverner par les instruments*. Paris: Presses de Sciences Po, 2004.

Lavabre, Marie-Claire. "Du Poids et du Choix du passé." *Cahiers de l'IHTP* 18 (1991): 177–185.

Lavabre, Marie-Claire. *Le Fil rouge. Sociologie de la mémoire communiste*. Paris: FNSP, 1994.

Lazare, Lucien. *La Résistance juive en France*. Paris: Stock, 1987.

Lazare, Lucien. *Le Tapissier de Jérusalem. Mémoires*. Paris: Le Seuil, 2015.

Lefranc, Sandrine, Lilian Mathieu, and Johanna Simeant, eds., "Les Victimes écrivent leur histoire." *Raisons politiques*, no. 30 (2008): 5–19.

Lehn, Walter. *The Jewish National Fund*. New York: Kegan Paul International, 1988.

Letourneau, Jocelyn and Bogumil Jewsiewicki. "Politique de la mémoire." *Politique et Sociétés* 22, no. 2 (2003): 3–15.

Levene, Marc. "Nationalism and Its Alternatives in the International Arena: The Jewish Question at Paris, 1919." *Journal of Contemporary History* 28, no. 3 (1993): 511–31.

Lindenberg, Daniel. "Guerres de mémoire en France." *Vingtième Siècle. Revue d'Histoire* 42 (April–June 1994): 77–95.

Lopez, Gérard, Serge Portelli, and Clément Sophie. *Les Droits des victimes: victimologie et psychotraumatologie*. Paris: Dalloz, 2003.

Ludi, Regula. "Waging War on Wartime Memory: Recent Swiss Debates on the Legacies of the Holocaust and the Nazi Era." *Jewish Social Studies* 10, no. 2 (2004): 116–52.

Macdonald, Sharon. "Accessing Audiences: Visiting Visitor Books." *Museum and Society* 3, no. 3 (2005): 119–36.

March, James G. and Johan P. Olsen. *Rediscovering Institutions. The Organizational Basis of Politics*. New York: Free Press, 1989.

Martiniello, Marco. *Culturalisation des différences, différenciation des cultures dans la politique belge*. Les Cahiers du CERI, 20. Paris: CERI, 1998.

Mesnard, Philippe. *La Victime écran: la représentation humanitaire en question*. Paris: Textuel, 2002.

Michman, Jozeph, and Bert Jan Flim, eds. *The Encyclopedia of the Righteous among the Nations: Rescuers of Jews during the Holocaust. The Netherlands*. Jerusalem: Yad Vashem, 2004.

Michnik, Adam. "Poles and the Jews: How Deep the guilt?" *New York Times*, 17 March 2001. Republished in Antony Polonsky and Joanna B. Michlic, eds. *The Neighbors Respond. The Controversy over the Jedwabne Massacre in Poland*. Princeton: Princeton University Press, 2004, 438–39.

Mieszkowska, Anna, ed. *Matka dzieci Holokaustu. Historia Ireny Sendlerowej* [Mother of the Children of the Holocaust. A History of Irena Sendlerowa]. Warsaw: Muza Sa, 2004.

Muller, Pierre. "L'Analyse cognitive des politiques publiques: vers une sociologie politique de l'action publique." *Revue française de science politique* 50, no. 2 (2000): 189–208.

Muller, Pierre. "Esquisse d'une théorie du changement dans l'action publique. Structures, acteurs et cadres cognitifs." *Revue française de science politique* 55, no. 3 (2005): 155–187.

Muller, Pierre and Yves Surel. *L'Analyse des politiques publiques.* Paris: Montchrestien, 1998.

Niewiedzial, Agnieszka. "Figure du Juste et politique publique de la mémoire en Pologne: entre relations diplomatiques et structures sociales." *Critique Internationale* 34 (January–March 2007): 127–48.

Nissim, Gabriele. *Il tribunale del bene: la storia di Moshe Bejski, l'uomo che creò il Giardino dei giusti.* Milan: Mandadori, 2003.

Nizard, Lucien, *Planification et Société.* Grenoble: Grenoble University Press, 1974.

Nora, Pierre, ed. *Realms of Memory: Rethinking the Past.* 3 vols. New York: Columbia University Press, 1996. First published in French as *Les Lieux de mémoire.* Paris: Gallimard, 1984.

Nora, Pierre. "Between Memory and History: Les Lieux de mémoire." *Representations,* 26, *Special Issue: Memory and Counter-Memory* (Spring 1989): 7–24.

Nora, Pierre, ed. "L'Ère de la commémoration." Vol. 3 in *Les Lieux de mémoire.* By Nora. Paris: Gallimard, 1997, 4687–718. Coll. "Quarto."

Novick, Peter. *The Holocaust in American Life.* New York: Houghton Mifflin, 2000.

Ofer, Dalia. "The Strength of Remembrance: Commemorating the Holocaust during the First Decade of Israel." *Jewish Social Studies* 6, no. 2 (2000): 24–55.

Olick, Jeffrey K. "Memory and the Nation—Continuities, Conflicts, and Transformations." *Social Science History* 22, no. 4 (1998): 385.

Olick, Jeffrey K. ed. *States of Memory: Continuities, Conflicts, and Transformations in National Retrospection.* Durham: Duke University Press, 2003.

Olick, Jeffrey K. *Politics of Regret: On Collective Memory and Historical Responsibility.* New York: Routledge, 2007.

Olick, Jeffrey K., Vered Vinitzky-Seroussi, and Daniel Levy, eds. *The Collective Memory Reader.* Oxford: Oxford University Press, 2011.

Ozouf, Mona. "Le Panthéon. L'Ecole normale des morts." In *Les Lieux de Mémoire.* Vol. I: *La République,* ed. Pierre Nora, 139–66. Paris: Gallimard, 1984.

Passeron, Jean-Claude and Jacques Revel, eds. *Penser par cas.* Paris: Editions de l'EHESS, 2005.

Paxton, Robert O. "La Spécificité de la persécution des Juifs en France." *Annales* 3 (May–June 1993): 605–19.

Paxton, Robert O. "Jews: How Vichy Made It Worse." *The New York Review of Books,* 61, no. 4, 6 March 2014.

Poche, Bernard. "La Belgique entre les piliers et les 'mondes linguistiques.' Quelques réflexions sur la question des formes sociales." *Recherches sociologiques* 23, no. 3 (1992): 43–68.

Poliakov, Léon. *L'Auberge des musiciens. Mémoires.* Paris: L'Harmattan, 1981.

Pollak, Michael. "Mémoire, oubli, silence." In *Une Identité blessée. Etudes de sociologie et d'histoire.* By Pollak. Paris: Métailié, 1993: 15–39.

Polletta, Francesca. "Legacies and Liabilities of Insurgent Past: Remembering Martin Luther King, Jr., on the House and Senate Floor." *Social Science History* 22, no. 4 (1998): 479–512.

Poznanski, R. "Comment les trois quarts de Juifs de France ont-ils survécu?" In *Les Juifs en France pendant la Seconde Guerre mondiale.* By Poznanski, 579–83. Paris: Hachette, 1997 [1st ed. 1994].

Prost, Antoine. "Monuments to the Dead." In *Realms of Memory*, edited by Pierre Nora, 307–32. Vol. 2. Columbia: Columbia University Press, 1996.

Raimond, Pierre-François. *Un Exemple de politique de la mémoire: la délégation à la mémoire et à l'information historique.* Paris: Mémoire de l'Institut d'Etudes Politiques, 1994.

Rémond, R. *Un Fichier juif: rapport de la Commission présidée par René Rémond au premier minister.* Paris: Plon, 1996.

Rémond, René. *Quand l'état se mêle de l'histoire.* Paris: Stock, 2006.

Ricoeur, Paul. *La Mémoire, L'Histoire, L'Oubli.* Paris: Seuil, 2000.

Rosoux, Valérie. *Les Usages de la mémoire dans les relations internationales.* Brussels: Bruylant, 2001.

Rousso, Henry. *Le Syndrome de Vichy.* Paris: Seuil, 1990.

Rousso, Henry. "Pour une histoire de la mémoire collective: l'après-Vichy." In *Histoire politique et sciences sociales*, edited by Denis Peschanski, Michael Pollack, and Henry Rousso, 243–64. Cahiers de l'IHPT, no. 18. Paris: Centre national de la recherché scientifique, 1991.

Rousso, Henry. "Une Justice impossible. L'Épuration et la politique antijuive de Vichy." *Annales. Histoire, Sciences Sociales* 3 (May–June 1993): 745–70.

Rozenblum, Thierry. "Une Cité si ardente. L'Action communale de Liège et la persécution des Juifs, 1940–1942." *Revue d'histoire de la Shoah. Le Monde Juif* 179 (September–December 2003): 9–49.

Saerens, Lieven. *Vreemdelingen in een wereldstad. Een geschiedenis van Antwerpen en zijn joodse bevolking (1880–1944).* Lannoo: Tielt, 2000.

Sandler, Shmuel. "Towards a Conceptual Framework of World Jewish Politics: State, Nation and Diaspora in a Jewish Foreign Policy." *Israel Affairs* 10, nos. 1–2 (2003): 301–12.

Schochat-Rebibo, Jacqueline. "Etrange Malaise." *Site Primo, Jerusalem*, 29 January 2007.

Schreiber, Jean-Philippe. "L'Israélitisme belge au XIXe siècle: une idéologie romano-byzantine." In *Un Modèle d'intégration: Juifs et Israélites en France et en Europe, XIX–XXe siècles*, edited by Patrick Cabanel and Chantal Bordes-Benayoun, 77–89. Paris: Berg, 2004.

Schwartz, Barry. "Memory as a Cultural System: Abraham Lincoln in World War II." *American Sociological Review* 61, no. 5 (1996): 908–27.

Schwartz, Barry and Robin Wagner-Pacifici. "The Vietnam Veterans Memorial: Commemorating a Difficult Past." *The American Journal of Sociology* 97, no. 2 (1991): 376–420.

Segev, Tom. *The Seventh Million: Israelis and the Holocaust.* Jerusalem: Keter Publishing, 1991.

Selznick, Philip. *TVA and the Grass Roots: A Study in the Sociology of Formal Organization.* Berkeley: University of California Press, 1949.

Sémelin, Jacques. *Sans armes face à Hitler.* Paris: Payot, 1998 [1989].

Shapira, Anita. "The Eichmann Trial: Changing Perspectives." *The Journal of Israeli History* 23, no. 1 (2004): 18–39.

Simoncini, Gabriele. "The Polyethnic State: National Minorities in Interbellum Poland." *Nationalities Papers* 22, no. 1 (1994): 5–28.

Stauber, Roni. "Realpolitik and the Burden of the Past: Israeli Diplomacy and the 'Other Germany.'" *Israel Studies* 8, no. 3 (2003): 100–122.

Steinberg, Maxime. *Le Livre des homes. Enfants de la Shoah. AIVG 1945–1959.* Brussels: Didier Devillez, 2004.

Steinlauf, Michael C. *Bondage to the Dead: Poland and the Memory of the Holocaust.* Syracuse: Syracuse University Press, 1997.

Surel, Yves. "Idées, intérêts, institutions dans l'analyse des politiques publiques." *Pouvoirs* 87 (1998): 161–78.

Sweet, Alec Stone, Neil Fligstein, and Wayne Sandholtz. *The Institutionalization of Europe.* Oxford: Oxford University Press, 2001.

Szurek, Jean-Charles. "Juifs et Polonais (1918–1939)." *Les cahiers de la Shoah,* no. 1 (1994): 67–78.

Terray, Emmanuel. *Face aux abus de la mémoire.* Arles: Actes Sud, 2006.

Terzi, Cédric. "'Qu'avez-vous fait de l'argent des Juifs?' Problématisation et publicisation de la question 'des fonds Juifs et de l'or nazi' par la presse suisse, 1995–1998." Ph.D. dissertation, Ecole des hautes études en sciences sociales, Paris, 2004.

Thelen, Kathleen. "How Institutions Evolve. Insights from Comparative Historical Analysis." In *Comparative Historical Analysis in the Social Sciences,* edited by James Mahoney and Dietrich Rueschemeyer, 208–40. Cambridge: Cambridge University Press, 2003.

Tilly, Charles. "Mechanisms in Political Process." *Annual Review of Political Science* 4 (2001): 21–41.

Todorov, Tzvetan. *Les Abus de la mémoire.* Paris: Arléa, 1995.

Todorov, Tzvetan. *Facing the Extreme: Moral Life in the Concentration Camps.* New York: Holt Paperbacks, 1997.

Tomaszewski, Irene and Tecia Werbowski. *Zegota: The Council to Aid Jews in Occupied Poland 1942–45.* Westmount: Price-Patterson, 1994.

"Trend Reports, Poles' Opinions about the Crime in Jedwabne—Changes in Social Consciousness." *Polish Sociological Review* 1, no. 137 (2002): 117–28.

Vidal, Claudine. "La Commémoration du génocide au Rwanda. Violence symbolique, mémorisation forcée et histoire officielle." *Cahiers d'Etudes Africaines* 175 (2004): 575–92.

Vinitzky-Seroussi, Vered. "Commemorating a Difficult Past: Yitzhak Rabin's Memorials." *American Sociological Review* 67 (2002): 46.

Voye, Liliane. "Belgique: crise de la civilisation paroissiale et recompositions du croire." In *Identités religieuses en Europe,* edited by Grace Davie and Danièle Hervieu-Leger. Paris: La Découverte, 1996: 195–213.

Wagner, Meir. *The Righteous of Switzerland. Heroes of the Holocaust.* Hoboken: Ktav, 2001.

Waintrater, M. "Touvier contre les Juste." *L'Arche,* May 1994.

Weitz, Yechiam. "Political Dimensions of Holocaust Memory in Israel." *Israel Affairs* 1, no. 3 (1995): 129–45.

Weitz, Yechiam. "The Holocaust on Trial: The Impact of the Kasztner and Eichmann Trials on Israeli Society." *Israel Studies* 1, no. 2 (1996): 1–26.

Wieviorka, Annette. *Le Procès Eichmann.* Brussels: Editions Complexe, 1989.

Wieviorka, Olivier. *Divided Memory: French Recollections of World War II from Liberation to the Present.* Stanford: Stanford University Press, 2012.

Winock, Michel. "La Part des Justes." In *La France et les Juifs. De 1789 à nos jours.* By Winock. Paris: Seuil, 2004: 103–135.

Winter, Jay and Emmanuel Sivan. *War and Remembrance in the Twentieth Century.* Cambridge: Cambridge University Press, 1999.

Zawadzki, Paul. "Transition, Nationalisme et Antisémitisme: l'exemple polonais." In *Théories sociologiques du nationalisme,* edited by Pierre Birnbaum, 103–19. Paris: PUF, 1997.

Zawadzki, Paul. "Juifs de Pologne: malaise dans la filiation." *Les Cahiers du judaïsme,* no. 1 (Spring 1998): 32–42.

Zawadzki, Paul. "Le Temps de la re-connaissance: ruptures dans la trame du temps et re-composition des subjectivités juives en Pologne." In *Ecriture de l'histoire et identité juive. L'Europe ashkénaze. XIXᵉ–XXᵉ siècle,* edited by Delphine Bechtel, Evelyne Patlagean, Jean-Charles Szurek, and Paul Zawadzki, 95–130. Paris: Les Belles Lettres, 2003.

Zerubavel, Yael. *Recovered Roots. Collective Memory and the Making of Israeli National Tradition.* Chicago: University of Chicago Press, 1995.

Zerubavel, Yael. "The Forest as a National Icon: Literature, Politics and the Archeology of Memory." *Israel Studies* 1 (Spring 1996): 60–99.

Zubrzycki, Geneviève. *The Crosses of Auschwitz: Nationalism and Religion in Post-Communist Poland.* Chicago: University of Chicago Press, 2006.

Zubrzycki, Geneviève. "What Is Pluralism in a 'Monocultural' Society? Considerations from Post-Communist Poland." In *After Pluralism: Re-imagining Models of Interreligious Engagement,* edited by Courtney Bender and Pamela Klassen, 277–95. New York: Columbia University Press, 2010.

Zubrzycki, Geneviève. "Religion, Religious Tradition and Nationalism: Jewish Revival in Poland and 'Cultural Heritage' in Quebec." *Journal for the Scientific Study of Religion* 51, no. 3 (2012): 442–55.

INDEX